The Practice of Perspective

THE
PRACTICE
OF
PERSPECTIVE.

THE

PRACTICE

OF

PERSPECTIVE,

On the PRINCIPLES of

Dr. BROOK TAYLOR:

IN

A series of examples, from the most simple, and easy, to the most complicated, and difficult cases.

In the course of which, his method is compared with those of some, of the most celebrated writers, before him, on the subject.

Written many years since, but now first published,

By JOSEPH HIGHMORE.

LONDON,
Printed for A. MILLAR, and J. NOURSE, in the Strand.
MDCCLXIII.

THE

PREFACE.

THERE are, already, ſo many treatiſes on perſpective, that perhaps it may ſeem needleſs to add to the number; and it might juſtly be thought impertinent to offer any thing to the public, on this ſubject, after Dr. Brook Taylor; *unleſs the end propoſed were different from his, and conſequently different means neceſſary.*

He has invented, and, in a very ſhort compaſs, exhibited an univerſal theory; the truth, and excellence, of which is acknowledged by all who have read, and conſidered it, at the ſame time that they complain of its obſcurity. The attention, and application which the reading, and underſtanding this little book require, eſpecially with ſuch as are but little converſant in geometry, has diſcouraged the generality of thoſe, for whoſe ſervice it was chiefly deſigned, from the attempt; ſo that very few have profited by the beſt treatiſe that has been publiſhed on the ſubject.

It was firſt printed in 1715, *and again in* 1719, *with ſome difference, in order to render it leſs difficult, objections having been made to the former edition, on account of its intricacy: neither of the impreſſions is entirely ſold, if we are rightly informed *. But though this author has been ſtudied by few, yet with theſe he is in the higheſt eſteem, as the inventor of the true univerſal ſyſtem.*

Now if that, (the moſt excellent of all books on the ſubject,) has been liable to ſuch objections, as to make the labours of later

* Since the above was written, there has been another edition of Dr. *Brook Taylor*, publiſhed in 1749, ſaid to be reviſed, and corrected by Mr. *Colſon*, of *Cambridge*.

writers,

writers, on the ſame principles, acceptable to the public, the author hopes that this tract (the firſt written after Brook Taylor's, *as he has reaſon to believe, though laſt publiſhed) will be received with candour: And eſpecially becauſe, though his deſign, in general, be the ſame with theirs, his manner of treating the ſubject has been very different, as he had conceived it might be more naturally adapted to the comprehenſion of learners, for whoſe uſe it was principally intended.*

His purpoſe, and endeavour, has been to give the ſureſt, and ſhorteſt rules for repreſenting all ſorts of objects, and this in a popular, familiar manner, without conſtant ſtrict mathematical demonſtrations; although illuſtrations, and even demonſtrations, are not omitted, where they have been thought neceſſary.

He had, originally, intended to ſupply only what was wanting in the old perſpective, which might have been acceptable to thoſe already experienced in the art, but would have been wholly uſeleſs to others. And ſince many have been diſcouraged from the ſtudy, by hearing of the deficiency of the old method, and the difficulty of comprehending the new, he judged it better to make his work as complete in its kind, as he could; ſo as to enable any one, with a common application, to repreſent objects, in all poſſible ſituations, with the feweſt lines that the nature of the thing will admit, and without the aſſiſtance of any other book.

With this view he hath, in the firſt part, given a few examples in a manner common to the old, and new ſyſtem, and has endeavoured to explain even this as clearly, and comprehenſively as poſſible, both to render it eaſy to the learner, and alſo to prepare him more effectually for the other method.

In the ſecond part, objects are repreſented in both methods, ſeparately, to ſhew the advantage of the new, not only where the old is falſe, but alſo where it is incumbered with unneceſſary lines, and points, for want of the true, univerſal principles: here, examples are taken from Pozzo, *and the* Jeſuit, *the two moſt celebrated, and moſt ſtudied authors; as alſo from* A. Boſſe, *an old*

old French writer, by ſome, much eſteemed, from whom the Jeſuit *has borrowed, with proper acknowledgment to the merit of Monſ.* Deſargues, *on whoſe principles* Boſſe *profeſſes to have written. And in the courſe of this part, ſeveral miſtakes of theſe authors are remarked.*

This ſecond part may be conſidered as a comparative perſpective, and will be acceptable to thoſe who are already acquainted with moſt of the methods of projection, though they may not have taken the pains to make ſuch compariſon; but it is principally deſigned to ſhew the great advantages of the new method, and to excite the ſtudents, in this ſcience, to render themſelves maſters of it; which, although it may require more application at firſt, will enable them, afterwards, to execute whatever they undertake with more certainty, and expedition, than any other.

Thoſe whoſe curioſity may not detain them to examine the ſeveral ſchemes of this ſecond part, may paſs directly from the firſt, to the third part; wherein the five regular ſolids are projected; which examples are choſen, as furniſhing occaſion for almoſt every caſe that has any difficulty, in perſpective; inſomuch, that whoever fully comprehends the diagrams, and can project theſe objects, will (it is apprehended) find the projection of all others eaſy.

In this, and the following parts, are many things which the author preſumes are entirely new, at leaſt, he has never met with them elſewhere.

The learner, however, is adviſed, not to content himſelf with a mere inſpection of the diagrams, nor even with performing the problems as here exhibited, only, but to project the ſame objects in various ſituations, till he finds himſelf perfect both in the principles and practice; he is alſo adviſed, to begin theſe operations with a ſmall diſtance, that ſo all, or moſt, of the vaniſhing points may be found within the limits of his paper; but when he ſhall have acquired a facility in the execution, he may take what diſtance he pleaſes, and if any difficulties ariſe, on that, or any other circumſtance, he will find in the next,

And fourth part, expedients for them, this being the place frequently referred to, in the course of the treatise, for obviating several inconveniencies that may happen from want of space, as well as for many other schemes, of great utility in practice; these were reserved for this part on purpose, that the learner, by having gradually advanced thus far, might be more sensible of their usefulness, and so apply himself with the more eagerness, and pleasure, to comprehend them.

The fifth, and last part, treats of the manner of finding the shadows of objects on divers planes, and the images of objects in reflecting planes, but briefly, as being of less use than the former parts, which are absolutely necessary. Both shadows, and reflections, are wholly omitted by Pozzo, *though so great a master in the practice of perspective. The* Jesuit *has examples of shadows cast on planes, but is strangely mistaken in some of them, as well as in the precepts with which they are accompanied, as is shewn, where they are particularly mentioned.*

ADVERTISEMENT.

As the Author was near sixty miles from London, while this Work was printing, it is hoped the following errors of the press will be the more easily excused: And the Reader is particularly desired to correct them, with his pen, before he begins the book, because the smallest errors, in these Subjects, perplex the sense, and in some cases entirely pervert it; especially where letters of reference are mistaken.

Page	Line	ERRATA.
8	5	from the bottom, for *f*, read f,
15	6	——— for *distance* o, read *distance*; o,
	10	——— for *from which*, read *and*
	11	——— for *having been*, read *method was*,
20	5	from the top, for D, read *D*,
22	8	from the bottom, read, *by drawing from* S, *through* 4, *to the ground*,
64	4	from the top, dele *To*, and begin the sentence with *Find*
	5	——— after the words, *of this vanishing line*, insert, *Then*
	19	——— after 3, 2, 10, make a full stop, and then read, *As*
65	11	from the bottom, for *Fig. I. Below is*, read *Fig. I. Is*
87	6	——— for *e*, read e,
93	14	from the top, the last letter in the line, for *B*, read B,
94	1	*for* V, *read* U,
98	24	*for* V, *read* U,
99	8	from the bottom, for *(which will be perspectively perpendicular to the vanishing line a*, C, *b, and) of* 1, P, *and all its parallels, draw* U, P, *cutting the line a*, C, *b, in* V, Read, *of* 1, P, *and of all its parallels; draw* U, P, *which will be perspectively perpendicular to the vanishing line a*, C, *b, and will cut it in* V,

THE

THE

PRACTICE

OF

PERSPECTIVE, &c.

THIS treatiſe, being chiefly intended for thoſe who are verſed in *Deſigning*, begins immediately with the practice of perſpective; though the utmoſt care has been taken to render every thing as clear, to any attentive reader, as the nature of the ſubject will admit. With this view, as many of the known terms are preſerved, as poſſible, that all may be readily underſtood by thoſe to whom theſe terms are familiar; though others might have been invented that would have been preferred as more ſignificant, if the author had intended to exhibit a theoretic ſyſtem.

His aim is to render the practice intelligible and eaſy, to ſuch as above mentioned; for whoſe ſake, the terms and methods in common uſe are employed, ſo far as is conſiſtent with the improvement propoſed; and in thoſe caſes where others become neceſſary, they are introduced and explained, and not before; by which means they will be more readily underſtood, and more eaſily remembered.

The reader is ſuppoſed to be acquainted with ſome of the firſt elements of Geometry, otherwiſe he wants the very language of the ſcience.

The letter S, is every where uſed for the point commonly called *The point of ſight*, which is the ſame point that Dr. Taylor (more properly) calls *The center of the picture*, it being *that* wherein the picture is interſected by a right line from the eye of the ſpectator, perpendicular to the picture (or to its plane continued, if need be) which line is the diſtance of the picture; and that end of it, ſuppoſed to be at the eye of the ſpectator, is always marked D, whether placed on the horizontal line, or elſewhere, and is called *The point of diſtance.*

The point S, may very properly be conſidered as the center of the picture, for if a circle be deſcribed round it, with a radius equal to the diſtance, the point D, may be placed any where in the circumference of that circle.

Fig. 1. S, d, is *the horizontal line*, or *vaniſhing line* of the horizontal plane, it being the interſection (with the picture) of a plane paſſing from the eye, parallel to the horizon. S, *the point of ſight*, or *center of the picture*. D, the *point of diſtance*; as are alſo d, and *D*, (in the circumference of the ſame circle.) G, H, is the *ground line*, or interſection (with the picture) of an original plane, *which is here* the plane of the horizon. A, is an original point, on that plane, ſuppoſed to be beyond the picture, ſo far as it is placed below the *ground line*, that is, from A, to a; and therefore (once for all) it may be proper to remark, that whatever is ſo ſituated, ſhould be conceived to be turned back, behind the *ground line*, and D, to be turned forwards, on the point S, in ſuch manner, that A, a, and D, S, be parallel to each other, and (in the preſent caſe) both perpendicular to the picture; then ſuppoſing the picture tranſparent, the point A, will be ſeen through it at *a*, by an eye placed at D; or, to explain it otherwiſe, the viſual ray from D, to A, (when in the ſituation above) will interſect the picture in *a*. For ſuppoſe a plane paſſing through the lines D, S, and A, a,) when both are perpendicular to the picture) that plane will cut the picture in the line S, a. Now the point *a*, muſt be ſomewhere in the viſual ray, D, A, and it muſt alſo be ſomewhere in the line S, a; therefore it muſt be in their interſection *a*, the only point

point common to both lines. And the ſame line S, a, would be the interſection of a plane paſſing through D, S, and A, a, though theſe two lines were not perpendicular, but in any other direction *(not parallel to the picture)* provided they were ſtill parallel to each other; and therefore the ſame point *a*, will be as truly found in whatſoever direction A, a, and D, S, are drawn, if ſtill parallel to each other, as here A, is tranſpoſed to *A*, on the *ground line*, and D, to d, on the *horizontal line*; then drawing d, *A*, and a, S, interſecting it in *a*, that will be the ſame perſpective repreſentation of A.

It is evident alſo that a, *a*, is the *perſpective* of a, A, (an original line) and the whole line a, S, is the *perſpective* of the ſame original, continued infinitely, of which a, *a*, is a limited part, and all lines terminating in S, repreſent originals perpendicular to the picture; for S, repreſents a point infinitely diſtant, to which all ſuch lines tend, or (which is the ſame thing in perſpective) ſeem to tend; and is called their *vaniſhing point*. Hence it appears, that the perſpective repreſentation of every original right line, *not parallel to the picture*, is included between its *interſection* with the picture, and its *vaniſhing point*:—that is, having continued that original line *(whether perpendicular, or oblique)* till it cuts the picture, as here in a, and having drawn a parallel to the original line, from the eye, cutting the picture, as here in S, the line drawn from a, the *interſection*, to S, *the vaniſhing point*, will be the whole repreſentation of the original line; though that line be infinitely continued beyond the picture. The repreſentation of the more diſtant parts of which will approach to S; but the moſt diſtant point, ſhort of infinite, will not reach S; therefore that is very properly named the *vaniſhing point* of ſuch line.

A, is here tranſpoſed to *A*, and a, *A*, becomes by that means parallel to *S*, d; it is ſo tranſpoſed, becauſe in this, and moſt caſes, it is eaſieſt for the operation; but though it is neceſſary that theſe two lines ſhould be parallel, yet they may be *ſo* in any direction; for ſuppoſe D, tranſpoſed to *D*, and A, to j, the viſual ray, *D*, j, will cut a, S, in the ſame point *a*, as is evident.

It is recommended to thoſe readers who have not yet begun this ſtudy, to re-conſider what has been ſaid, till they fully conceive every part of it, before they proceed; and if they draw the ſchemes themſelves, they will apprehend the reaſons of the ſeveral operations much better, and even ſave time by ſo doing.

In like manner may be found the *perſpectives* of any number of points, and conſequently of lines, and ſuperficies: for inſtance,

Fig. 2. C, B, is a line in the ſame original plane (whoſe interſection e, is found by continuing it to the ground line) the extremities of which, being points, are ſet off, (in the ſame manner as was A) on the ground line, to f and g; from each of which, by drawing a line to d, and then drawing e, S, are found the points c, and b, the perſpectives of C, and B, and thus c, b, is the *perſpective* of the original line, C, B.

Fig. 3. E, F, is a line lying oblique to the *ground line*, whoſe *perſpective* is found in the ſame manner, *viz.* by drawing perpendiculars from E, and F, to the *ground line*, and from each interſection drawing a line to S; then transferring the diſtances of E, and F, to the ſame line, and thence ſeverally drawing to d, cutting the two lines (tending to S,) in e, and f, and drawing e, f, this line becomes the *perſpective* of the original line, E, F.

Thus any right line, however ſituated, may be repreſented, by finding the *perſpective* of its two extremities. Hereafter a ſhorter, and better method will be ſhewn of projecting any oblique lines, but it was neceſſary to begin with points.

Fig. 4, 5, 6, 7. It is obvious, that the perſpective repreſentations of the ſquare, and parallelograms are found the ſame way, and that the reaſon why the ſquare needs no pricked arch, is, that having all its ſides equal, the diagonal from d[2], determines the perſpective depth, without any farther trouble.

Fig.

Plate I.

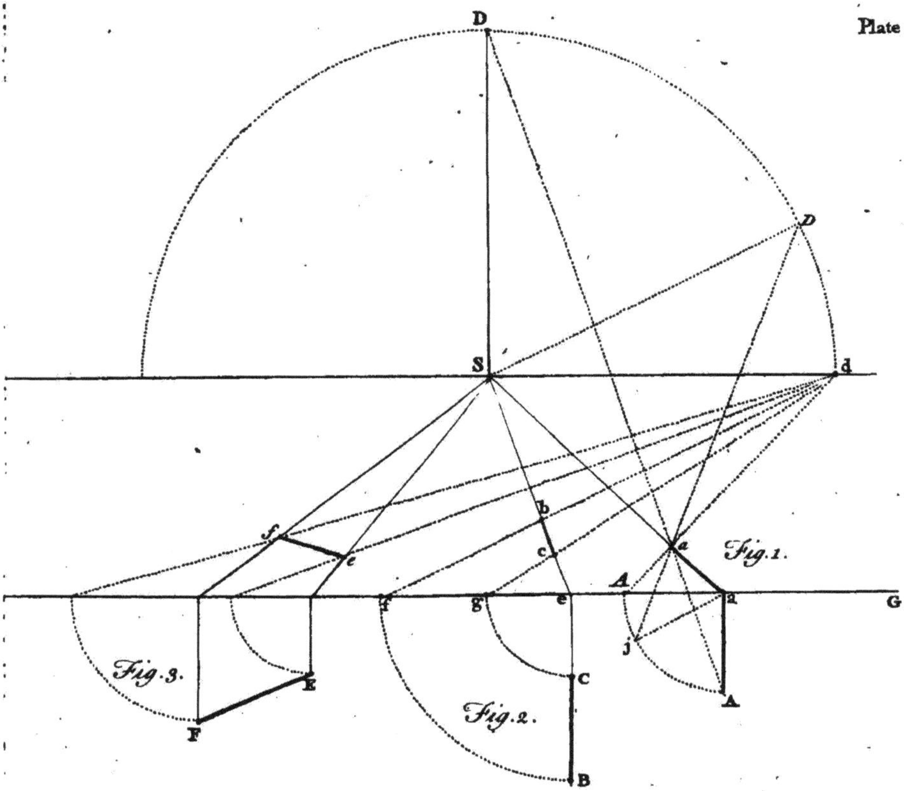

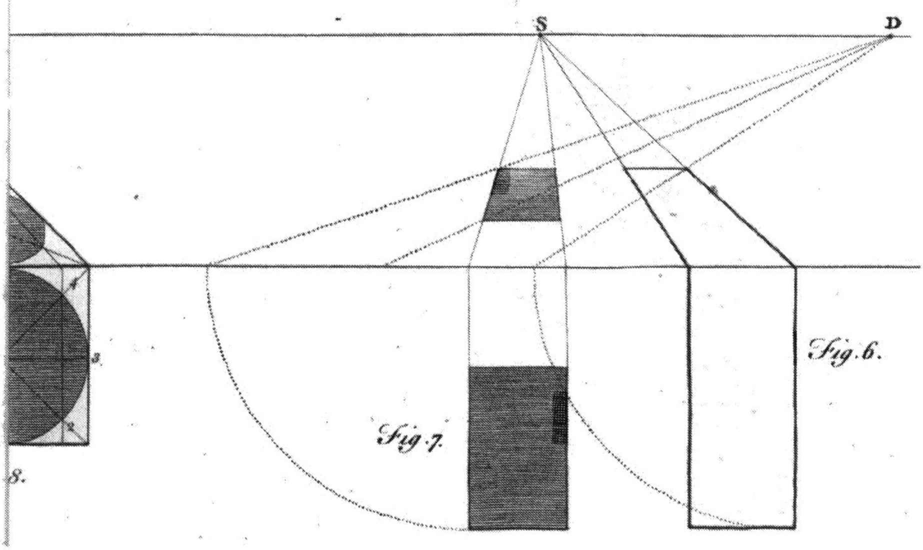

Fig. 8. And for the ſame reaſon, the eaſieſt way of deſcribing the perſpective of a circle, is by including it in a ſquare, and finding the eight points marked 1, 2, 3, 4, 5, 6, 7, 8.

Fig. 9. The perſpective of any irregular plan, as A, B, C, &c. may be found by the ſeveral points, as is evident. It is to be remarked, that the pricked arches by which the diſtances are ſet off to the ground line, ſhould always be on the ſide oppoſite to d, *(i. e.)* when d, is to the right of S, they ſhould be transferred to the left, and ſo *vice verſa*.

Fig. 10. When a ſquare is placed touching the ground line, in one point, ſo as to make, with that line, an angle of 45 degrees on each hand, continue the ſides, as A, B, and A, C, to the *ground line*, and draw from the points b, and E, to d^{1}, and from the points c, and E, to d^{2}, which will give the *perſpective*; (d^{1}, and d^{2}, being equally diſtant from S.) But in the ſecond part, an univerſal rule will be given for all ſituations of original figures.

SOLIDS.

Fig. 11, 12. THE plans are firſt reduced to perſpective, as here of the cube, and parallelopiped, by the rules above, then perpendiculars raiſed on the ground line equal to their true, or geometrical heights, and from the tops, lines drawn to S; then other perpendiculars from the remaining angles of the perſpective plan (meeting the lines drawn to S, from the firſt perpendiculars) complete the ſolids.

Fig. 13. This figure is a Tuſcan pedeſtal, whoſe geometrical plan, and elevation, are firſt deſcribed, then the plan in perſpective, which may be either in its place, on the picture, or (as here,) below it, this being choſen that it may not incumber the work above, and alſo that it may be more diſtinct, by being leſs crouded in ſpace. This is performed as the ſquare at Fig. 4, and the inner ſquares are determined by the diagonals, croſſing the rays drawn to S, from the loweſt line taken from the geometrical plan with its divisions. After this operation, continue the several parallel lines of the geometrical elevation, to the line of section F, G, by pricked lines, and from all those intersections draw to S: Then set off from G, on the ground line, the divisions of the geometrical *plan*, taken from the base of the pedestal, (*viz.* 1, 2, 3, 4—5, 6, 7, 8,) and from these divisions draw lines to d, which lines will cut the line G, S: from which intersections, raise perpendiculars to the respective members of the pedestal; these perpendiculars will complete the perspective elevation marked E.

The perspective plan might have been made nearer to S, or any where on, or below the ground line, beyond the numbers 1, 2,——8, so as not to interfere with them, or on the other side of S, (*e. g.*) as far as Fig. 14; for the perspective elevation E, would have served for *that*, by means of parallels.

Then the whole is completed, by raising perpendiculars from the several angles of the perspective plan, and cutting them by parallels from the corresponding angles of the perspective elevation; and lastly, by tracing the figure thro' these intersections; as for instance, a perpendicular from 9, in the perspective plan, Fig. 13, and a parallel from 9, in the perspective elevation, will meet at 9, in the finished pedestal, and so of the rest.

N. B. When the perspective plan is, at once, represented in its proper place, (*i. e.*) on or above the ground line, as at No. 14. then parallels drawn from the several members of that plan, will cut the lowest line G, 9, of the perspective elevation E, in the true points, from which the perpendiculars are to be raised to complete that elevation; but when it is found more expedient to make the plan below the ground line (as at No. 13.) it is necessary to set off the geometrical breadth of the plan from G, on the ground line, with its divisions, which must be then drawn to d, as before directed, and thereby the perspective figure completed; for perpendiculars from this last perspective plan, tho' below the ground line, will meet the parallels from the perspective elevation in the same points.

These

These ſeveral ways are explained, that the principles may be more clearly underſtood; but the beſt of all methods to conceive them thoroughly, will be to perform theſe operations at the time of reading, and not to paſs on to another figure, till all the former are fully comprehended: it is alſo recommended to ſuch as are not practiſed in the art, to perform this Fig. 13, in the ſeveral ways mentioned, before they read farther: they will then proceed with more facility and pleaſure.

Fig. 14. This figure is projected in the ſame manner as the laſt, except that, inſtead of the plan and elevation drawn geometrically, the breadths only of the plan, and heights of the elevation, are marked with their ſeveral diviſions; all which are drawn to S, and a diagonal from d[a], gives the ſquares of the plan; then from the ſeveral diviſions of this perſpective plan, parallels are drawn to the loweſt line of this ſubſtituted elevation, and from theſe interſections, perpendiculars to the heights of the ſeveral members: By means of this preparation, the whole is completed in its place; tho', as hath been ſaid, the plan, and line of elevation, may be ſeparated, to avoid confuſion.

Fig. 15. This example is of a rough pedeſtal without mouldings.

After having made the geometrical elevation and plan, draw from every angle of both to S, thro' the line d, A, which is to be conſidered as the ſection of the picture; with this diſtinction, that d, G, part of it, is the perpendicular edge of the picture, and conſequently will determine the heights of all the points, by means of parallels to the horizontal line, drawn from the interſections of the rays, as 1, 2, 3, *&c.* but from *b*, to A, (incluſive) the interſections are ſuppoſed to be on the bottom of the picture touching the ground; and are therefore to be tranſpoſed to G, H, the ground line, as at h, g, G, *&c.*—a, repreſenting A; for ſetting one foot of your compaſſes at A, and extending the other to h, on the line of ſection, the whole is transferred to the ground line, from a, to h, together with the intermediate diviſions, from which laſt points, perpendiculars being drawn, will meet the reſpective parallels in the true perſpective points, which being joined will form the figure.

N. B. In

N. B. In the ground line, the point h, muſt be placed exactly at the ſame diſtance from *f*, as h, is from d, on the line of ſection; otherwiſe the pedeſtal will not be ſeen in the picture, as the ſpectator ſtanding at S, ſees the original. *This method of projection is* Pozzo's, *in his ſecond volume, and is introduced for reaſons which will be explained hereafter.*

Fig. 16. The next is without geometrical plan, or geometrical elevation.—Having firſt drawn the baſe line, *a*, *b*, and divided it geometrically at *c*, and *d*, (for the body or trunc of the pedeſtal) project the whole baſe perſpectively, by means of a diagonal from D, then any where apart on the ground line, as at k, erect a perpendicular, the height of the whole pedeſtal, and divide it geometrically at the heights of the ſeveral members; and from theſe diviſions draw to any point in the horizon, as *f*: after which, draw parallels from all the angles of the perſpective plan to k, *f*, (the loweſt line of the perſpective elevation,) and, from theſe interſections, erect perpendiculars, cutting the ſeveral lines drawn to *f*, and, by theſe laſt interſections, form the perſpective elevation, then, by means of parallels, from the ſeveral members (cutting perpendiculars, raiſed from the ſeveral angles of the perſpective plan) complete the figure.

Fig. 17. Here is added one object more, leſt any difficulty ſhould ariſe from ſuch figures whoſe ſides are not ſimilar, but whoever has underſtood thus far, will perceive how this is performed on inſpection; the method being the ſame as at Fig. 15, except that inſtead of drawing all the lines of the geometrical * to the point S, in the horizontal line. In this ſcheme, thoſe of the plan are drawn to another point below, as T, to avoid confuſion, but then it muſt be remarked, that as T, f, is equal to S, D, (the diſtance) ſo R, *b*, muſt be equal to *f*, B, for the reaſon given above at Fig. 15, and here the line of diviſions taken from 1 B, &c. tranſpoſed to 1 *b*, was ſet off on the ground line, the contrary way to that of Fig. 15, (the rays being drawn to T, the contrary way to S,) that the rays in the finiſhed figure may run to S[4].

* The term *geometrical* here, and elſewhere, (when without a ſubſtantive) is uſed ſubſtantively for the original object, as the term *perſpective* is frequently uſed for the repreſentation.

Fig.

THE

INTRODUCTION.

SINCE the completion of this treatiſe in the order propoſed, it has been thought proper to prefix a few of the firſt principles of geometry, to facilitate the progreſs of ſuch readers who may not have been converſant in theſe ſtudies.

Definitions from *Euclid's* Elements.

Fig. 1. A point is conſidered as having no parts, as A.

2. A line is conſidered as having no breadth, as A, B.

3. The extremities of a line are points.

4. A right (or ſtraight) line, is that which lies equally between its points, or is the ſhorteſt that can be drawn from point to point, as A, B, fig. 2.

5. A ſuperficies is that which hath only length and breadth, without depth, or thickneſs, as A, B, C, D, fig. 3.

6. The extremes or ends of a ſuperficies are lines.

7. A plain ſuperficies is that which lies equally between its lines.

8. A plain angle, B, A, C, is an inclination of two lines in a plane to each other, as A, B, and A, C, the one touching the other, as in the point A, fig. 4.

N. B. The ſecond, or middle letter, is always the angular point.

9. When the lines which contain the angle are right (or ſtraight) lines, it is called a right-lined angle.

If both be curved, it is a curve-lined angle; if one be curved, and the other right, it is a mixed angle.

Fig. 10. When a right line, as A, B, ſtanding upon a right line, as C, D, makes the angles on each ſide equal, then both of them are right angles, and the right line A, B, is called a perpendicular to C, D, fig. 5.

11. An obtuſe angle is that which is greater than a right angle, as E, B, C, fig. 5.

12. An acute angle is that which is leſs than a right angle, as E, B, D, fig. 5.

13. A circle is a plain figure comprehended by one line, which is called a circumference, to which all right lines drawn from the point in the middle of the figure (called its center) are equal, as C, A,—C, B,—C, D, fig. 6.

14. The diameter of a circle is a right line, as A, B, drawn through the center C, and being terminated by the circumference, on either ſide, divides the circle into two equal parts.

15. A ſemicircle is contained by the diameter, and half the circumference, as A, D, B, fig. 6.

16. Of trilateral, or three ſided figures, that which hath three equal ſides, is called an equilateral triangle, as A, B, C, fig. 7.

17. That which hath only two ſides equal is called an iſoſceles triangle, as A, B, C, fig. 8.

18. And that which hath all the three ſides unequal, is called a ſcalenum, as A, B, C, fig. 9.

19. But that which hath one angle right is called a right-angled triangle, as A, B, C, fig. 10.

And the ſide oppoſite to the right angle is called the hypothenuſe, as A, B.

20. Of quadrilateral figures, the ſquare is that which hath the four ſides equal, and the four angles right, as A, B, C, D, fig. 11.

21. An oblong, or long ſquare, is rectangled, but not equilateral, as A, B, C, D, fig. 12.

22. A rhombus, is a figure equilateral, but not right-angled, as A, B, C, D, fig. 13.

Fig.

Fig. 23. A rhomboides, hath the oppofite fides and angles equal, but is neither equilateral, nor right angled, as A, B, C, D, fig. 14.

24. All other quadrilateral figures (being irregular) are called trapeziums, as A, B, C, D, fig. 15.

25. Parallels are right lines in the fame plane, which being infinitely prolonged on both parts, would never meet, as A, B and C, D, fig. 16.

26. A parallelogram is a quadrilateral figure, whofe oppofite fides are parallel, as A, B, C, D, fig. 12, and 14.

27. When in a parallelogram, as A, B, C, D, fig. 17. there is drawn a diameter (or diagonal) A, C, and two right lines G, H, and F, E, parallel to the fides, cutting the diameter in the fame point I, fo that the parallelogram be divided into four parallelograms, thofe two, I, E, D, H, and I, F, B, G, through which the diameter doth not pafs, are called *complements*, but the two others, I, E, A, G, and I, F, C, H, through which it doth pafs, are faid to be *about the diameter*.

Some Propofitions from the firft, fecond, third, and fixth, books of *Euclid*'s Elements.

PROP. I. PROBLEM.

Upon a given right line A, B, (fig. 18.) to make an equilateral triangle A, B, C.

On the center A, at the diftance A, B, defcribe the circle B, C, D, and on the center B, at the fame diftance B, A, defcribe the circle A, C, E, and from the point C, where the circles interfect one another, draw the two right lines C, A, and C, B. Then A, B, C, will be an equilateral triangle.

For A, C, and C, B, are each equal to A, B, by conftruction.

PROP. IX. PROBLEM.

To divide a given right-lined angle B, A, C, (fig. 19.) into two equal parts.

 Let

Let there be taken, in the line A, B, a point at pleaſure, D, and on A, C, cut off A, E, equal to A, D, (by ſetting one foot of the compaſſes on A, and with the other deſcribing the arc D, E;) draw the right line D, E, and on it make an equilateral triangle D, F, E, and draw A, F, which will divide B, A, C, into two equal angles. Or the points D, and E, being found, the right line D, E, may be omitted; and inſtead of whole circles (as at the firſt Prop. fig. 18.) only mark the interſection at F, as in this figure.

PROP. X. PROBLEM.

To divide a given right line A, B, (fig. 20.) into two equal parts. *Euclid* directs here alſo to make an equilateral triangle A, C, B, on the given line, and then to divide the angle C, as in the laſt propoſition; that is, by means of another equilateral triangle below the line; but if the angular points above and below are found by interſection, it is ſufficient.

PROP. XI. PROBLEM.

On a given right line A, B, (fig. 21.) and from a given point therein C, to raiſe a perpendicular C, F.

In the part C, A, take any point D, and let C, E, be taken equal to C, D; then, on D, E, deſcribe the equilateral triangle D, F, E, and draw C, F, which will be perpendicular to A, B.

To raiſe a perpendicular at the end of a line A, D, fig. 11. With any opening of the compaſſes A, D, deſcribe the arc D, *e*, *f*, and with the ſame opening the arc D, *e*, and again with the ſame opening *e*, *f*; laſtly, with the ſame *e*, *g*, and *f*, *g*, now draw *g*, A, which will be perpendicular to A, D.

PROP. XII. PROBLEM.

On a given right line A, B, (fig. 22.) and from a given point C, which is not in it, to draw a perpendicular line C, F.

Let any point H, be taken on the other ſideof A, B, and from the point C, as a center, at the diſtance C, H, deſcribe the circle D, H, E, cutting

cutting A, B, in the points D, and E, and divide D, E, into two equal parts in F, and draw C, F, which will be perpendicular to A, B.

PROP. XIII. THEOREM.

When a right line E, B, (fig. 5.) falls on another right line C, D, either it makes two right angles, or two angles equal to two right angles.

DEM. For if the angle E, B, D, be equal to E, B, C, they ſhall be both right angles; but if it be unequal, let A, B, be drawn at right angles to C, D, then A, B, D, and A, B, C, ſhall be right angles. Now ſince E, B, D, and E, B, A, (taken together) are equal to the right angle A, B, D, if the common angle A, B, C, be added, then the three angles E, B, D,—E, B, A, and A, B, C, ſhall be equal to the two right angles A, B, D, and A, B, C. And ſince the angle E, B, C, is equal to the two angles E, B, A, and A, B, C, if you add the common E, B, D, the two angles E, B, D, and E, B, C, ſhall be equal to the three angles E, B, D,—E, B, A, and A, B, C. But theſe three have been ſhewn to be equal to two right angles; therefore E, B, D, and E, B, C, ſhall be alſo equal to two right angles. Which was to be demonſtrated.

PROP. XXII. PROBLEM.

To conſtitute a triangle F, G, K, (fig. 23.) of three right lines equal to three given right lines A, B, and C.

Draw an indefinite right line D, E, and on it make D, F, equal to A,—F, G, equal to B, and G, E, equal to C; and from F, as a center, with the length F, D, deſcribe a circle D, K, L: again, from the center G, with the length G, E, deſcribe the circle E, K, L, and draw F, K and G, K; then the triangle F, G, K, is made of three lines equal to A, B, and C.

PROP. XXIII. PROBLEM.

On a given right line A, B, (fig. 24.) and at a point given, A, to make an angle F, A, G, equal to a given angle D, C, E.

Set one foot of the compaſſes on C, and with the other foot, at any diſtance, deſcribe the arc E, D; then, with the ſame opening, ſet one foot on A, and deſcribe the arc G, F. Take, with the compaſſes, the diſtance D, E, and ſet it off from G, to F, and draw A, F; then the angle F, A, G will be equal to E, C, D.

PROP. XXXI. PROBLEM.

Through a given point A, (fig. 25.) to draw a parallel to a given right line B, C.

From A, draw an oblique line A, D, to the line B, C, and from D, with the diſtance D, A, deſcribe the arc A, B; then from A, with the ſame diſtance, deſcribe the arc D, E, make D, E, equal to A, B, and draw A, E, which will be parallel to B, C.

PROP. XXXII. THEOREM.

Of every triangle, as A, B, C, (fig. 26.) (one ſide B, being prolonged) the exterior angle A, C, D, is equal to the two interior, and oppoſite angles A, and B.

And the three angles of any triangle, as A, B, C, are equal to two right angles.

For having drawn C, E, parallel to A, B, it is evident that E, C, D, muſt be equal to A, B, C, and alſo that the angle A, C, E, muſt be equal to C, A, B. *This is not* here *ſtrictly demonſtrated, nor is that neceſſary in this introduction, but the reader is referred to the preceding propoſitions, in* Euclid, *for farther ſatisfaction.* Therefore the exterior angle A, C, D, (compoſed of them both) muſt be equal to A, and B; which is the firſt aſſertion.

Again. Since the angle A, C, D, and the angle A, C, B, taken together, are equal to two right angles (by Prop. XIII.) and ſince the angle A, C, D, is equal to the angles A, and B, (as above) it follows that the angles A, B, and A, C, B, which is common, (the three angles of any triangle,) are equal to two right; which was the ſecond aſſertion.

PROP.

PROP. XXXV. THEOREM.

The parallelograms A, C, D, B, and F, C, D, E, (fig. 27.) conſtituted on the ſame baſe C, D, and between the ſame parallels A, B, and C, D, are equal to one another.

For the demonſtration of this, and the three following propoſitions, the reader is referred to Euclid.

PROP. XXXVI. THEOREM.

Parallelograms on equal baſes, and between the ſame parallels, are equal.

PROP. XXXVII. THEOREM.

Triangles (being the halves of parallelograms) conſtituted on the ſame baſe, and between the ſame parallels, are equal.

PROP. XXXVIII. THEOREM.

Triangles on equal baſes, and between the ſame parallels, are equal.

PROP. XLVI. PROBLEM.

On a given right line A, D, (fig. 11.) to deſcribe a ſquare. Draw the right line A, G, perpendicular to A, D, make A, B, equal to A, D, through B, draw a parallel to A, D, and through D, draw a parallel to A, B.

PROP. XLVII. THEOREM.

In any right-angled triangle, (fig. 28.) the ſquare of the hypothenuſe, (*i. e.*) the ſide oppoſite to the right angle, is equal to both the ſquares of the other ſides taken together.

For demonſtration, the reader is referred to *Euclid*; but to aſſiſt the imagination, a regular figure is here exhibited, which will make the propoſition evident, on inſpection only.

PROP. XXXI. of the third book of *Euclid*. THEOREM.

The angle in a ſemicircle (fig. 6.) is a right angle. For demonſtration, ſee *Euclid*.

DEFI-

DEFINITION III. BOOK VI.

A right line is ſaid to be cut in mean, and extreme proportion, when the whole is to the greater ſegment, as the greater ſegment is to the leſs.

LEMMA. Fig. 29.

To divide a given line A, B, in extreme and mean proportion.

Through the extremity A, draw F, D, perpendicular to it, biſect A, B, in X, take A, D, equal to A, X, and from D, as a center, with the radius D, B, deſcribe the arc B, F; then from A, as a center, with the radius A, F, deſcribe the arc F, C, and C, will be the point ſought. *Euclid*, Prop. XI. of the ſecond book.

PROP. II. BOOK VI. THEOREM.

If a right line *a*, *c*, be drawn parallel to one of the ſides A, C, of a triangle A, B, C, (fig. 9.) it ſhall cut the ſides of the triangle proportionally. See *Euclid*.

THE

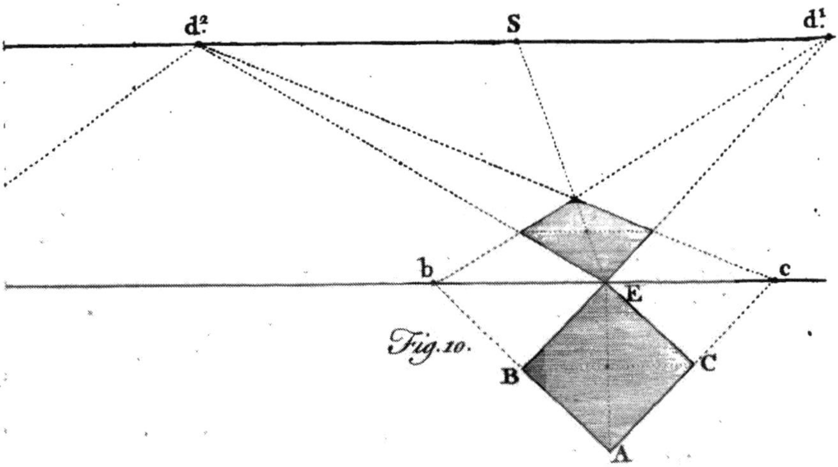

Fig. 10.

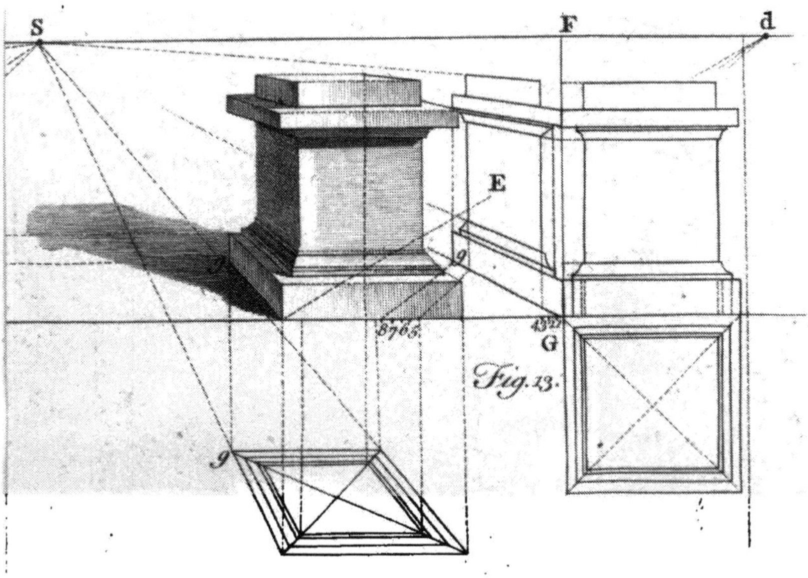

Fig. 13.

Fig. 18. Is performed in the ſame manner as 14, but in this, the lines which form the perſpective plan, are left viſible, that the operation may more eaſily be underſtood. The meaſures for the perſpective plan are taken from the geometrical, and ſet off on o, p. From thence rays are drawn to S^3, and the diagonal from p, to D^1, cuts the ray q, S^3, in the point z, which determines the perſpective ſquare, that repreſents the ſquare B, Z, in the geometrical plan, and, by means of this, the whole plan is put into perſpective. On the perpendicular o, 7, mark the geometrical heights of the ſeveral members, and from theſe diviſions draw rays to S^3, and then draw parallels from all the angles of the baſe, to o, S^3, the loweſt ray; and from the ſeveral interſections, raiſe perpendiculars to the uppermoſt, and ſo form the perſpective elevation, as at Fig. 14, *but which is more apparent at Fig.* 16, *becauſe the elevation is there ſeparated from the body of the pedeſtal, tho' the method is the ſame).* Now raiſe perpendiculars from all the angles of the plan, and, by means of parallels from all the members of the elevation, meeting theſe perpendiculars, complete the whole figure, in the ſame manner as was done at Fig. 14, and 16.—*Particular care muſt be taken that each parallel, from the elevation, meet its correſpondent perpendicular from the plan, to determine the ſame member*, and this is, perhaps, the eaſieſt, and ſhorteſt method of all: for the perſpective plan is made with as few lines, and in as little, time as the geometrical, which is unneceſſary here; and inſtead of the whole geometrical elevation, the geometrical diviſions, or heights only (on the firſt line o, 7) are neceſſary: ſo that the meaſures may be taken from a book of architecture, without drawing any thing geometrically; and if their meaſures (in ſuch book) be on a larger, or ſmaller ſcale, it is eaſy to ſet them off in any proportion required for the perſpective; as in this very figure, the meaſure for the baſe is limited to o, p, wherefore firſt draw o, p, in its place; but as the meaſures here, are equal to the original at B, and this expedient (for that reaſon) unneceſſary in the preſent figure, it is more convenient to ſhew it apart. —Suppoſe then, o, p, drawn in its place Fig. 18. (as directed above) draw from o, any other line, o, t, and on it mark all the geometrical diviſions of the plan from the book; then lay a parallel ruler from t, to p, drawing t, p, and parallel to it, all the rest of the divisions from o, t, to o, p, and the line o, p, will thus be truly divided; whether o, t, be longer or shorter than o, p.

And also having drawn in its place a perpendicular to o, p, as o, 7, for the elevation, draw any other line from o, as o, r, on which mark the divisions of the geometrical elevations from the same piece of architecture in the book, and (in order to preserve the proportion of the base) set off the measure of o, p, on the perpendicular o, 7, reaching to v, and the measure of o, t, on o, r, reaching to t², then lay the ruler from v, to t², drawing that line, parallel to it, transfer all the divisions from o, r, to o, v, which will give them in the same proportion as those on o, p.

In this first part, the several methods proposed by writers before Dr. *Taylor* are exhibited, any of which will answer the purpose, when objects are placed directly in front, and on the horizontal plane; but when objects are in an oblique situation, even on the horizontal plane, and especially when they are on an oblique plane, or when the figures to be represented on any plane are themselves irregular, the new method will appear preferable beyond all comparison.

SECOND PART.

THESE few examples are sufficient for the first part, that being intended only to exhibit the common methods, with some improvements; which methods, tho' useful in many cases, are no more proper for some, than the rule of addition, in arithmetic, is proper for finding the product of a sum in multiplication; and notwithstanding a person, ignorant of multiplication, might find, by addition, how much 300 times 278 makes; yet, in order to ascertain it, he must set down 278 three hundred times, and add all together; whereas, if he understood multiplication, he would do it in an instant, and be much less liable to mistake: It is not pretended that the cases are exactly parallel, but a few examples will shew that this may not improperly serve

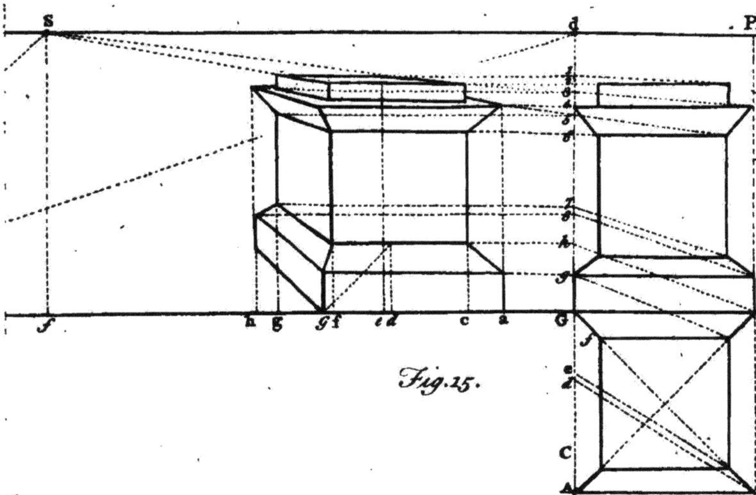

Fig. 15.

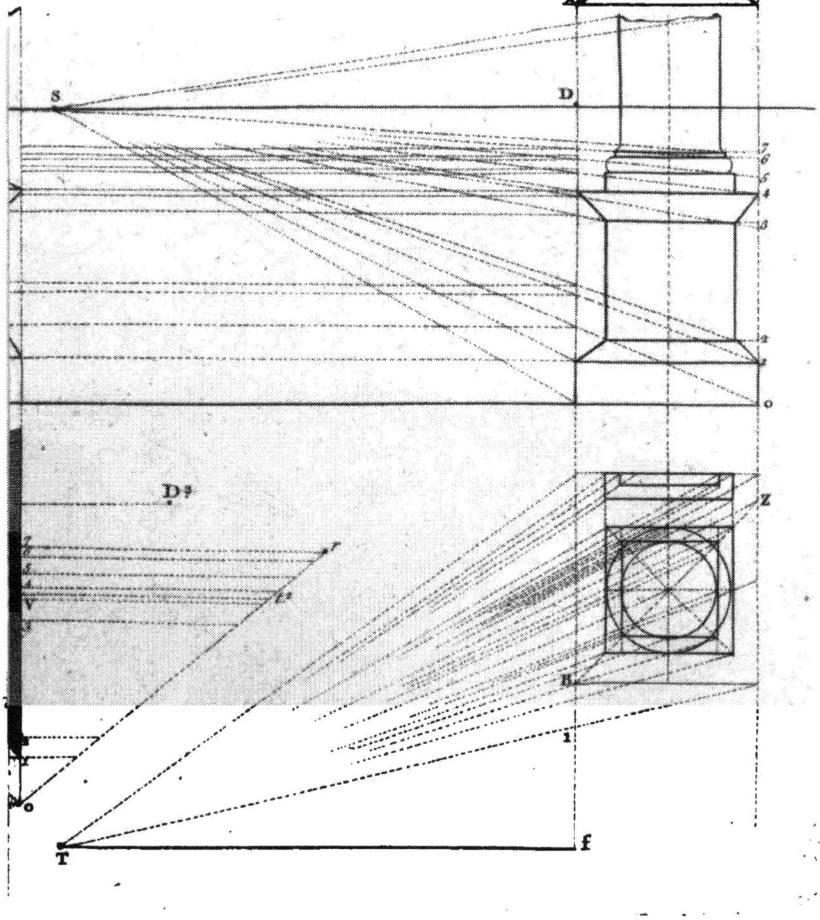

for illuſtration, and that the common methods are attended with ſuch tedious operations, ſuch a multitude of unneceſſary lines, and, in ſome ſituations, with ſuch perplexed and intricate ſchemes, as require more than human patience to execute, and, after all, render miſtakes almoſt unavoidable, of which any one will be convinced who ſhall examine the plates of *Pozzo*, even in his ſecond volume, where he has publiſhed his ſhorter method, which he had promiſed in his firſt, as well as in other authors; eſpecially when they exhibit objects in oblique poſitions, not only on oblique planes, but even on that of the horizon.

In this ſecond part, therefore, it is propoſed to ſhew the advantages of the new method, by comparing it with the old, in ſeveral inſtances: and here it may be proper to obſerve, that thoſe readers, whoſe leiſure or curioſity may not permit, or incline them to examine the ſeveral compariſons propoſed, may neglect the examples of the old methods, and go regularly thro' thoſe of the new, and ſo arrive at the knowledge of the practice the ſhorteſt way at once: thoſe however who are already acquainted with the old methods, will be better ſatisfied on ſeeing the different manners of operation, in the ſame examples; and it is preſumed that much the greater number of readers may be of this claſs.

Fig. 19. A, B, C, E, a parallelogram, making a given angle with the ground line G, H, repreſented, in perſpective, by the common method before explained.

Fig. 20. The ſame parallelogram by the new method. And here, inſtead of placing the diſtance on the horizontal line, it is proper to raiſe it perpendicularly, as S, D; then continue the ſides of the plan C, A, and C, E, till they cut the ground line in G, and H; from D, draw D, a, parallel to A, B, and C, H, cutting the horizontal line in a, and draw D, e, parallel to E, B, and C, G, cutting the horizontal line in e; then draw B, a, and H, a, and alſo B, e, and G, e, which complete the perſpective repreſentation: the lines themſelves forming the figure, without the trouble of finding points, or riſque of miſtake, or of inaccuracy in joining them when found.

N. B. A, B, and C, E, H, being parallel, D, a, is parallel to both; as is D, e, to E, B, and C, A, G; and it is an universal rule, that all original lines parallel to each other, (and not parallel to the picture) run to the same point in perspective; which, when not the point of sight, is called by the old writers an accidental point, or more generally a point of concourse; but by *Taylor, a vanishing point,* whether it lies in the horizontal line, or elsewhere: Thus a, is the vanishing point of A, B, and C, H, and B, and H, being their intersections, their perspectives are found between B, and a, and between H, and a; and so, universally, the perspectives of all original lines (not parallel to the picture) lie between their intersections with the picture, and their vanishing points, as was observed before.

Fig. 21. A, B, C, E, the plan of a cube placed obliquely to the ground line.---It is required to find the perspective of the whole cube in that situation.

According to the old method: After having found the perspective of the plan, and raised perpendiculars from all the angles, set off the geometrical height any where on the ground line, as at *f*, and draw from the extremities *f*, and *g*, to any point in the horizontal line h; then draw parallels from all the angles of the perspective plan, to the lower line *f*, *h*; and, from the intersections, raise perpendiculars to the upper line; and then, from these perpendiculars, draw back other parallels to the corresponding perpendiculars raised from the angles of the perspective plan, which will complete the cube.

Fig. 22. To represent the same according to the new method: After having found the perspective plan, (as at No. 20.) raise perpendiculars from all the angles of the perspective plan, and make c, 1, (which touches the ground line) of the true geometrical height; then from 1, the top of this line, draw to e, and k, (as before for the plan,) and from 2, to K, and from 3, to e, intersecting each other at 4, and so finish the upper square, as the lower, which completes the figure.

After

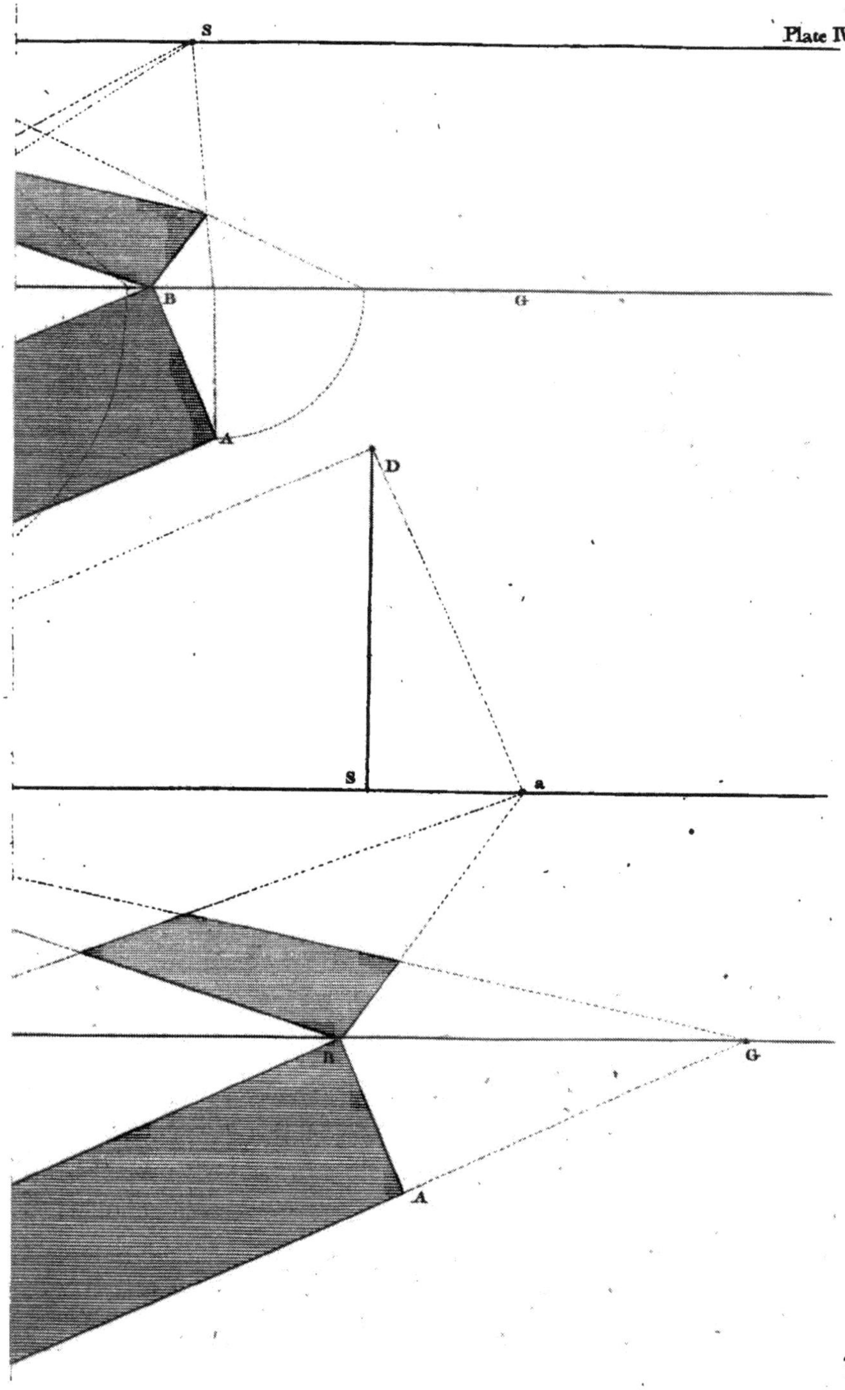
S
B
G
A
D
S
a
B
G
A

After what has been ſaid (at Fig. 15. and 17.) of *Pozzo*'s ſecond method, it would not be neceſſary here to add any thing more in explanation of it, if it were not, that there will be ſeveral occaſions for the ſame kind of operation; wherefore, to render it as clear as poſſible, the following example is propoſed.

Fig. 23. A, is an original parallelogram, ſuppoſed to be placed on the horizontal plane, behind the picture, whoſe interſection with that plane is G, h, the ſpectator ſtanding at d; wherefore firſt draw lines from each angle to d, which will cut G, h, then transfer thoſe interſections to the proper ground line of the picture G, H; begin by ſetting one foot of the compaſſes in o, (which is the interſection of d, o, with G, h, perpendicular to it,) and ſo transfer the ſeveral diviſions from the line G, h, to the line G, H, beginning at O, in this laſt line; and from 1, 2, 3, 4, on G, H, raiſe perpendiculars.

After this operation, raiſe perpendiculars alſo from all the points of the original figure A, to the line G, H, (continued behind G,) and from their interſections with this line, draw lines to S, which will cut G, D, the ſection (or upright edge) of the picture, and from theſe interſections (*viz*. of the lines to S, with G, D,) draw parallels, which meeting with the perpendiculars raiſed from 1, 2, 3, 4, determine all the points of the perſpective; but here care muſt be taken that each parallel determines its correſponding perpendicular; as for inſtance, the perpendicular 3, correſponds with the loweſt parallel, marked alſo 3, and their interſection repreſents the neareſt point of the object marked 3, and ſo of the reſt, which are all marked with their correſponding numerical figures: this, and the examples before referred to, are performed by the ſhorter method of *Pozzo*, exhibited in his ſecond volume, which he propoſed as the moſt expeditious manner of all; and for that reaſon it has been thought proper here, and in ſome following examples, to make the compariſon between this method and the new.

This example is the ſame kind of object, and ſituation, as is above ſhewn at Fig. 19, in the common method, and Fig. 20, in the

the new, to which the reader is referred, who may compare them together.

Here is alſo added the ſame object, according to the method of *A. Boſſe*, (a famous French engraver and author, who wrote about one hundred years ago) not only becauſe he aſſerts his to be the eaſieſt, ſhorteſt, and moſt exact of any to that time, or that ever could be invented *, but alſo becauſe it is ſtill ſo eſteemed by ſome moderns; he propoſes two methods little different from each other, both of them are ſhewn in this example.

Fig. 24. And firſt at Fig. 24, where the original object is encloſed in ſquares of feet (or any known meaſure) geometrically, the diſtance is ſet off in the ſame meaſure, as from p, to D, eight feet, and the height of the eye, as from D, to O, five feet.

In order to put this in perſpective, as below at Fig. 25, draw the ground line G, H, and divide it into feet; draw S, S, for the horizontal line, parallel to G, H, and the height of D, O, from it; and having placed S, on that line perpendicularly over P, (which correſponds with P, above,) draw rays from all the diviſions to S; then, in order to reduce the ſquares into perſpective, (inſtead of ſetting off the diſtance from S,) make a perſpective ſcale, or *echelle fuyante*, (as he calls it,) by marking from any point of the horizontal line eight parts of any opening of the compaſſes for the eight feet: as here from a, to b, and take one of theſe parts from G, to d, draw d, a, and G, b, which will cut d, a, in c, draw the parallel through c, and from the point where that cuts G, a, as at e, draw again to b, and ſo on, till you have as many parallels as are wanted. G, a, d, is what he calls the ſcale, the peculiar advantage of which is, that you may always divide the ſquares perſpectively within the picture, whatſoever diſtance be taken, becauſe any opening of the compaſſes may anſwer to your foot, the truth of

* *His words are,*—laquelle maniere s'eſt treuvée, ſans contredit, la plus familiere, et abregée, juſte, & preciſe qu'aucune qui ait encore parue, et j'oſe bien dire qui pareſtra. *Avertiſſement.*

His book is intitled, "Moyen univerſel de Pratiquer la Perſpective ſur les Tableaux ou "Surfaces irregulieres, &c. A Paris, MDCLIII. Par A. Boſſe."

And again Chap. I. J'ay dit que j'avois mis en lumiere un traité de perſpective que je crois, avec pluſieurs, etre le meilleur qui ſe ſoit fait, et, ſe fera, &c.

the

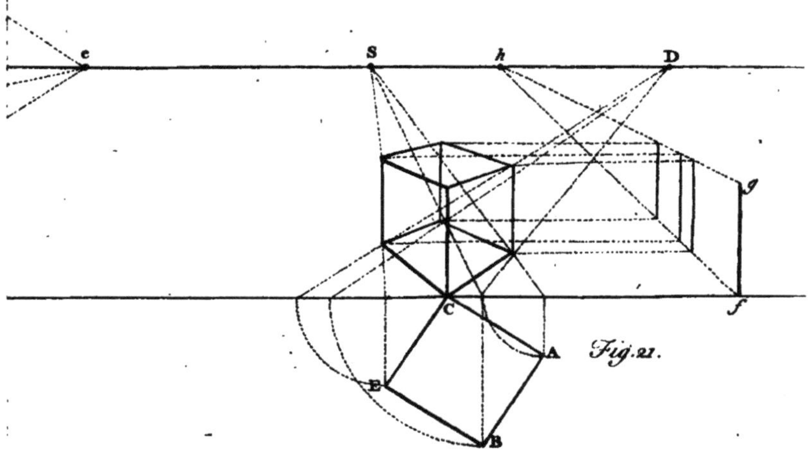

Fig. 21.

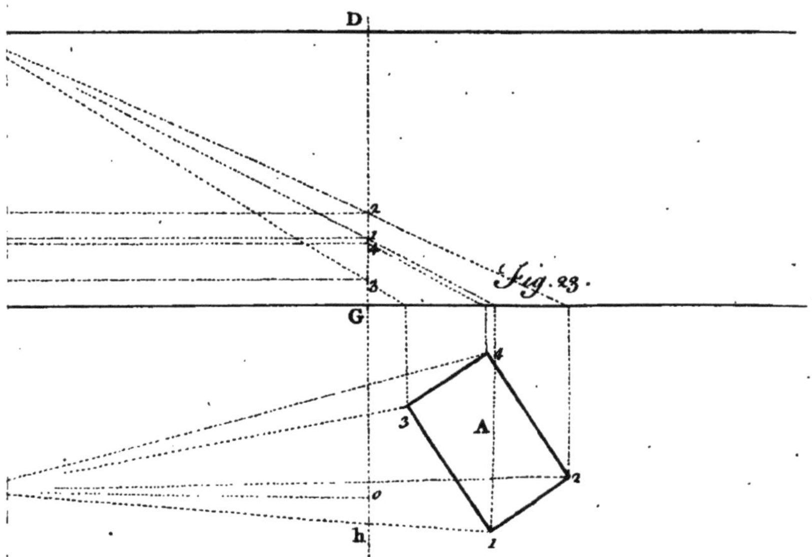

Fig. 23.

the operation depends only on making G, d, equal to one ſuch opening, or diviſion. Now find the ſeveral points, of the object in theſe perſpective ſquares, correſponding to the original in the geometrical plan, join theſe points, which complete the work.

His other manner differs in nothing from this, except that inſtead of drawing the rays and the parallels quite through them. You need only make the perſpective ſcale, and divide the perpendicular S, P, by that ſcale, and ſo meaſure the depths of the ſeveral points by the line S, P, and the breadths from the ſame line on both ſides, correſponding to the original: but then, in order to ſet off the parallel feet, it is neceſſary to add the line e, a, placing e, one real geometrical foot diſtant from G, which will determine the perſpective parallel feet, all the way up.

The performance of all theſe particulars will convince any one of the tedioufneſs, as well as uncertainty, of this manner of working; it will be found almoſt impoſſible to aſcertain the exact place of the ſeveral points, even with the utmoſt care; not to mention the neceſſity of making all that preparatory geometrical work, if not in ſquares, yet in diviſions *.

Fig. 26. Next follows the ſame object, according to the new method, in order to be compared with thoſe above, which having been before explained at Fig. 20, from which this differs only, in that the neareſt angle touches not the ground line. It is to be obſerved, that the lines here form the object, without the poſſibility of miſtaking, and with the utmoſt exactneſs, and in the tenth part of the time. The perpendicular S, D, is the diſtance o, and d, the two vaniſhing points, found by drawing D, o, on one ſide, and D, d, on the other ſide parallel to A, B, and E, B, reſpectively.

Fig. 27. This pedeſtal is repreſented in perſpective by *Pozzo's* ſhorter method, as explained at Figures 15, and 17, to which nothing need be added, except that the geometrical elevation muſt be formed by

* To do juſtice, however, to the author, it is acknowledged that this ſcale is, in ſome caſes, a very uſeful expedient; though it will by no means juſtify what he ſays of his general method.

perpendi-

perpendiculars from all the angles of the plan, as placed obliquely, which, in a complicated design, makes sometimes a very odd, and intricate figure, scarcely intelligible, as appears in several instances in *Pozzo's* second volume; whereas, according to the new method, this never happens; but, on the contrary, how complicated soever the original may be, the plans and elevations always make the same kind of figures as the original geometrical objects. This will be shewn hereafter.

The operation is the same as at Figure 23. And here, besides the great number of lines, much time, patience, and care, are necessary to find the corresponding points, (after having drawn all the perpendiculars, and parallels of the plan, and elevation,) which renders the work very liable to errors.

Fig. 28. Here is also added the same pedestal, in the same position, according to *A. Bosse's* method, by means of squares, (which is shorter than his other mentioned before, because the measuring is avoided, which requires more time than making the squares;) but, besides so many needless lines, there is great danger of mistaking the points by the perspective measures, and much time is necessary to complete the figure with any exactness.

N. B. The small plan above is, (in this method,) a necessary preparation, and the several points of the perspective plan are determined by marking them in the same parts of the perspective squares below, as in this, respectively. The perpendicular e, f, on the side of the small plan above, is divided geometrically for the height of the members, which are to be transferred also to the perspective; for instance, the top of the capital is four feet; therefore, on the ground line take four feet, and with that measure turn the compasses from the nearest angle l, which touches the same ground line, to h.——Again, for the same height at i, take four feet on the parallel at i, and turn the compasses up to k; and so for every other point; after which they must all be joined.

Fig.

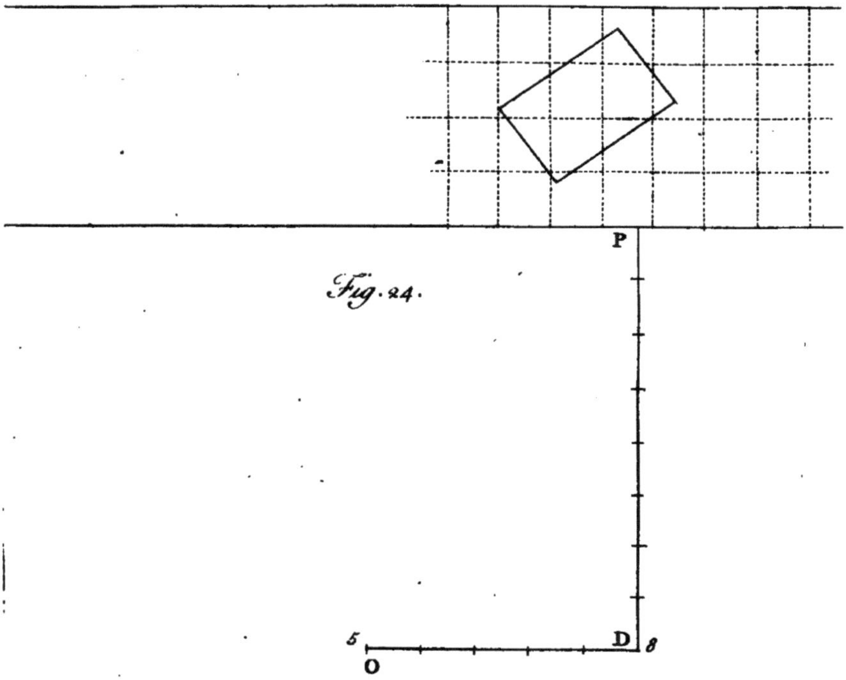

Fig. 24.

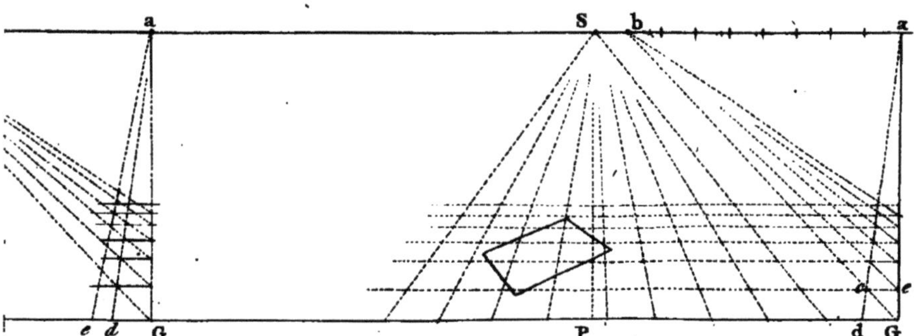

Fig. 25.

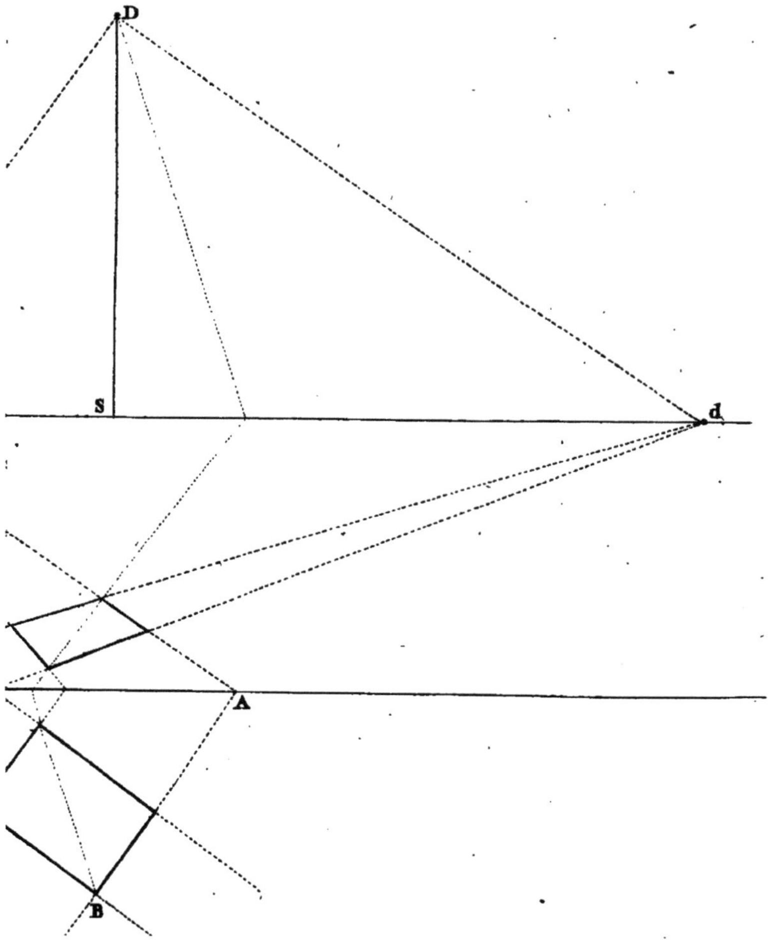
D
S
d
A
B

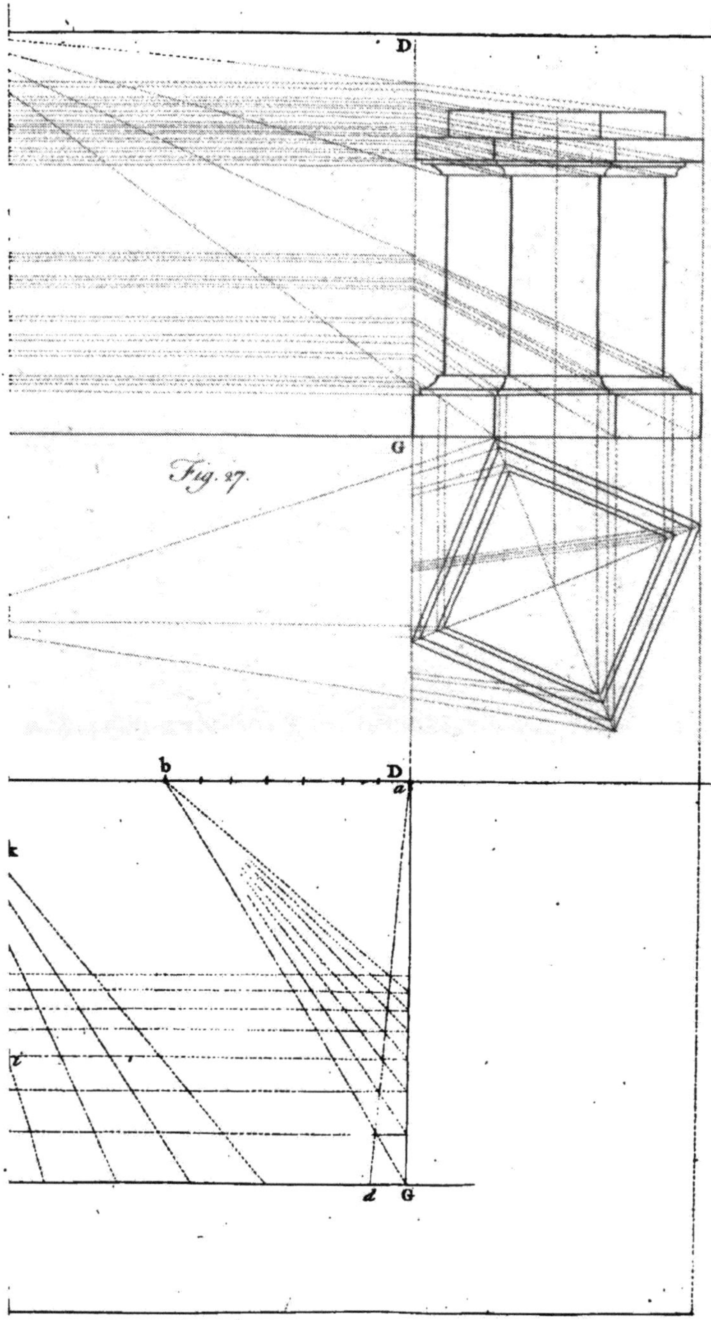

Fig. 27.

Fig. 29. But in the reprefentation of the fame pedeftal, by the new method, the whole work is performed by means of three points only, a, b, and c, to which all the lines are drawn, and thefe lines form the figure itfelf; fo that having fixed one end of the ruler at a, the lines of two fides, *(i. e.)* all that are parallel in the original, are drawn without taking it off, and by placing it at c, the lines of the other two fides are all drawn, without moving the end from thence, and, with the utmoft exactnefs; b is the vanifhing point of one of the diagonals, found by drawing D, b, parallel to d, b, in the geometrical plan.

If what has been hitherto faid of this method be underftood, (efpecially at Fig. 22.) this will not need farther explanation; however, to leave no difficulty; After having raifed perpendiculars from all the inward and outward angles of the perfpective plan, the geometrical meafures of the heights are marked on the perpendicular of the neareft outward angle, (which is pricked, or dotted;) and, from thefe divifions, lines drawn to b, cutting the perpendiculars of the neareft and fartheft angles of the die, or body of the pedeftal, determine the feveral points of the die; and drawing from thefe interfections to a, and c, the reft of the die is completed, and fo of the mouldings.

Fig. 30. The next figure reprefents two bafes leaning one againft the other, taken from the 28th of *Pozzo*'s fecond volume, both of them raifed from the horizontal plane; for which reafon he fays, "*he could* "*not affign a point of fight, and therefore was obliged to transfer all the* "*points one by one with his compaffes, that he might find the termination* "*and curvature of each line* *." And although (in the plate referred to) he has not left the lines by which thofe points were determined, yet whoever underftands his method will perceive the neceffity of them, and that in fuch oblique fituations, they muft be almoft innumerable, as will appear throughout his book, on infpection of the odd plans

* *His words are,*—defcendendo cum lineis occultis, ad perpendiculum, ab fingulis projecturis limborum defcribuntur totidem circuli in veftigio, ut unufquifque aptè collocetur, atque ab utrifque fierunt bafes opticè adumbratæ: *pro quibus certum oculi punctum ftatuere non potui, eò quod horizontales non fint. Sed transtuli, circino, fingillatim, puncta, ut finem, ac finuationem cujufque lineæ invenirem,* &c.

he was obliged to make, which of themſelves are extremely difficult to form, and intricate when formed.

The pains of ſo tedious an operation, as this method requires, might have been ſpared; but that *Pozzo*'s books (eſpecially the ſecond volume) are not in every one's poſſeſſion; and that, of thoſe who have them, very few (if any) may have given themſelves the trouble to project theſe, or ſubjects of the ſame kind, by his rules; and, therefore, may not be ſenſible of the neceſſity of uſing ſo many lines. It was, therefore, thought expedient to project theſe baſes in his way firſt.

The manner of working is the ſame as at Figures 15, 17, 23, and 27, above explained. And firſt the profiles A, and B, are geometrically drawn, then the plans C, and D, by dropping perpendiculars from every point of the profiles, and from the ſeveral points of the axes A, E, and B, F, (which cut the members of the baſes) in order to find the ſeveral centers on the line C, D, which line receives all the tranſverſe diameters, as *f*, *d*, and its parallels of the baſe A, and likewiſe thoſe of the baſe B; but the perpendicular diameters are transferred from the profiles geometrically, thus; C, repreſents the center A; d, repreſents the point *d*; and f, the point *f*; all three found by the perpendiculars; then from C, upwards and downwards, the geometrical length A, *d*, or A, *f*, is ſet off from C, both ways, to h, and g, for the perpendicular diameter g, h; which completes this circle; the ſame operation forms each circle, &c. After the profiles and plans are completed, lines muſt be drawn from every point of both to O, cutting the line 1, 5, part of which, *viz.* from 1, to 3, repreſents the interſection of the bottom of the picture with the ground, and muſt be transferred, with all its diviſions, to the proper ground line of the picture, and perpendiculars raiſed from all theſe diviſions. Another part of 1, 5, *viz.* from 4, to 5, repreſents the perpendicular, or upright ſection of the picture; and, therefore, from all its diviſions, parallels muſt be drawn, meeting the perpendiculars raiſed from the diviſions of the ground line, and theſe interſecting, will determine the points of the perſpective; but the number and confuſion of lines is ſo great, that it will be neceſſary to fix every point with the compaſſes, or (as *Pozzo* himſelf adviſes) with a pair

Plate IX.

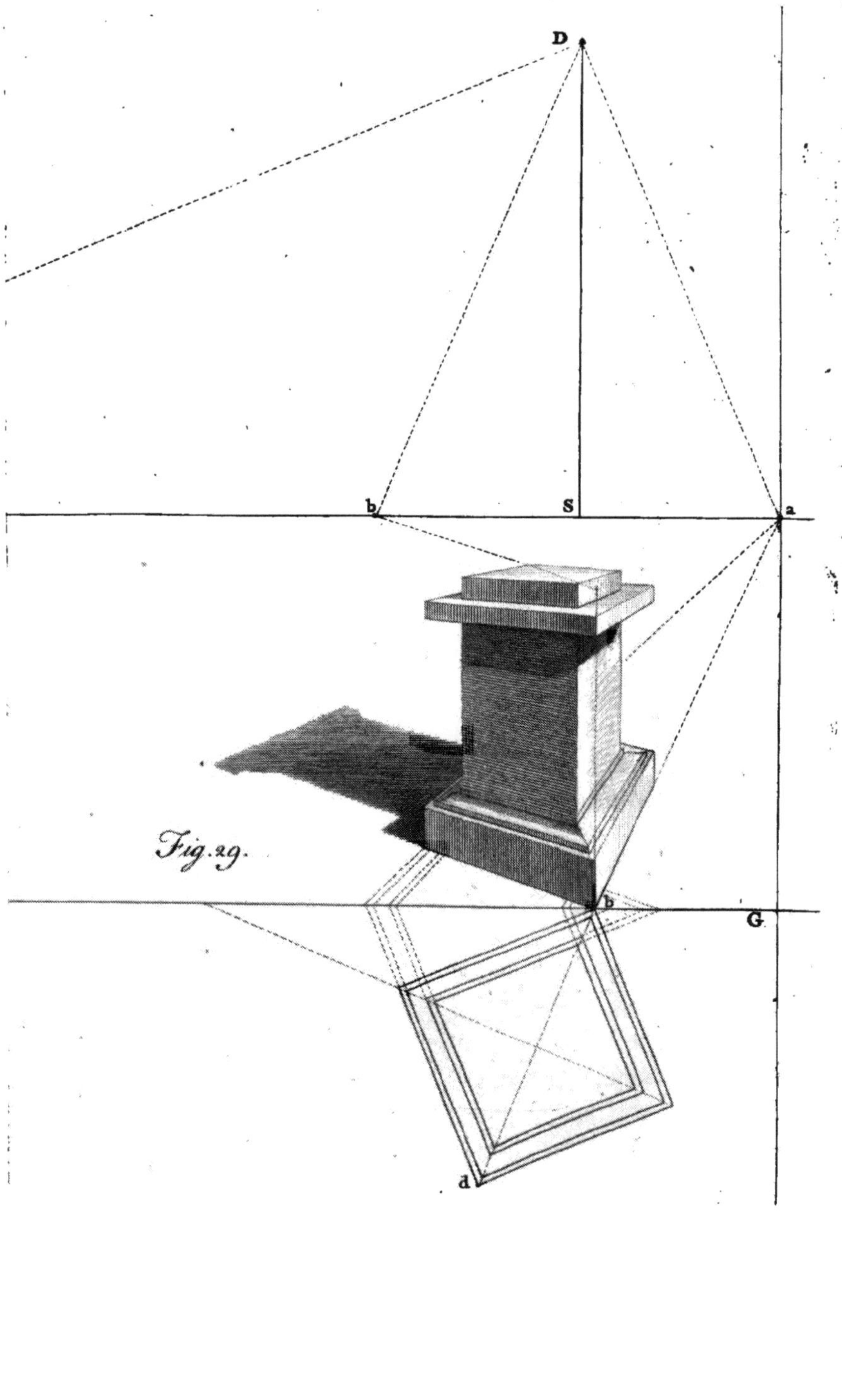

Fig. 29.

a pair in each hand, as thus; place one foot of your compasses in 1, on the line of section, and extend the other to 6, which is the intersection of the visual ray from D, to O, and transpose this measure to the picture, setting one foot there in 1, and the other foot will rest on the perpendicular marked 6, in which the center D, is to be found: at the same time, set one foot of the other pair of compasses in 2, on the line of section, and extend the other to the point where the ray B, O, cuts that line, as at 7, and transfer that height to the perpendicular 6, on the ground line, (found by the other compasses,) which will mark 7, on that perpendicular, the perspective of the center sought; and this double operation must be repeated for every point, till all the points in the perspective are found, which must afterwards be joined: in doing all this, great care must be used not to mistake; and when completed, can never be so true as by the other method; because here the several lines, which should be drawn to the same vanishing point, must be drawn from point to point only. Here are used five points only for each circle, *viz.* the center, and extremities of two diameters, to avoid adding more lines.

As to the parallels and perpendiculars, which inclose the perspective, they might have been omitted, if the two pair of compasses be made use of; and especially if the person using them has got into the habit: but these lines are left, that every thing may be clearly understood; but as the parallels are in themselves necessary to mark the line of section, they are only continued on to the bases, and do not increase the number of lines.

All the other lines are absolutely necessary in *Pozzo's* second, or shorter method. The great number of lines, and the confusion arising from thence, has caused even him to mistake, the lower base being false in his plate; for the lines representing the thickness of the plinth, which are perpendicular to the ground line, and parallel to each other, ought to run towards a certain point, and so be neither perpendicular, nor parallel: if the fault be not his, it may be the engraver's; but whosesoever it be, the print is apparently wrong.

Fig. 31. In order to repreſent this according to the new method, it was neceſſary to find the centers and diſtance, both of the vaniſhing line, and picture, by continuing the two ſides of the lower plinth till they met in a point, (as here in C,) and then drawing C, *D*, parallel to the ground line: Thus, C, D, becomes the vaniſhing line of the oblique plane, which the lower baſe forms by being raiſed, and C, its center.

N. B. *This line is always to be uſed for objects obliquely ſituated, as the horizontal line is uſed for objects on that plane.*

The point of diſtance *D*, of this vaniſhing line, was alſo found, by drawing a line through the diagonal of the ſquare of this plinth, from the angle 3, to the vaniſhing line C, *D*. *Thus far, from* Pozzo's *book, for otherwiſe, theſe are circumſtances always given.*

Theſe points being found, half the meaſure of *Pozzo*'s was taken, and ſo the ſame proportions were preſerved.

The reſt is all performed as before explained; but the ſituation of the objects being new, a more particular detail may be uſeful, and will ſhew the univerſality of the principles.

As the center of the picture, found, by a line, perpendicular to it, from the ſpectator's eye, is that point to which all original lines, perpendicular to the picture, tend; ſo every vaniſhing point being found by ſome line from the eye of the ſpectator to the picture, is alſo the vaniſhing point of all other lines parallel to that; and every line from the ſpectator's eye cutting the picture, (or plane of the picture how far ſoever extended,) makes ſuch a vaniſhing point; thus C is the vaniſhing point of the line 1, 2, and of all original lines parallel to it.

S, D, is the horizontal line, found by making the angle *D*, C, D, equal to that which the plinth makes with the ground, and deſcribing an arc from *D*, to D, with an opening of the compaſſes, or radius, equal to C, *D*, (the diſtance before found,) and drawing D, S, parallel to *D*, C; then drawing through C, a line perpendicular to *D*, C, cutting D, S, in S, that point S, becomes the center of the picture, and D, S, the diſtance of it.——D, C, is the diſtance of the vaniſhing

2 point

Plate X.

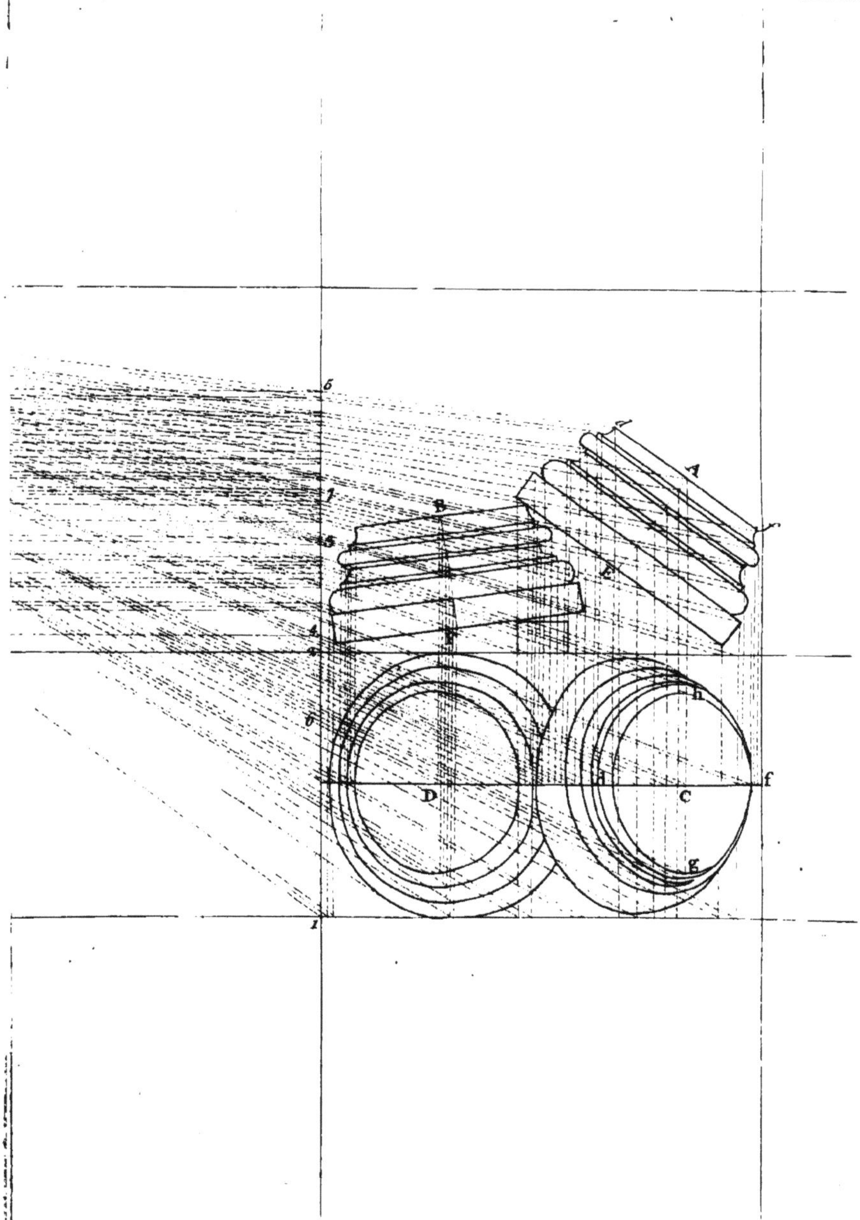

point C, and of the vaniſhing line *D*, C; and D, is to be conſidered as the eye of the ſpectator; therefore (if D, C, finds the vaniſhing point C,) a line from D, perpendicular to D, C, muſt find the vaniſhing point of lines perpendicular to 1, 2, as D, *d*, finds *d*, cutting C, S, *b*, beyond the limits of the paper, which will be the vaniſhing point of the line 1, 3; and all others parallel to it, as are thoſe at all the angles of this plinth, which muſt therefore be drawn to *d*, as the line D, *d*, cuts the line C, S, beyond the limits of the picture; but it is not neceſſary to ſtop here to explain the manner of drawing lines to an inacceſſible point, (which is done in the fourth part:) then, for the thickneſs of this plinth, draw a line through 1, parallel to C, S, (which is the vaniſhing line of the planes 1, 2, 3, and 4, 5, 7,) for that point 1, is ſuppoſed to touch the picture, (where all objects are of their true, or geometrical ſize,) and on that line, from 1, downwards, mark the geometrical thickneſs of the plinth, and having tranſpoſed the diſtance of the vaniſhing point *d*, from D, to d*d*, draw a line from d*d*, to the point marked, which will cut 1, *d*, in the point 3; this determines the thickneſs of the plinth, by which it may be completed. The reſt of the members are determined exactly in the ſame manner, as if the baſe was on the horizontal plane, uſing C, *D*, the vaniſhing line, as an horizontal line.—The heights, and breadths of the circles are determined in ſquares, as hath been taught in the firſt part, and the circles drawn through the eight points there ſpecified.

For the other baſe, draw firſt the pricked line 3, S, which marks the ground or horizontal plane, perpendicularly under 3, k, C; then ſet off from 3, to *f*, the geometrical diſtance, that the angle of the other plinth is from the point 3, and from D, draw a line to *f*, cutting S, 3, in 4, and that interſection will be the point ſought, in which this plinth touches the ground; and having drawn D, *b*, making the angle S, D, *b*, equal to that which this plinth makes with the ground, *(i. e.)* 38 degrees, *b*, is the vaniſhing point of the line 4, 5, and its parallels; therefore draw *b*, 4, 5; then to find the length of that line, make uſe of the parallel to the vaniſhing line C, S, before drawn, *viz.* 1, 3, e,

by

by drawing first a line from d*b*, (the distance of D, *b*,) through 4, to that line, cutting it in e; and from e, upwards, mark the geometrical length to g, and from g, draw back again to d*b*, which gives the perspective length of 4, 5; from which points 4, and 5, parallels to the ground line are drawn; and the length of the parallel at 4, is found by drawing a line from S, to the point 6, cutting that parallel, and drawing a line from *b*, through this last intersection, it will cut the parallel 5, 8, in 8, and so complete the bottom, or lower square of the plinth.

Or this square may be determined (without making use of the line 1, 3, e,) by first finding the length of the parallel at 4, as last directed, and then drawing a line through the intersection which marks that length, from D[2], (the distance of the vanishing point *b*,) to the line *b*, 4, cutting it in 5. This line D[2], 5, gives the diagonal of the square, by which it may be completed.

> *N. B.* The distance *b*, D[2], is brought down to D[2], by fixing one foot of the compasses in *b*, and the other in D, and describing an arc, till *b*, D[2], is parallel to the ground line; and so it becomes the vanishing line of the plane, or square of this base.

D, *a*, being drawn perpendicular to D, *b*, finds *a*, the vanishing point of 4, 7, and its parallels; wherefore draw from 4, 5, and 8, to *a*, and having found the perspective height of any one of them, by the same operation as for the other plinth, this is completed. And to find that height, draw a parallel to S, C, *a*, from 4, upwards, and on that mark the proportional height or thickness, which is found by drawing from S, through 4, to 4, the ground line, making another parallel, as 3, 1, there, of the geometrical height, and from 1, the top of that, a line drawn back to the same point, S, will cut the parallel drawn from 4, in the true proportion. Now, from d a, (the distance of *a*,) draw a line to this last intersection, cutting 4, 7, in 7, and from *b*, through 7, a line cutting 5, *a*, and from that intersection, a parallel to 5, 8, by which the plinth is completed. The other members are determined, as those of the first base.

Or

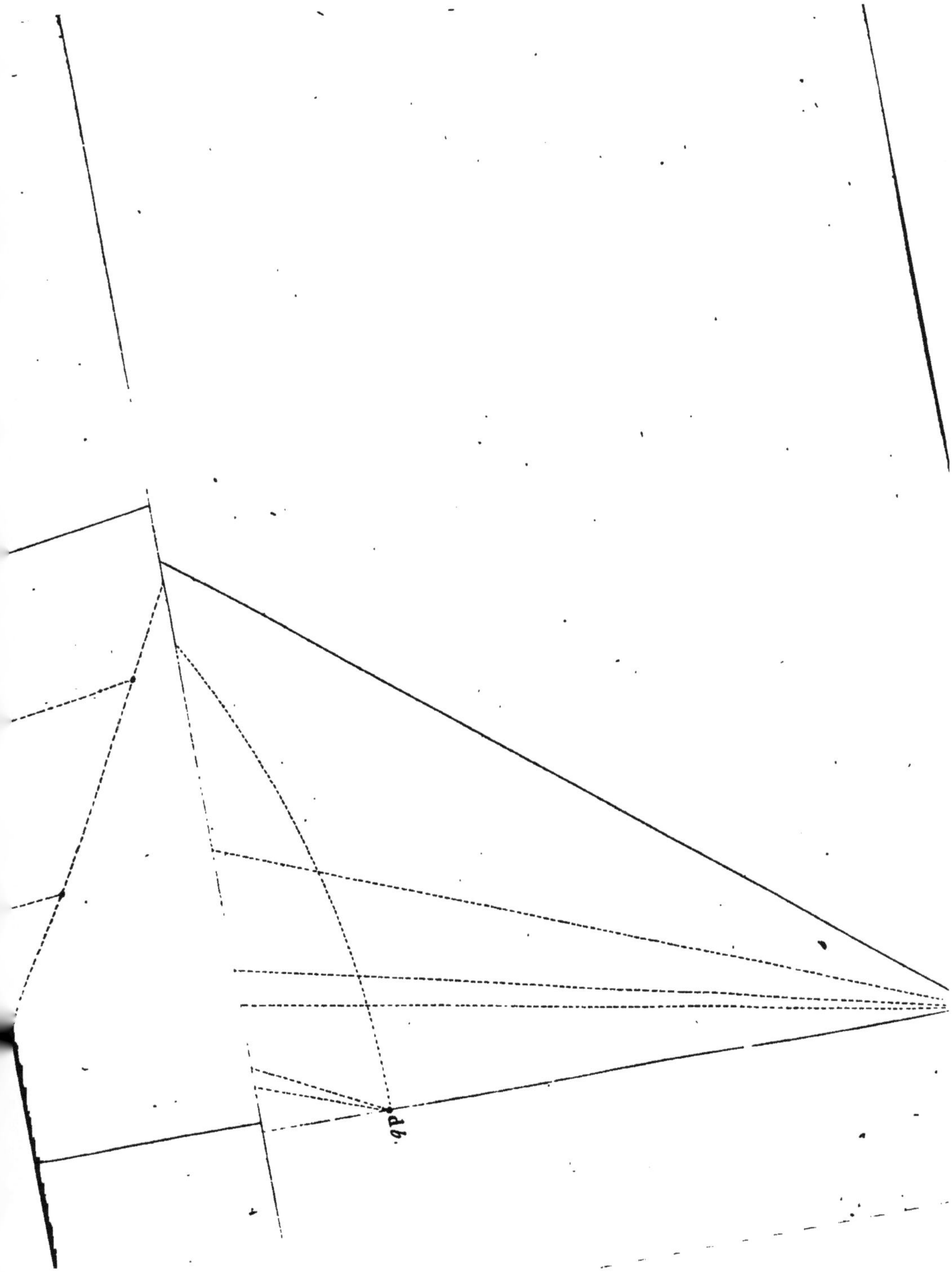

Or (omitting the parallel to S, C, *a*, drawn from 4,) continue the line 3, 1, upwards, and then produce the line *b*, 4, till it cuts that line (3, 1, continued) as at 9, and there mark the true geometrical height 9, 10, and draw *b*, 10, which will cut the line 4, *a*, in 7, and so finish the base. By this, the trouble of finding the proportional height at 4, is saved.

That the whole operation may be more easily comprehended, it is again represented apart from the picture, in pricked lines, drawn from the same points, and marked by the same numerical figures.

This explanation is lengthened by the necessity of shewing how the scheme was prepared from *Pozzo*, the intention being to represent these bases exactly in the same situation, as he had placed them; for otherwise, (*i. e.* without any reference to him,) the description would have been more simple; it is also very minutely particular, that nothing material might be left unexplained, it having been said at the beginning, that these things should be referred to the occasions that might require them, in order to avoid unnecessary definitions, &c. Though this method is less regular, yet it is much more easy, because the explanation attends the use.

Those who may not readily comprehend every particular, at the first reading, are advised to draw, in perspective, the two plinths only, in these, or the like situations, and to place them at such angles with the ground, that all the vanishing points may fall within the limits of the picture.——By this disposition, they will better see the reason of every operation; and the next figure is added to assist them in it.

Fig. 32. Here the vanishing points are all within the paper, and nothing completed but the two plinths, the lower of which is raised higher from the ground than in the preceding example, not only to bring the vanishing point *d*, within compass, but also to shew, evidently, that the lines 1, 3, and 6, 9, cannot possibly be perpendiculars to the ground line, nor parallel to each other (as they are in *Pozzo*) when the base does not lie flat on the horizontal plane.

In

In this scheme 3, 6, touches the ground line; and is therefore the true geometrical length. C, *D*, is the vanishing line of the oblique plane, to which the base is raised, or on which it may be supposed to lie. The lower square is therefore projected by means of C, the center of that vanishing line, and *D*, its distance; as readily as, if it was on the horizontal plane, it would be, by means of S, and D, the center and distance of that plane.

Now draw from *d*, (found as in the foregoing example) through 3, and 6; then raise a perpendicular from either of them, as here from 6, on which mark the geometrical height, or thickness of the plinth, at e, and having set off the distance *d*, D, to d*d*, from thence draw through e, which will cut *d*, 6, in 9, and 6, 9, will be the perspective height; from 9, draw a parallel which will determine the point 1, and so complete the plinth, by drawing 1, C, and 9, C, and from *d*, draw through the other two angles of the lower square, meeting 1, C, and 9, C. It is needless, here, to repeat what was before said of the other plinth in the last scheme.

The circles which are here barely traced, are done in the manner explained at the beginning, just as if they were on the horizontal plane.

It is apparent how much work is saved by this method; neither geometrical plan, nor profile are necessary, if the measures are but known; and if not, the plan and profile, in their common geometrical situation, will answer the purpose of the most oblique positions; so that a printed book of the several orders may be referred to, without the trouble of drawing the particular parts that may be occasionally wanted.

Fig. 33. A figure in *A. Bosse*'s perspective, for the representation of which, he makes use of several schemes. First, that at No. 1, where m, e,—n, a, is, by him, designed for the profile of the seat of the object: z, e, is the inclination of the picture: o, the spectator's eye: a, his station, or feet: o, z, the distance: o, a, height of the eye. If (says he) the object be only a plan, as b, c, d, on the geometrical squares at No. 2, find those several points in the corresponding perspec-

Plate XII.

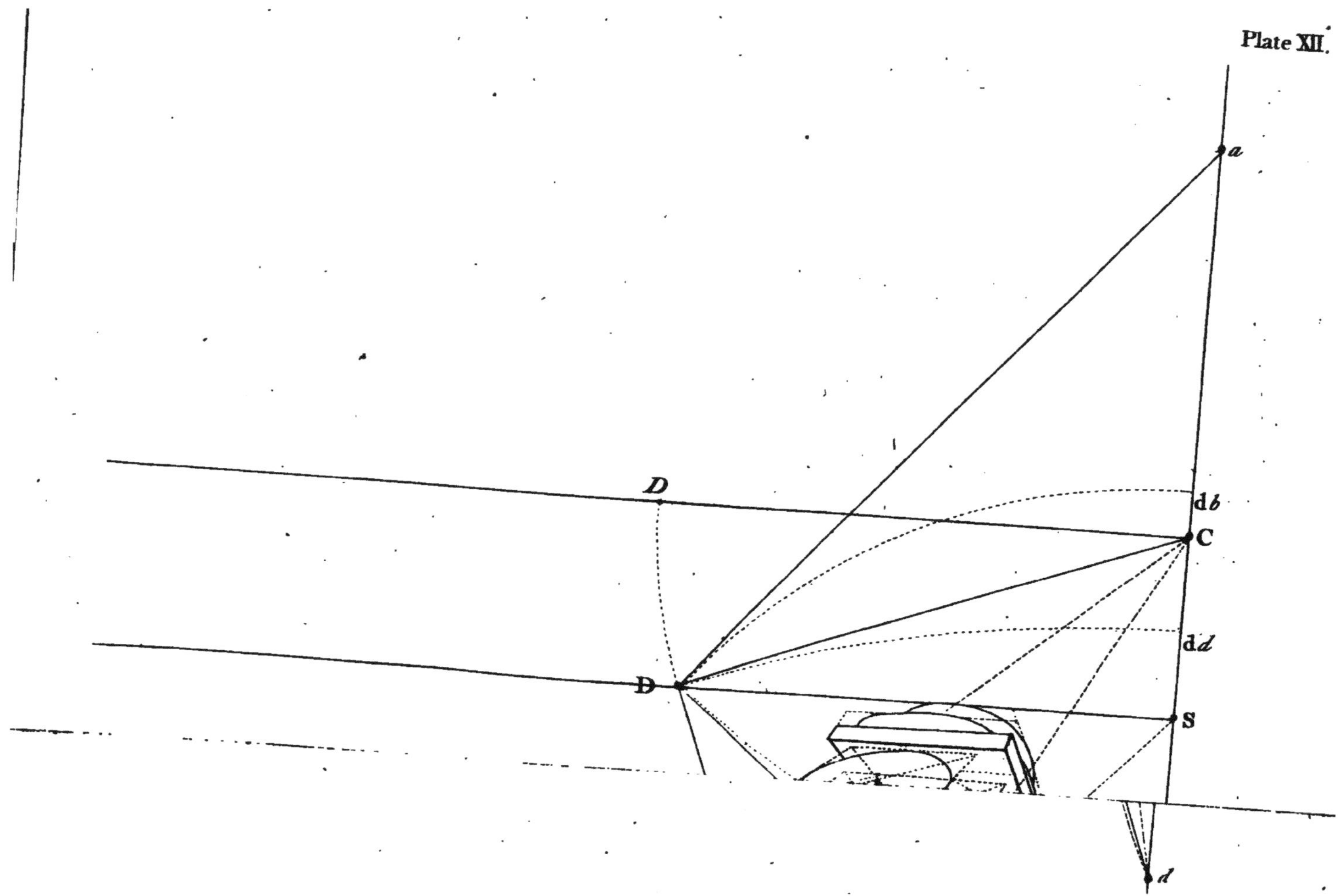

tive squares below at No. 3. (as has been taught before at Figure 25.) But if the object be above the plane of the seat, as the Fig. f, r, s, (in the said geometrical squares, No. 2.) then by means of the elevations b, f,—c, r,—d, s, perpendicular to the seat b, c, d, draw those elevations parallel to q, u, and from the ends of them b, c, d, drop perpendiculars b, 1,—c, 2,—d, 6; and from their other ends f, r, s, draw f, 1,—r, 2,—s, 6, making (with them) angles b, f, 1,—c, r, 2,—d, s, 6, equal to n, o, a, above at No. 1, and draw 1, 2,—1, 6,—2, 6, you will have another seat 1, 2, 6, and other elevations f, 1,—r, 2,—s, 6. Then find below, at No. 3, the perspective 1, 2, 6, of this other seat, as B, D, C, was found, and make the perpendiculars 1, F, 2, R, 6, S, in proportion to their respective plans; that is, on the perspective chequer take the same measures along the several parallels of 1, 6, and 2, as they have above in the geometrical chequer; then join F, R, F, S, R, S, by this means you will complete the perspective of f, r, s; and, lastly, join F, B, S, D, and R, C, which finish the whole prism.

Fig. 34. Now, in order to represent the same object in the same situation, nothing more is necessary than to describe, either geometrically, or in words, the form and situation of the object, or to give one side of it, whose form and situation are known, or described, and require the rest; as here, let E, F, be given, it is required to represent a triangular prism, whose base is similar to the triangle *D*, *f*, g, (above this Fig. 34,) and whose height is in proportion to the side *D*, *f*, of that triangle, and on a picture inclined to the plane of the seat in the angle o, a, n, Fig. 33, No. 1. The picture is as *Bosse*'s.

Continue E, F, Fig. 34, till it cuts the vanishing line [C, D, Z, X,] as in i, which will be its vanishing point; then from C, raise C, *D*, equal to C, D, or [Z, X,] the distance given; draw i, *D*, and at *D*, make the given triangle *f*, *D*, g, continue *D*, g, to the vanishing line, which finds k, the vanishing point of E, G; therefore, draw k, E; then in order to find the length E, G, which is geometrically equal to E, F, bring down the distance i, *D*, to the vanishing line at d, draw E, b, parallel to the vanishing line, and draw d, F, which

E will

will cut E, b, in b; then is E, b, the geometrical length ſought, which ſet off from E, to a; bring down (in like manner) k, *D*, to e, and draw e, a, which cuts E, k, in G; then draw G, F, which finiſhes the baſe.

And in order to complete the priſm in this ſituation, having deſcribed the arc D, *d*, with the radius C, D, draw C, *d*, ſo as to make the angle D, C, *d*, equal to the inclination of the original plane, with a plane perpendicular to the picture; that is, to the angle z, o, S, (Fig. 33, No. 1;) and cutting the arc D, *d*, in *d*, draw *d*, S, parallel to D, C; then S, will be the center of the picture, and the angle C, *d*, S, equal to D, C, *d*; draw *d*, N, perpendicular to C, *d*, cutting C, S, (continued) in N, below, which will be the vaniſhing point of lines perpendicular to the original plane; ſo that drawing from N, through the points G, E, and F, the lines G, H, E, I, and F, K, are got. And to determine their lengths, the diſtance N, *d*, is ſet off on C, S, at N[a]; and E, *l*, being made parallel to S, C, and equal to E, b, (the geometrical height) draw N[a], *l*, which cuts E, I, in I, the length ſought; whence drawing to i, and k, the points H, and K, are determined, which, on joining H, K, completes the whole figure.

> *N. B.* Leſt the reader ſhould not readily conceive the reaſon of this operation, there are repreſented on the profile of *Boſſe's* figure, No. 1, the lines made uſe of in this; for inſtance, S, is there the center of the picture (as formerly explained;) and *o*, S, properly the diſtance of the picture, *e*, *y*, (being parallel to o, S,) repreſents the profile of the plane, perpendicular to the picture; and e, h, being the original plane, on which the object is placed, *h*, *e*, *y*, is the angle of inclination of theſe two planes, equal to z, o, S, in the ſame ſcheme, which is ſuppoſed to be given for working the problem; and is the ſame angle as D, C, *d*, and S, *d*, C, in the picture, Fig. 34.

Though

Though the work is ſimple and ſhort, the text may appear ſomewhat long; but that is only becauſe the reaſons of the operation are taught, and becauſe every particular is explained in the moſt familiar manner for the ſake of learners.

It might have been remarked before, that this method of *Boſſe* is exceedingly operoſe, and very uncertain; for in order to tranſpoſe the ſeveral points from the ſmall geometrical chequer to the larger perſpective ſquares, the rays Z, B, 1, 8, (Fig. 33.) Z, D, 6, and Z, C, 2, ſhould be drawn, and theſe croſſed by lines from the point of diſtance X, to find each point, as Z, 8, and X, 7, are neceſſary to find the point 1, only, (the diſtance 8, 7, being the geometrical depth or diſtance of the point 1, from the ground line;) unleſs there were ſo many ſquares in the geometrical plan as to croſs every point, which would not only be exceſſively tedious to perform, both there, and in the perſpective, (where all muſt be repeated;) but the multitude of lines would neceſſarily produce confuſion; and if the operation be performed without theſe lines, then the ſeveral places of the points in the perſpective plan can only be gueſſed, by inſpection of thoſe in the geometrical plan; and whatever is done by gueſs muſt be uncertain. Whereas, in the new method, there is not a line, or point, neceſſary, more than are here exhibited, and no poſſibility of miſtake, or occaſion of uncertainty, becauſe the lines form the figure of themſelves.

Fig. 35. In this figure, which is alſo *Boſſe*'s own, he propoſes to repreſent the priſm F, S, R, P, O, G, on a picture, whoſe profile z, e, above, inclines forward, (as the laſt did backwards:) the profile of the original plane is n, a, m, e; the whole operation is the ſame as his laſt, except that the pricked lines in his geometrical plan, on the chequer, which in the former were drawn downwards, are here drawn upwards, on account of the different kind of inclination: the correſpondence of the perſpective plan with the geometrical, is evident, therefore needs no farther explication.

Only it may be remarked, to what a confuſed ſcheme he was reduced, by his limited principles.

Fig. 36. And how ſimple and eaſy the other figure appears, which repreſents the ſame object, and is performed by exactly the ſame operation as Fig. 34, with this only difference, that *D*, N[a], runs upwards; whereas *d*, N, in the other, runs downwards, on account of the different inclination of the object at 34, and 36, (N, in 34, and N[a], in 36, are the vaniſhing points of lines perpendicular to the original planes of their reſpective objects;) and that *this* may, if poſſible, be more eaſily conceived, the points S, N, and S, N[a], are marked with the ſame letters in the geometrical ſchemes, Fig. 33, No. 1, and Fig. 35, No. 1. It is true *Boſſe* confines himſelf to the compaſs of his picture, and undertakes to repreſent all objects by means of lines terminating within it. This is very well, if it be always the ſhorteſt, and ſureſt way; but if there are caſes which require more room; that is, if ſome objects can be repreſented with greater certainty, by taking more ſpace, or on a ſmaller ſcale, and can then be transferred by the picture; and all this done in leſs than a quarter of the time, that would be neceſſary to produce them by his method; where is the advantage of confining the operation always to the picture? Beſides, the ſcheme formed to be transferred, remains, and may be very uſeful another time. Though this object, however, might have been repreſented by an operation within the picture (with the addition of a few more lines,) on the new principles, *as ſhall be ſhewn hereafter.* To all which may be added, that this very figure of *Boſſe's* is falſe, though very neatly engraved by his own hand, which muſt be owing to what was hinted before, *viz.* that his method requires ſo much gueſſing, as to make it almoſt impoſſible not to fall into ſome error from thence. And if, to avoid theſe errors, a greater number of lines ſtill are drawn, in order to aſcertain every point, the confuſion would be ſo much increaſed, that it would itſelf become a new cauſe of miſtake.

His error is in placing O, higher than P, G, in Fig. 35, as by the pricked lines; and ſo repreſenting P, O, G, as above the eye, (and ſeen on the under part) which cannot poſſibly be, while it is below Z, X, the vaniſhing line. This will appear on inſpecting his own geometrical profile, Fig. 35, No. 1, where, o, z, repreſents Z, X,

(Fig.

Plate XIII.

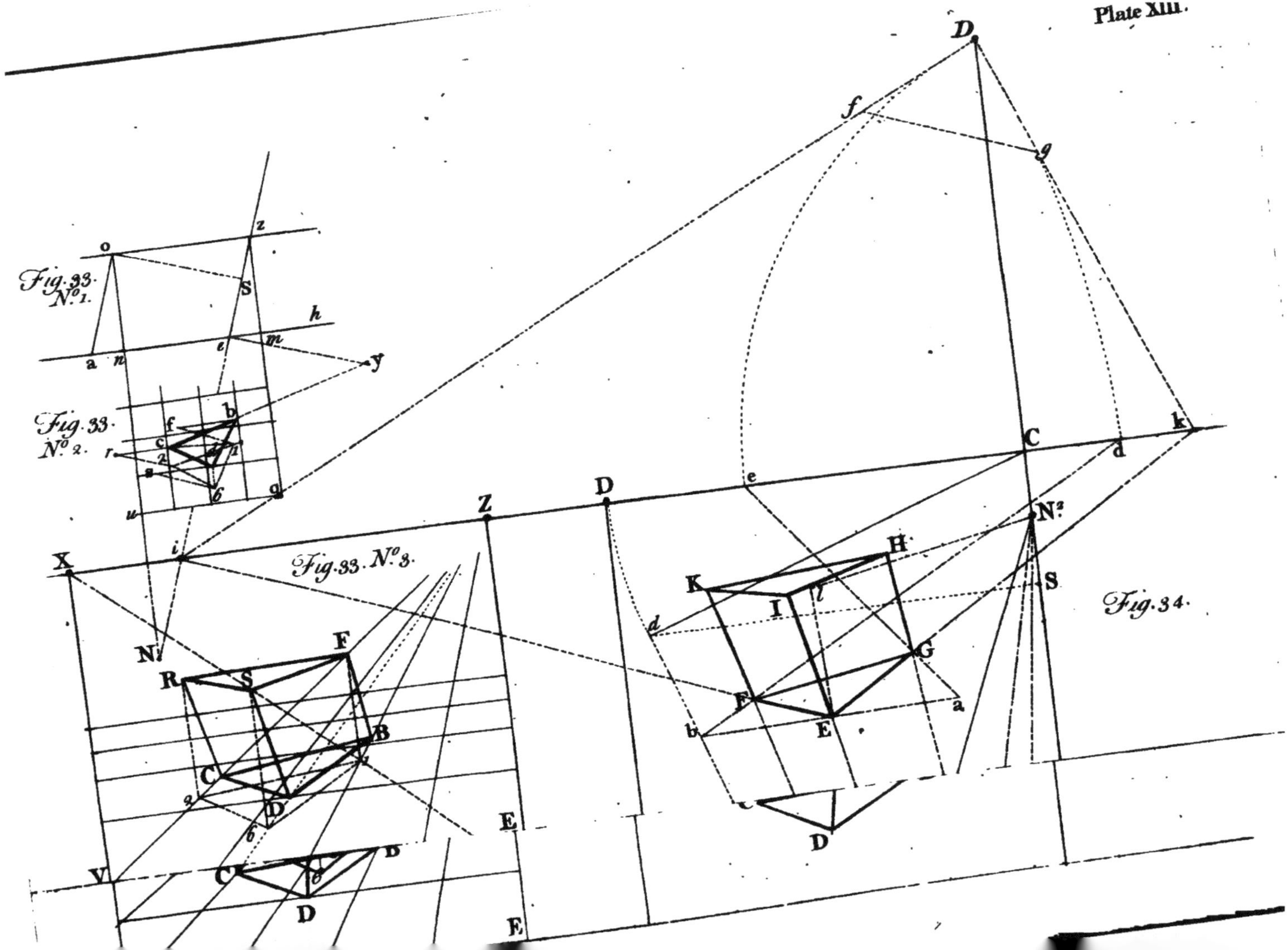

(Fig. 35, No. 3.) and ſhews that if P, O, G, was even with that line, it would be reduced to a ſingle line, and muſt be repreſented by it; that if it were ever ſo little under that line, as at 3, 4, (Fig. 35, No. 1.) then 4 would be ſeen (by the eye at o) higher on the picture z, e, than 3, which is nearer; and laſtly, that if it was above the line Z, X, Fig. 35, No. 3. (and not otherwiſe) the object would be ſeen as 1, 2, Fig. 35, No. 1. (*i. e.*) 2, would be ſeen lower than 1, which is nearer: thus he has falſly repreſented P, O, G, *being below the line* Z, X, having given it the ſame appearance as that in which it is truly exhibited, p, o, g, Fig. 36, where it is *above* the line C, D, which is the ſame with the line Z, X, Fig. 35. P, O, G, Fig. 36. is alſo a true repreſentation of the figure as it ſhould have been given by *Boſſe*.

Fig. 37. Here is added another figure of *Boſſe*, being a cube reſting on one of the ſolid angles, for which (by way of preparation) the geometrical ſcheme *above* is by him given, but not ſufficiently explained. Some lines therefore are added to render it more intelligible; 1ſt, the ſquare g, n, o, p, is made, then the diagonal n, p, drawn, which is transferred by the pricked arch p, b, to the point b, in the line n, g, and the line b, a, drawn parallel and equal to g, p, and then n, a, is drawn, and b, 7, perpendicular to, n, a, cutting it in 7, and from b, as a center, with the interval, or radius, b, 7, a circle is deſcribed, in which two regular equilateral triangles 1, 3, 5, and 2, 4, 6, are inſcribed; thus b, n, o, a, repreſents, geometrically, the cube ſtanding on the point n, b, n, and a, o, being profiles of two oppoſite faces ſeen anglewiſe; *(that is, repreſenting diagonals of the cube,)* b, a, and n, o, of two other faces ſeen laterally; b, 7, and o, 8, two ſemidiameters (together) equal to *l*, m, or (1, 4;) n, a, is the axis, to which are added the double line *l*, n, m, and the two perpendiculars b, *l*, and o, m; *l*, n, m, repreſents the profile or ſection of the ground or plane on which the cube is ſuppoſed to reſt, as on the point n; and n, b, (being equal to n, p, the diagonal of a face) is the profile of the face B, P, C, F, (repreſented below;) B, repreſenting n, and *l*, b, (equal to 7, n,) is the perpendicular height of the point b, in the geometrical ſcheme repreſented by C, 1, 3, G, and 5, H, in the perſpective; as o, m, equal to 7, a,

or

or 8, n, the perpendicular height of the most distant point, and two others represented by 4, I,—2, P, and 6, F, in the perspective; for n, a, is the greatest height, being the axis of the cube, represented in the perspective, by A, B; and these three are all the perspective heights.

The manner of performing the perspective, according to *Bosse*, has been before explained; and it is to be carefully remarked, that, in order to find these perspective perpendiculars, the measure must be first taken with the compasses, above, on the geometrical; the compasses thus open must be applied to that chequer, to see how many squares, and parts it contains, and then the same proportion must be taken along the parallel squares of the perspective, even with that point in the perspective plan, from which the perpendicular is required. For instance, to find the point c, in the perspective, take the measure *l*, b, with the compasses, apply them to the geometrical squares, where it appears, that this line *l*, b, is equal to r, s, in the geometrical chequer *(i. e.)* two squares, and a part of another; then from the point 1, in the perspective measure, take two squares and such part from 1, to 10, and make 1, c, equal to it, by applying the compasses, thus open, from 1, perpendicularly to C, and so for every height.

Fig. 38. No. 1. Is the same cube by the method so often explained; and here it is only necessary to require that a cube be represented perpendicularly on its axis, and after the center, and distance of the picture are given, to give, also, the point B, the pole of the axis, on which it stands: C, D, is the distance, wherefore make the angle C, D, W, equal to b, n, *l*, (Fig. 37, No. 1.) the inclination of the nearest face of the cube (b, n,) with the ground, n, *l*, and draw D, O, perpendicular to D, W; then draw B, O, and from B, draw B, i, parallel to D, O, and (in order to find the proportional length of B, i,) draw B, z, parallel to C, D; then make r, t, on the ground line, equal (geometrically) to a side of the cube, and draw t, Z, cutting z, B, in y; then y, z, is the proportional length, at B, which set off from B, to, i; now draw D, i, cutting B, O, in I, then B, I, is one line determined. Fix one foot of the compasses in W, and with the other, set off the distance W, D, to *D*, and also the same distance on each side of W, towards a, a, and b, which will be the vanishing points for the sides of the nearest (or front) face of the cube B, P, C, F, and its opposite face A, G, I, H; draw a, B, P, and b, B, F, and B, *f*, parallel to *D*, b, make B, *f*, equal to B, i, draw *D*, *f*, cutting B, F, in F, draw B, p, parallel to *D*, a, and equal to B, i, and draw *D*, p, cutting B, P, in P; draw a, F, and b, P, meeting in C, then B, P, C, F, will be one face determined; draw C, O, F, O, and P, O, and a, I, cutting P, O, in G, and b, I, cutting F, O, in H, and draw a, H, and b, G, meeting in A, which completes the whole cube.

Fig. 38. No. 2. The only difference between the operations to produce this figure, and the last, is, that here instead of finding B, I, B, P, and B, F, the diagonal B, C, is found, by drawing from W, its vanishing point, through B, and the length of it, by drawing B, c, parallel to D, W, and equal to the geometrical length of the diagonal *n*, *p*, (for this cube is supposed to stand on the ground line, and not within, as No. 1.) and drawing D, c, cutting W, B, in C.—Besides which, the length of B, I, is also found as before, so that this whole representation of the cube will be produced, by finding the length of two lines only, and these determine the lengths of all the rest, by means of the same vanishing points that served for the other. And in the same manner, many other cubes might be represented by the points already found.

> *N. B.* The length of this diagonal B, C, No. 2, as well as of the line B, I, in both the cubes, might be found by other ways, which are sufficiently explained elsewhere; however, to give an instance, as W, D, is set off to *D*, the line B, c, might have been drawn parallel to W, *D*, and then drawing from *D*, through c, would find the point C; for it is shewn, in the beginning of this treatise, that the truth of these things depends on the parallelism of the original line with its line of distance, and not on their direction.

And at No. 1, if the distance O, D, had been turned up on the point O, till that line became parallel to C, D, then B, i, might have been also drawn parallel to C, D, and if a, *D*, had been turned down

on

on the point a, and b, *D*, on the point b, both to the line a, W, b, then B, p, and B, *f*, might alſo have been drawn parallel to C, D.

Fig. 39. Is alſo from *Boſſe*; the geometrical is above, which needs no explication:——And for the perſpective (according to him) the horizontal plane in the picture muſt be chequered, perſpectively, by means of the point of ſight, or center of the picture X, and diſtance Z, the ground line E, V, being divided into ſix equal parts by the numerical figures, above that line, for feet, correſponding to the ſame number in the geometrical; then the line o, X, below, in the perſpective, which is the ſeat of the line 3, a, muſt be divided perſpectively (to repreſent the geometrical lines above, o, 9,) and marked with the ſame figures from o, to 9, incluſive: to effect which, ſet it off geometrically on the ground line from o, to V, dividing o, V, by the figures below that line, and from the ſeveral diviſions draw to Z, cutting the line o, X, in 1, 2, 3,—4, 5, 6,—7, 8, 9. Then from each of thoſe diviſions erect perpendiculars, which muſt be made (perſpectively) equal to their correſpondent perpendiculars in the geometrical ſcheme above; for inſtance, the perpendicular 9, above, being taken by the compaſſes, and one foot ſet on E, V, at E, the other foot reaches to the middle of the ſquare between 4, and 5, *(i. e.)* four feet and a half; wherefore, on the parallel at 9, in the perſpective line o, X, take $4\frac{1}{2}$ feet, and at 9, turn the compaſſes up, with that opening, perpendicularly over 9, which reaches to *a*, and determines the length of the line 3, *a*, and 3, touching the ground, its place is thereby determined; ſo that drawing *a*, 3, finds that line, and the perpendicular at 7, is found in the ſame manner, *(i. e.)* by taking its meaſure from the geometrical above, which applied to E, V, appears to be 5 feet $\frac{1}{4}$; and then on the parallel 7, in the perſpective, taking $5\frac{1}{4}$, and turning up the compaſſes (as before) the point b, is found; and thus is found the point c, below; then by joining c, b,—b, a,—and 3, c, one ſide of the beam *a*, *b*, *c*, 3, is found; then from b, and c, and alſo from 1, in the perſpective line o, x, draw parallels towards E, Z, and from the parallel of the laſt, raiſe a perpendicular to e, and draw e, *f*, and raiſe another perpendicular from the parallel of 7, *(i. e.)* at k, (in the

 line

Plate XIIII.

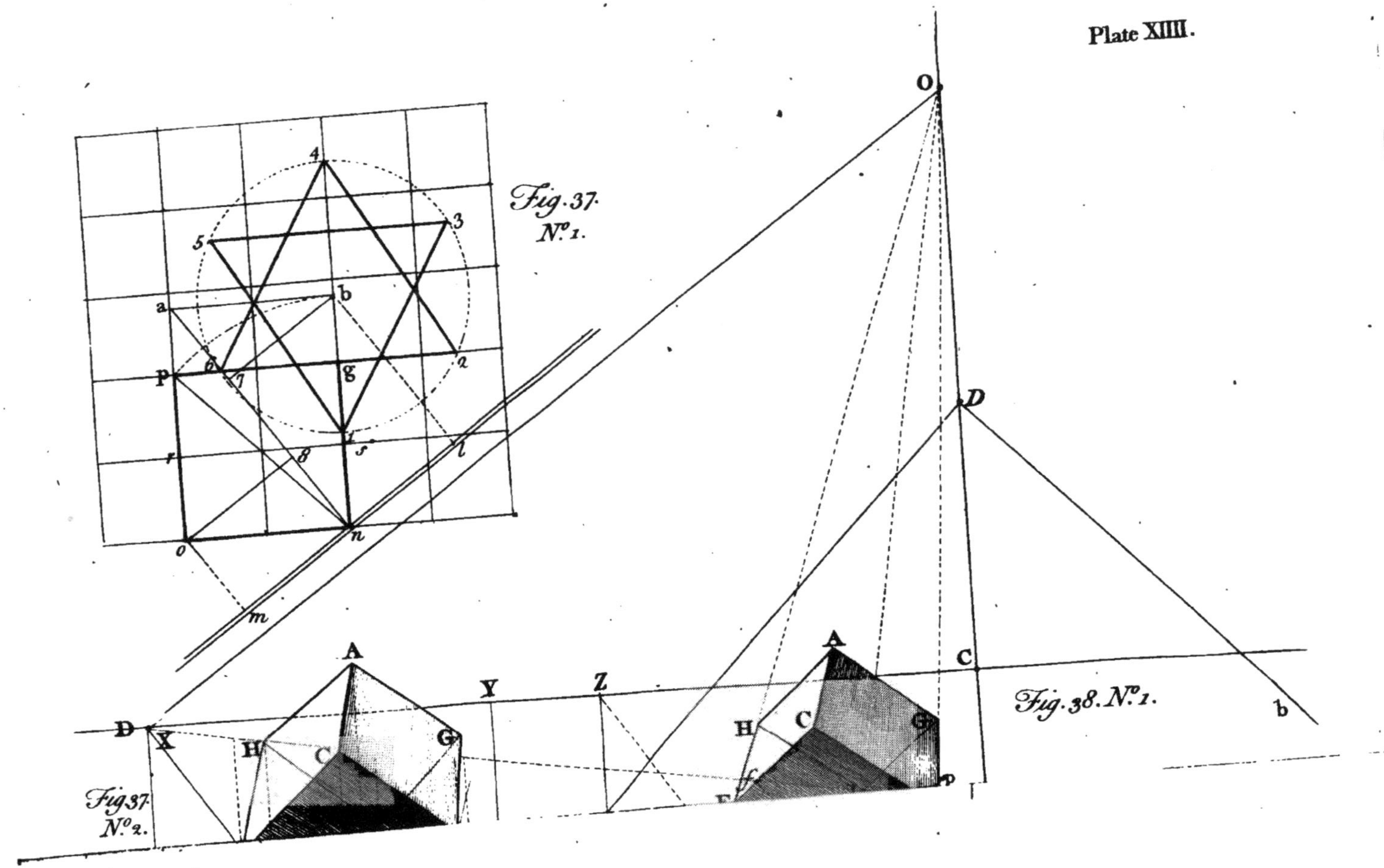

Fig. 37. Nº. 1.

Fig. 37. Nº. 2.

Fig. 38. Nº. 1.

line E, *f*, X,) equal to 7, *b*, which finds the point g; draw e, g, which completes this beam: the parallels, found on this, being continued, will ſerve for thoſe of the other beam, and with correſpondent perpendiculars, it may be completed.——Then for the croſs bar, perpendiculars from 4, 5, and 6, in the perſpective line o, X, reſpectively meaſured, firſt in the geometrical, then on the perſpective parallels, will find all the points neceſſary, by which the whole is completed.

Fig. 40. Is the ſame object repreſented by the method herein propoſed. Let the geometrical be either drawn as above, or only the form, and meaſures given in words, with the poſition, in conſequence of which, draw h, i, (or any other known, or given line); and having found S, the center of the picture, and D, the diſtance, by means of the terms given, ſet off the ſame diſtance, upwards, from S, to d, and downwards from S, to b, then the angle d, D, b, will be a right angle, and the angles S, D, d,—S, D, b, each of them 45 degrees, as will alſo the angles D, b, S, and D, d, S, which is the angle of inclination of the original object with the ground, (as well as with the perpendicular 9, 10, in the geometrical above) wherefore d, is the vaniſhing point for i, k, and all its parallels, and b, for *l*, i, and all its parallels. Draw m, p, on the ſame line as h, i, equal to it, and at the diſtance given, from it; then draw i, d,—h, d,—m, d,—and p, d, all to the ſame point d. And for the length of them, firſt draw from D, through m, to M, in the ground line, then draw M, a, (which is to be conſidered as an original line) parallel to D, d, and equal to the geometrical length of the originals, which are all equal. Now divide M, a, as 3, 10, (the original above) is divided, (*i. e.*) in z, and q, and draw z, D,—q, D, and a, D, cutting m, d, in Z, Q, and n, which will be the perſpective points anſwering to z, q, and 10, in the geometrical. Through Z, and Q, draw from b, two lines Z, r, and Q, s, and then cut theſe laſt lines from the perſpective diviſions of 4, m, found by like means, (explained a few lines lower); and thus the four points, for the croſs beam, are determined, in the plane 4, m, n.

N. B. o, S, *is the ſeat of* A, d, *on the plane of the horizon, which two lines cut each other in angles of* 45 *degrees perſpectively, as their originals do geometrically.*

For the squares at the bottoms, and tops, draw b, i,—b, h,—b, m, and b, p, also b, k,—b, n; then from g, draw g, h, cutting b, i, in *l*, and g, p, cutting b, m, in 4; drawing also from g, through the divisions of p, m, are got those of 4, m; *for* g, *is the distance of the vanishing point* b, *(equal to* D, b,) *and therefore is the vanishing point of the diagonals* p, 4, *&c. on* b, g, *the vanishing line of the plane* b, *l*, i,—p, 4, m, *and their parallels.* Now draw *l*, d, and 4, d, &c. Lastly, the cross beam is finished, by drawing its parallels, having before found the several points by means of the vanishing points b, and d; and this completes the whole.

Fig. 41. At the end of this treatise of *Bosse* a figure is proposed, which he calls a cage, and which is also inserted in the Jesuit's perspective borrowed from this; and, in both, said to be by the universal method of Mons. *Desargues*. Its excellence consists in this, that by it the object may be projected as large as the picture, by lines and points all within the compass of it;—now, besides that it might be more accurately done apart, and transferred to the picture with much less than one quarter of the work, and in less than one quarter of the time, it may also be done within the same compass, in a shorter, and less complicated way, and with fewer lines, as follows.

The same circumstances, *viz.* shape, size, and particular measures, are given, as are given by *Bosse*, with its situation, height of the horizon, distance, and vanishing points; all which are expressed geometrically on the side, in a small scale from him. The same letters are also used throughout, as many at least as are necessary here, that the two schemes may be more readily compared. Having marked G, the point of sight, or center of the picture, take so much of the true distance as comes conveniently into the picture; for instance one fourth, which is 6 feet (the distance given being 24) set it off from G, to Z, on the horizontal line.

A, B, is the ground line divided into 12 feet, draw A, G, and B, G, and rays to G, from 12, to 7, inclusive.

Now in order to find any point, as M, which is 17 feet within the picture, and 1½ from A, G, towards B, G, as appears by the small geometrical ſcheme above, take from A, towards B, $\frac{1}{4}$ of 17, that is, $4\frac{1}{4}$ feet, and thence draw to Z, cutting A, G, in R, which will be 17 feet within the picture, (for if Z, was 24 feet from G, and 17 feet had been taken from A, towards B, a line drawn from Z, *ſo placed* to 17, would have cut A, G, in the ſame point R, the proportion being exactly the ſame. Then through R, draw a parallel to A, B, and, on that parallel, meaſure 1 foot $\frac{1}{2}$ between 7, and 12, (which is a perſpective ſcale;) transfer that meaſure to R, and ſet it off from R, to M; thus the point M, is found.

K, is 29 feet within the picture, and $7\frac{1}{2}$ behind A, G; therefore from A, towards B, take $\frac{1}{4}$ of 29, which is $7\frac{1}{4}$, and draw from thence to Z, cutting A, G, in e, which will be 29 feet within;—through e, draw a parallel, and on that parallel meaſure 7 feet $\frac{1}{2}$, which meaſure carry to e, and ſet it off to K;—then for L, which is 26 feet deep, draw from $6\frac{1}{2}$ (on A, B,) being one quarter of 26, to Z, which finds a point in A, G, 26 feet within; and on the parallel drawn through that point, ſet off 13 feet $\frac{1}{2}$, being its diſtance from A, G, meaſured as before; that is, on this parallel take the whole line from e, to its interſection with G, B, which is 12 feet, and add $1\frac{1}{2}$ of the ſame meaſure, which will determine the point L.

In like manner for the point I, which is 38 feet within, draw from $9\frac{1}{2}$, the middle point between 9, and 10, to Z, which will cut A, G, 38 feet deep, and from this laſt interſection ſet off on the parallel in which it lies $4\frac{1}{2}$ perſpectively, as before for the others; join M, K,—M, L,—L, I, and I, K, which completes the lower ſquare of the cage.

The perpendicular ſides are all 17 feet high, wherefore take 8 feet $\frac{1}{2}$, (the half of 17) on the *parallel of each point*, M, K, L, and I, and doubling them over each point, reſpectively, the four corners, above, are determined, and by a like means the apex is found; *(i. e.)* after having drawn the diagonals of both ſquares, draw an indefinite perpendicular through both centers upwards; then take, on the parallel of the center of the lower ſquare, 13 feet $\frac{1}{4}$, being the height of the apex, above the upper ſquare, and mark it on the perpendicular drawn, to which draw lines from the four corners, this completes the whole object.—The work is apparently less than his, for besides that he makes use of a double operation for three of the four angles, merely to find their depth, which are found here by a single one, and all the four by the same method; this double series of numerical figures, which in his method is necessary, is apt to confound, and it requires much time, and great care, to divide the lower series with exactness, which is wholly unnecessary in the method here used.

Fig. 42. In the second Volume of *Pozzo*, Plate 9, these eight pilasters placed circularly are represented by his shorter method, which has been before sufficiently explained. The lines are all left, that the quantity of work may be seen, and none are drawn, but such as are necessary, those tending to O, are drawn only on one side of B;—because the other side exactly corresponds; so that having placed one foot of the compasses on the point B, the other is to be extended to the several divisions, and to be transferred each twice, that is, on both sides of the point C, as the objects are placed at equal distances from it on either side; for instance, B, 1, is set off from C, both ways, and so of the rest.

Fig. 43. The same subject according to the new method. And here the double circle is first made perspectively, as has been taught, then at the point of distance $D^{\frac{1}{2}}$, a geometrical double circle is drawn with one square, A, B, in its plane, as a plan of one pilaster, and $D^{\frac{1}{2}}$, A, $D^{\frac{1}{2}}$, B, drawn, which find a, and b, on the vanishing, or horizontal line; these would be the true vanishing points, if $D^{\frac{1}{2}}$, was the true distance, but it being only half, the distance C, a, is doubled to a^2, and C, b, to b^2, which become the vanishing points, (for the triangle C, $D^{\frac{1}{2}}$, a, being half of, and similar to, what the true distance would produce, c, a^2, is the base of that triangle); wherefore drawing a^2, S, and b^2, S, the perspective plans of the pilasters 1, and 5, are found, and setting off the same measures from C, on the other side, and thence drawing through S, as before, the plans of 4, and 8, two more of the pilasters, are also found; but there not being room for the vanishing points of E, F, the next pilaster in the geometrical plan, (which would complete the whole) another operation becomes necessary,

Plate XV.

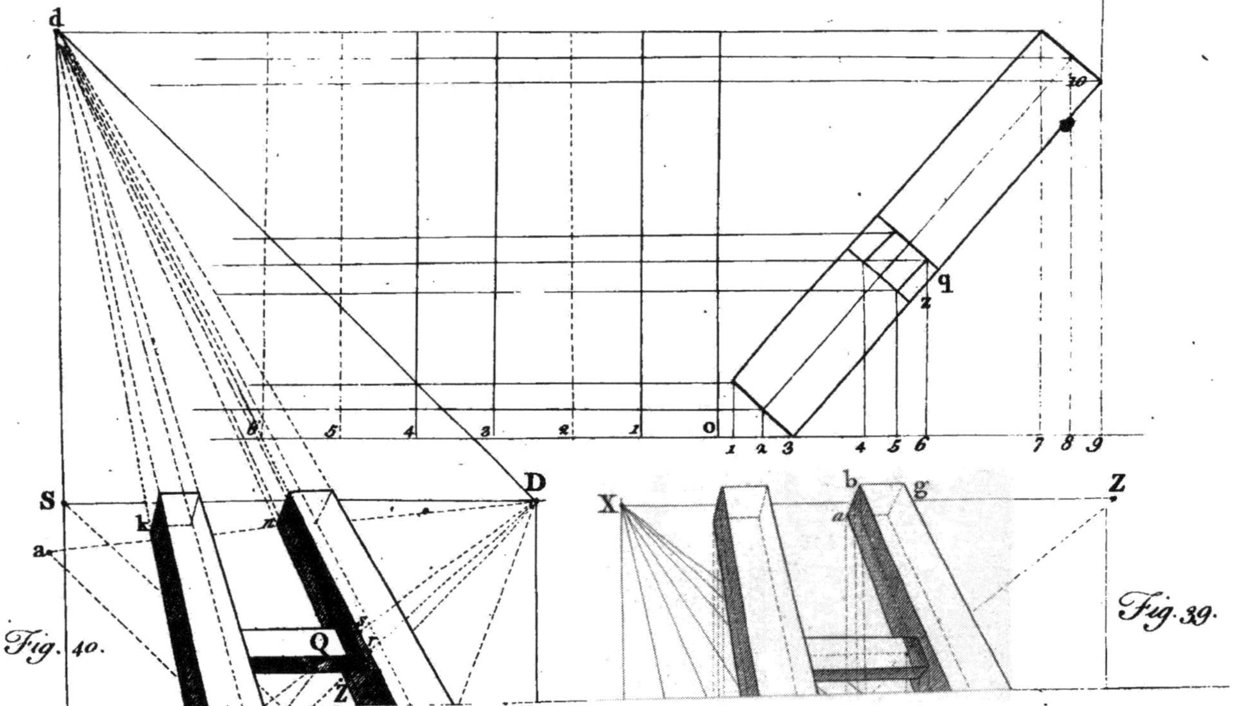

Fig. 40.

Fig. 39.

cessary, *viz.* the geometrical place of that pilaster, or its opposite, must be found below, as at G, and represented, as was explained in the first plate of this treatise; the plan of No. 2, will then be found, the sides of which being continued through S, finds also the plan of 6; the remaining two are found by parallel lines from those already done; for 3 is parallel to 6, and 7 to 2; then the geometrical height is set perpendicularly from e, to f, and lines drawn from both to C, between which all the several heights are found by means of parallels drawn from the bases or plans cutting e, C; and perpendiculars from those intersections to f, C, and parallels drawn back from the intersections of f, C, complete the whole.

Fig. 44. This is another representation of the same pilaster, added merely to shew how little work is necessary, where room is not wanting for all the vanishing points; and this representation is so easy to be understood, merely by inspection, after what has been said above, that no explanation is necessary.

Indeed this alone might have been sufficient to have shewn the practice; but then it might have been objected, that the Fig. 43. was avoided, to conceal the difficulty of this method, when the space allotted is too small to receive all the vanishing points necessary; but for the future, such a distance will be taken, as may admit of all, or most of the vanishing points; both because the work will be clearer, and shorter, and also because a proper place is reserved in the fourth part, for the explanation of several expedients that may be used, in cases that shall require them.

The THIRD PART.

THE reader is ſuppoſed, by this time, to be ſufficiently convinced, that the new method is preferable to any former; therefore no more compariſons will be made, but the new principles conſtantly recommended in this treatiſe will be regularly purſued.

Perſpective is principally exerciſed in projecting points and lines, and planes compoſed of lines; for ſolid bodies, of all kinds, are to be projected either by two planes perpendicular to each other, as the ichnography, and orthography, or by that number of planes which compoſe ſuch bodies reſpectively; in either caſe it is neceſſary, after having found the vaniſhing line of each plane, (the center and diſtance of the picture, on which it depends, being always given) to project the ſeveral lines which form ſuch plane. When the whole number of planes are projected, the body or figure is completed by ſuch projection, without any further operation; but when only the two planes of the ichnography, and orthography are choſen to be projected, it is neceſſary, afterwards, to join their correſponding points, by perpendiculars drawn from them reſpectively.

It is apprehended, that the following examples will be ſufficient to explain, and illuſtrate theſe two manners of projecting objects, perſpectively.

Here it may be proper, more explicitly, to deſcribe the nature of vaniſhing points, and lines, (hitherto occaſionally explained) and to ſhew how they are generated.

A vaniſhing point, is that point, wherein a line, paſſing from the eye, parallel to an original line, cuts or interſects the picture; and a vaniſhing line, is that line wherein a plane, paſſing from the eye, parallel to an original plane, cuts or interſects the picture. Thus the point, commonly called the point of ſight, or center of the picture, being determined by a line paſſing from the eye, at right angles, or perpendicular to the plane of the picture, is the vaniſhing point of all original

Plate XVI.

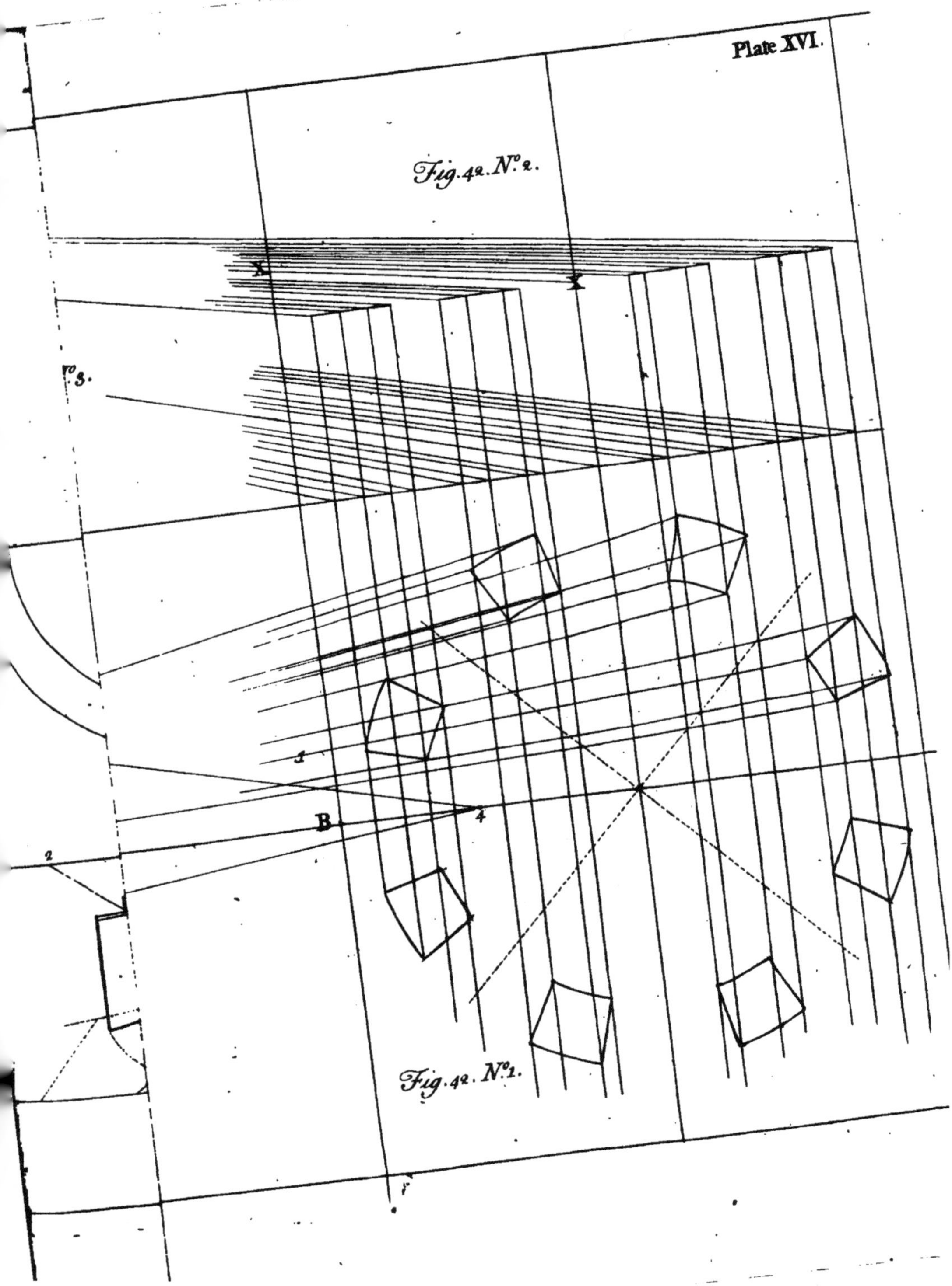

Plate XVII.

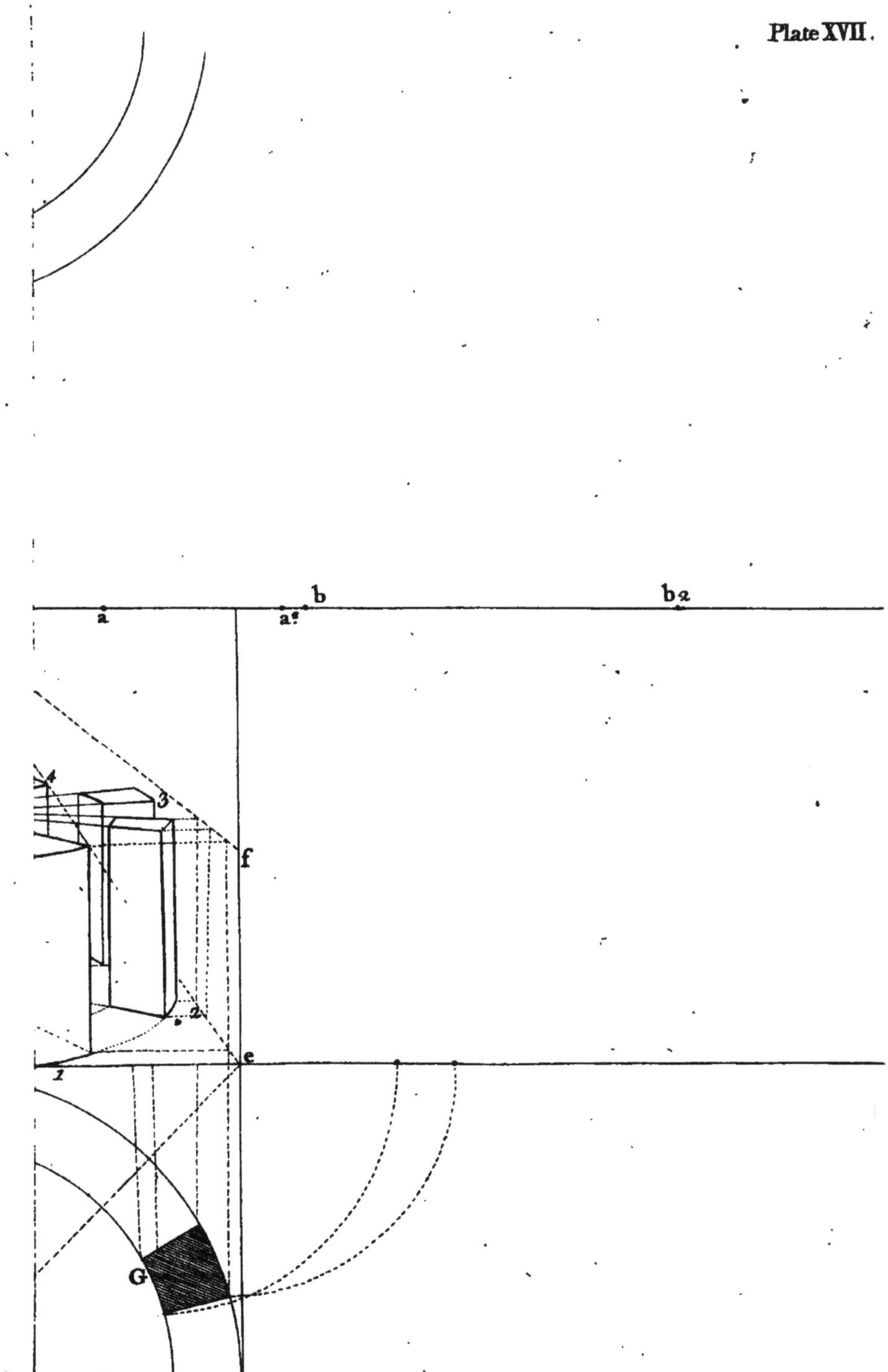

original lines, making right angles with, or which are perpendicular to, the plane of the picture. And when the picture is perpendicular to the plane of the horizon, which is the most ordinary situation, the line, commonly called the horizontal line, being formed by a plane passing from the eye, at right angles, or perpendicular to the picture, is the vanishing line of the horizon, as well as of all other planes parallel to the horizon; but when the picture is inclined to the horizontal plane, in any other than a right angle, then the vanishing line of the horizon will be higher or lower than the vanishing line of a plane perpendicular to the picture, according as the picture is inclined backwards or forwards, as shall be explained hereafter.

And thus, in general, the vanishing line of any original plane, is that line in which the parallel of such original plane (passing from the eye) cuts the picture.

Fig. 45. Let it be required to represent a cube standing on a plane, making a given angle with the horizon, (suppose thirty degrees) the point of sight, or center of the picture, and the distance being given. First mark the center of the picture S, and draw S, D, parallel to the intersection of the original plane with the picture, and equal to the distance given; through S, draw S, P, perpendicular to S, D, and from D, draw D, C, making the angle S, D, C, 30 degrees; and cutting S, P, in C, draw d, C, parallel to S, D, which will be the vanishing line of the plane on which the cube stands; draw D, P, perpendicular to D, C, cutting S, P, in P, and bisect the angle C, D, P, to X, and set off the distance (D, C,) of the vanishing line, d, C, from C, to d, then will the points C, P, X, and d, be all the vanishing points requisite for projecting the cubes No. 1. and 2, and as many more as may be required, with a situation, direct, on the plane, whose vanishing line is d, C; for draw at pleasure e, f, parallel to d, C, then e, C, and f, C, and d, f, cutting e, C, in g, and g, h, parallel to e, f, which finishes the lower square, then P, e,—P, f,—P, g, and P, h, after which draw X—h, cutting P, f, in *l*, and the diagonal h, *l*, will determine the length of f, *l*; then draw *l*, C, and *l*, u, parallel to e, f, then u, C, and the remaining parallel, by which the cube is completed.

The

The ſame points and operation are ſufficient for No. 2, or any others in a like ſituation.

For No. 3, the ſame lines, with very little addition, (on account of the different poſition of it) are ſufficient. This cube is in an oblique ſituation on the ſame plane; m, 6, is firſt drawn at pleaſure, and continued to a, its vaniſhing point, then the diſtance of the vaniſhing line, *viz.* D, C, is ſet off from C, to *D*, then a, *D*, is drawn, and *D*, *b*, at right angles to it, and ſo *b*, becomes the vaniſhing point of m, q, and its parallels; the length of m, q, is taken at pleaſure (as was e, f, of No. 1.) but by that all the other lines are determined. Draw q, a, and to find the length, q, 5, biſect the angle a, *D*, *b*, to X^2; draw X^2, m, cutting q, a, in 5; draw *b*, 5, cutting m, a, in 6, which finiſhes the lower ſquare; draw P, m,—P, q, and P, 6, and to find their lengths, the diſtance of P, *b*, the vaniſhing line (of the plane of m, q, n,) muſt be found; therefore draw through S, a perpendicular to P, *b*, cutting it in C^2, which will be the center of that line, and on P, *b*, as a diameter, deſcribe a ſemicircle, cutting that perpendicular in d^3, then P, d^3, *b*, will be a right angle (by 31. III. Eucl.) and conſequently d^3, C^2, the diſtance, of that vaniſhing line; or draw S, D^2, parallel to the vaniſhing line P, *b*, and equal to S, D, (the diſtance of the picture) and draw from D^2, to C^2, (the center of P, *b*,) and ſet off D^2, to d^3, by placing one foot of the compaſſes on C^2, and with the other foot deſcribing the arc D^2,—d^3, at d^3, biſect the right angle P, d^3, *b*, to X^3, and draw X^3, q, which will find the diagonal q, n, of the ſquare m, q, n; draw n, a, and n, *b*, &c. and ſo complete the cube.

No. 4. Is another cube repreſented by means of the ſame vaniſhing points, as No. 3, without the addition of one other point or line. But becauſe in ſome caſes it may not be ſo convenient to make uſe of the diagonals to determine the lengths of lines, the following method is added, which is univerſal. Having drawn from k, to the three vaniſhing points a, b, and P, in order to determine the length of any line, as for inſtance k, i, (whoſe vaniſhing point is b,) ſet off b, *D*, the diſtance of that vaniſhing point, on its proper vaniſhing line a, C, b, from

from *D*, to the point o, and parallel to that vanishing line draw k, r, equal to the original of k, i, in that place: Draw o, r, cutting k, b, in i, which will be its perspective length; make k, t, on the other side equal to k, r, and, in like manner, set off the distance of a, *D*, to u, on the same vanishing line; draw u, t, cutting k, a, in w.—The same is repeated at z, *(i.e.)* the distance P, *d*³, is set off to z, on the vanishing line *b*, P, to determine one line in that plane, *viz.* k, 7, for which purpose the same geometrical length is placed from k, to 8, parallel to *b*, P, and drawing z, 8, cuts it in 7, the perspective length.

If it were required to find the plan of one of these cubes on the horizontal plane, this might be done by dropping perpendiculars from every point of the cube, as at No. 4, and cutting those perpendiculars by lines drawn from vanishing points found in the horizontal line S, D, by means of perpendiculars from the corresponding vanishing points of the several lines of the projected figure; as for instance, S, is the vanishing point P, brought up to the horizontal line, wherefore draw from S, through 7, the lower angle of the cube (supposed to touch the ground) cutting the perpendicular from k, in the point a, which is the seat of the point k, on the horizon; from a, draw to the point perpendicularly (under *b*,) in the horizontal line, which determines the plan or seat of i; from a, draw to the point under *a*, which finds the seat of w; and from these two last found points, the seats of i, and w, draw to the same vanishing points, of the horizontal plane, which completes the plan of the upper face, of the cube; and in the same manner is the plan of the lower face found, and by joining the two extreme points on each side, the plan of the whole cube is completed.

That of No. 2. is also found in the same manner, but as one whole side of this cube touches the horizontal plane, it being placed parallel to the horizontal line, and only the point S, used, the plan is more simple. And if it were required to find the plan at any given distance below, on supposition of the object being above, and not touching the horizontal plane, the same method will answer the purpose; thus, at No. 3, drop a perpendicular as low as required, *(e.g.)* from N, to M, and proceed as at No. 4, beginning with M.

N. B. *The finding plans of objects already projected, is by no means an useless curiosity, but in some cases absolutely necessary, and particularly, in order to the projection of their shadows.*

Suppose it required to represent an object standing on a plane inclined to the horizon, in any given angle, as *(e. g.)* in an angle of 20 degrees, and on a picture perpendicular to the horizon.

Fig. 45. No. 5. Let S, be the center of the picture; S, D, the distance, marked on the horizontal line; S, C, drawn perpendicular to S, D; and D, C, drawn so, as to make with S, D, an angle of 20, (the required inclination of the original plane, with that of the horizon,) and cutting S, C, in C. Then the angle at C, will be 70, the complement of 20, to a right angle, and equal to that which the original plane makes with the picture.

By such original plane is to be understood a plane whose intersection, with the picture, is parallel to the horizontal line, in which case its vanishing line will necessarily be parallel also: wherefore C, D^a, drawn through C, parallel to S, D, is that vanishing line, and C, D, its distance, which may be raised up to its vanishing line C, D^a.

The object, or wedge A, is an example, shewing the use of such vanishing line, the base of it is a square on the horizontal plane, projected by means of the horizontal line F, S, D. But the upper face of it inclines to the horizon in an angle of 20, and is, therefore, projected by means of the vanishing line C, D^a, as appears by the lines of the operation, in the diagram.

But when the original plane (though with the same inclination to the horizontal plane) is oblique to the picture, then the vanishing line of that plane will be oblique also, and will intersect the horizontal line, as E, D, the vanishing line of the upper face of the wedge B, which object is, in all respects, similar to A, its position *only* being different, and is projected on its proper vanishing line E, D, by means of points exactly corresponding to those on the vanishing line C, D^a, for the upper face of the wedge A.

Now, here, though the inclination of the upper face of B, to the plane of the horizon, is still the same, yet, its inclination to the plane

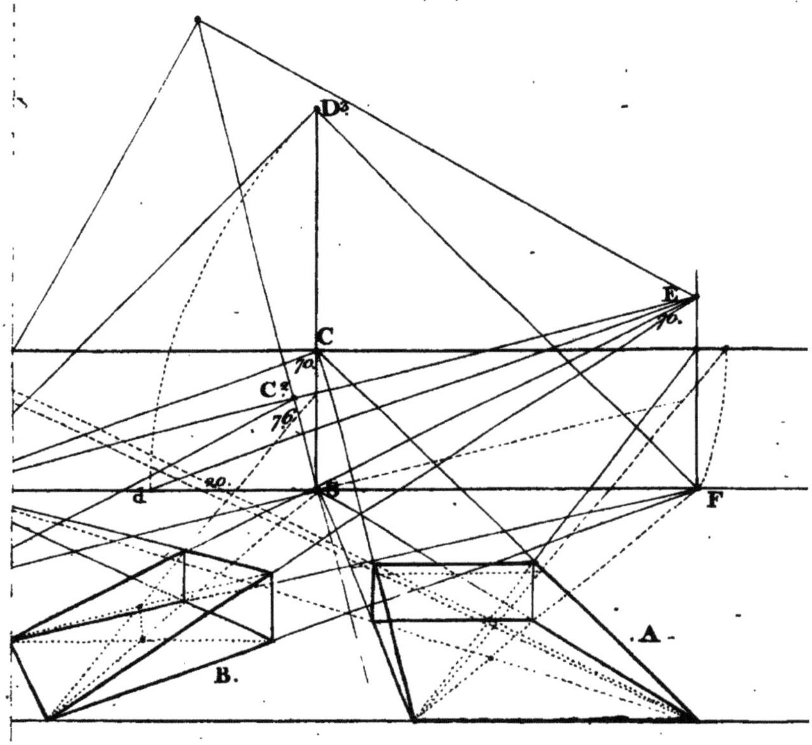
D2
E
70.
C
70.
C2
76.
d
20.
B
F
A.
B.

of the picture is altered by the obliquity of its position; and as the inclination of two planes is always measured on a third plane perpendicular to both (or which is the same thing) perpendicular to their common intersection; so it appears in the diagram, that the angle E, d, F, which measures the inclination of the upper face of the object B, with the horizon, is equal to C, D, S, which measures that of the upper face of A.—But that *d*, C², S, which measures the inclination of the upper face of B, *with the picture*, is larger than D, C, S, which measures the inclination of the upper face of A, *with the picture*.

And as the angle *d*, C², S, is larger than d, E, F, so the angle at *d*, (the complement of *d*, C², S,) is necessarily less than that at d, (the complement of d, E, F,) which angle at *d*, is the inclination of a plane, to another plane whose vanishing line would be *d*, S, continued, *(i. e.)* parallel to D, E, *and not to the* plane of the horizon.

The vanishing line E, D, for the upper face of B, is found by bringing down F, D³, (the distance of the vanishing line E, F,) to d, on the horizontal line, and drawing d, E, making F, d, E, an angle of 20, and then drawing E, D, which is the vanishing line required.

For if the triangle F, D³, D, be raised up on the line F, S, D, so as to become perpendicular to the picture, and the triangle E, d, F, raised up, with it, on the line E, F, till d, coincide with D³; (in that perpendicular situation,) then it will be evident that the plane E, d, F, will be perpendicular both to the plane of the horizon, and to the plane E, d, D, (when in such situation) which plane, being parallel to the original, oblique plane, and cutting the picture in E, D, that line becomes its vanishing line.

As this part, relating to oblique planes, and especially when obliquely situated with respect to the picture, is somewhat difficult, particular attention has been employed to render it as clear, as possible, and for that purpose the two principal parts of the last diagram, are again *separately* represented, and distinctly considered, in the two following schemes, and with a greater angle of inclination to the horizon.

Fig. 45. No. 6. F, D, is the horizontal line; S, the center of the picture; S, D, the distance of the picture; E, D², the vanishing line of a plane inclined

clined to the horizon in an angle of 40 degrees, and conſequently to the plane of the picture in 50, the complement of 40; C, the center of that vaniſhing line; C, D, its diſtance; C, D^2, the ſame diſtance raiſed up to its proper vaniſhing line. This wants no farther explanation.

Fig. 45. No. 7. F, D^2, the horizontal line; S, the center of the picture; S, D, the diſtance of the picture; E, D^2, the vaniſhing line of a plane inclined to the plane of the horizon in an angle of 40 degrees, *(as is* E, D^2, No. 6.*)* but in a different direction, *(i. e.)* obliquely, with reſpect to the picture. For it is inclined to the picture in an angle of 55, *(and not of* 50, *as* No. 6.)

Now to explain the reaſon of this difference, it is to be conſidered, that, in this ſcheme, No. 7, the circumſtances required are, to find the vaniſhing line of a plane inclined to the horizon, in an angle of 40, but with a certain given direction, *(i. e.)* ſo as to interſect the horizontal line in a given point, as D^2.—In order to effect which, the firſt ſtep to be taken is to find the vaniſhing line of a plane perpendicular to the line whoſe vaniſhing point is D^2, *(becauſe on ſuch plane the inclination is to be meaſured, as has been before mentioned,)* therefore from S, (the center of the picture) raiſe a perpendicular S, D^3, equal to the diſtance of the picture, and draw the line D^2, D^3, and then, perpendicular to it, draw D^3, F, cutting the horizontal line in F, at which point raiſe the perpendicular F, E, and this will be the vaniſhing line (ſought) of a plane perpendicular to the vaniſhing point D^2, firſt given.

F, is the center of this vaniſhing line, F, D^3, its diſtance; wherefore bring down that diſtance to d, on the horizontal line, and there make the angle of inclination required, by drawing d, E; and laſtly, draw D^2, E, which is the vaniſhing line of the oblique plane required. And this plane inclines to that of the horizon in an angle of 40; for if the triangle F, D^3, D^2, be raiſed up on the horizontal line, till it is perpendicular to the picture, and the triangle F, d, E, be raiſed up at the ſame time with it on F, E, till d, and D^3, coincide; then the plane F, d, E, will be perpendicular both to the horizontal plane, and to the plane whoſe vaniſhing line is E, D^2, *(for in the ſituation deſcribed,* E, D^3, D^2, *or which is the ſame,* E, d, D^2, *will be that plane)* and will

ig.45. N°. 6.

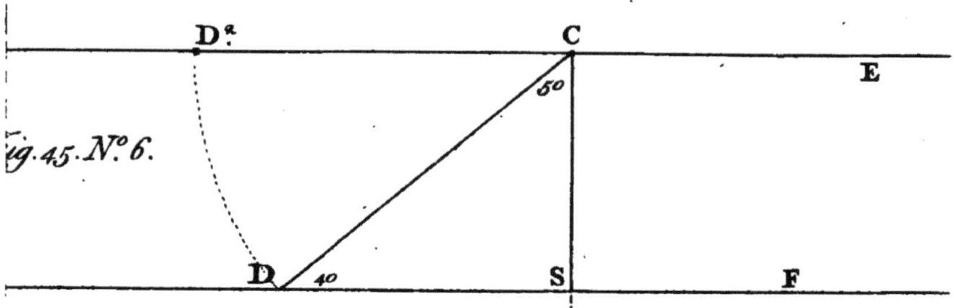

7.

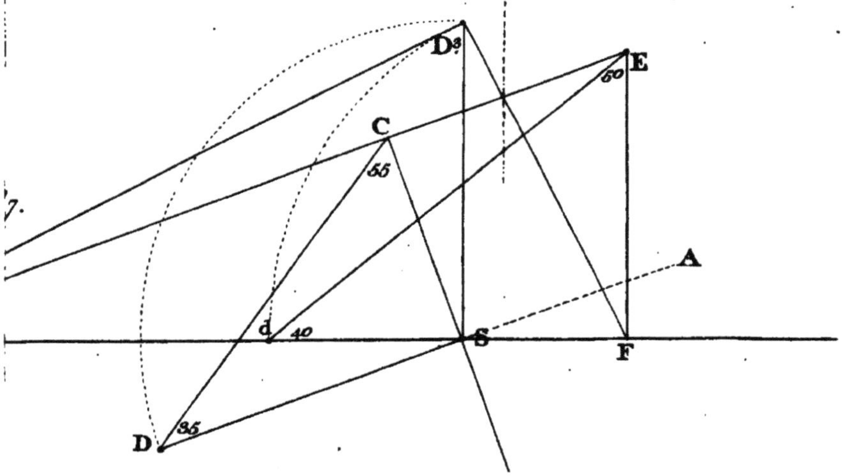

will truly meaſure their inclination; therefore thoſe two planes are inclined in an angle of 40, as required.

But as the plane F, d, E, is not perpendicular to the picture alſo, it cannot meaſure the inclination of the oblique plane with that of the picture.

And as this is to be found by means of a plane perpendicular to both, draw S, C, perpendicular to that vaniſhing line, and S, D, parallel to it, and equal to the diſtance of the picture, and draw D, C; then imagine the triangle S, D, C, raiſed up perpendicularly on the line S, C, and the other planes raiſed up with it (as before), and, in this ſituation, the plane S, D, C, will be perpendicular to both the picture, and the oblique plane, (*for* D, *will then coincide with* D^3, *and* d, *perpendicularly over* S,) and will therefore truly meaſure their inclination, which, thus, is found to be an angle of 55, and its complement 35, is the angle of inclination of the oblique plane, with a plane whoſe vaniſhing line would be D, S, continued, (*and not the horizontal plane*) but which would be inclined to the horizon in the angle D, S, D^2; for paſſing thro' the center, it is the ſame as the real, original, or geometrical angle of inclination. From the two laſt diagrams, appears the difference between the relations of an oblique plane, whoſe vaniſhing line is parallel to the horizontal line, and an oblique plane, whoſe vaniſhing line interſects the horizontal line.

For at No. 6, the plane S, D, C, (when raiſed perpendicularly on the line C, S,) is perpendicular to all the three planes, *viz.* of the horizon, of the picture, and of the oblique plane; and therefore meaſures the inclination of any two of them.

But at No. 7, the plane F, d, E, when raiſed, ſo that d, be perpendicularly over S, is perpendicular to two of them *only*, *viz.* to that of the horizon, and to the oblique plane, but *not* to the picture. And alſo, that the plane S, D, C, (when raiſed perpendicularly over the line S, C,) is perpendicular to two *only* of the three before mentioned; *viz.* to the picture, and to the oblique plane; but *not* to that of the horizon.

N. B. This

N. B. This laſt is alſo perpendicular to a third plane, *(though not one of the three here required)* *viz.* to a plane perpendicular to the picture, whoſe vaniſhing line would be D, S, continued, as was before obſerved.

Fig. 46. Here are ſome circumſtances explained, which were reſerved for this place, both that the learner might be prepared by what has preceded, and alſo that he might not be embarraſſed by too many lines in one diagram. S, is the center of the picture; S, D, the diſtance drawn in the direction of an original plane, with reſpect to the picture; or in which a vaniſhing line is required; S, C, drawn perpendicular to S, D; and D, C, drawn parallel to the inclination of the original plane, *(i. e.)* making with D, S, a certain given angle *(e. g.)* an angle of 24, and cutting S, C, in C; then the angle at C, will be 66, the complement of 24, and equal to the angle ſuch original plane makes with the picture.

Now thro' C, draw *a*, C, *b*, parallel to S, D, which will be the vaniſhing line of the original plane, and on which ſeveral cubes are ſuppoſed to be placed. Let C, S, be continued downwards; draw D, P, perpendicular to C, D, cutting C, S, P, in P; now ſuppoſing the plane C, D, P, to be raiſed up ſo, as that the point D, (which repreſents always the eye of the ſpectator) be perpendicular over S, then that plane C, D, P, becomes perpendicular to the picture, and P, the vaniſhing point of lines, perpendicular to the planes whoſe vaniſhing line is *a*, C, *b*; therefore any line, as *a*, P, paſſing thro' P, and cutting *a*, C, *b*, will be the vaniſhing line of a plane perpendicular to *a*, C, *b*; but in order to find a third vaniſhing line perpendicular to both theſe vaniſhing lines already found, the diſtance C, D, of *a*, C, *b*, is ſet off on C, P, at d'; then a, d', is drawn, and d', *b*, perpendicular to it; and thus *b*, P, being drawn, becomes the third vaniſhing line of planes perpendicular to both the others; for (as was remarked before) any line paſſing through P, meeting the vaniſhing line *a*, *b*, will be the vaniſhing line of a plane perpendicular to it; therefore P, *b*, is a vaniſhing line perpendicular to *a*, *b*, and it is perpendicular to P, *a*, by conſtruction, *a*, d', *b*, being made a right angle. This vaniſhing line P, *b*, might

might have been found, by drawing a, S, and S, *D*³, perpendicular to it, equal to S, D, (the diſtance of the picture) and drawing a, *D*³, and *D*³, C³, perpendicular to it; cutting a, S, in C³; then drawing P, C³, cutting *a*, *b*, in *b*; as is evident; and ſo of the reſt.

C, is the center of the vaniſhing line a, *b*, found by drawing a line through S, perpendicular to it, and the point ſo found in every vaniſhing line, is always called its center, which is to be uſed on ſuch vaniſhing line in the ſame manner, and for the ſame purpoſes with reſpect to the plane which it repreſents, as the center of the horizontal line with reſpect to the horizontal plane; and in the ſame manner are found C², the center of a, P, and C³, the center of *b*, P.—If a circle be deſcribed round S, the center of the picture, with the radius S, D, which is the diſtance of the picture, as all the radii are neceſſarily equal, any line from S, to the circumference will be equal to, or will be properly, the diſtance of the picture; therefore drawing S, *D*², at right angles, on the perpendicular *b*, C², of the vaniſhing line a, P, and drawing C², *D*², it will be the diſtance of that vaniſhing line.

In the ſame manner drawing S, *D*³, at right angles, on the perpendicular *a*, C³, of the vaniſhing line *b*, P, and drawing C³, *D*³, it will be the diſtance of that vaniſhing line; S, D,—S, *D*²,—S, *D*³; will all be ſeverally parallel to their reſpective vaniſhing lines *a*, *b*,—*a*, P,—and *b*, p. Now if D, S, be raiſed up perpendicularly over C, P,—*D*², S, over *b*, C²,—and *D*³, S, over *a*, C³, theſe three points D, *D*², and *D*³, will coincide over S.—Again, if C, D, (which is the diſtance of *a*, *b*,) be transferred to d¹, on C, P, the perpendicular of the ſaid vaniſhing line *a*, *b*, and C², *D*², the diſtance of *a*, P, to d², on its perpendicular *b*, C², and alſo C³, *D*³, the diſtance of *b*, P, to d³, on its perpendicular *a*, C³, the three points d¹, d², d³, being raiſed on their reſpective vaniſhing lines a, *b*,—a, P,—and *b*, P, ſo far as that each be perpendicular over S; theſe three points will all coincide, not only with each other, but alſo with the three firſt named D, *D*², *D*³.

The learner is adviſed to make all theſe points, and lines, as familiar to himſelf as poſſible, by drawing vaniſhing lines in ſeveral directions, and

and eſpecially three, to repreſent planes at right angles to each other, as in this ſcheme, for the projection of cubes, and cubical forms, in all poſitions; becauſe nothing is more neceſſary in the practice of perſpective: and if he has underſtood all the preceding part, it is apprehended this will not be difficult to him. In order to aſſiſt the imagination a little, let him conſider the two cubes, A, and B, one of which, A, is ſeen direct, the blank parts to be ſuppoſed on the other ſide of the picture, and the lines n, *l*,—*l*, m, and m, n, to interſect the picture; theſe three lines may be conceived to be the vaniſhing lines of the three planes which form the ſolid angle of a cube, and m, n, *l*, the vaniſhing points of its ſides, or legs. The ſame thing is repreſented in B, with this only difference, that it is oblique, as the large ſcheme, juſt explained; for which reaſon, two of the legs cut the picture on this ſide of the angles of the cube, and the lines a, *b*,—*b*, p, and p, a, repreſent thoſe three vaniſhing lines, in the large ſcheme, to which they are reſpectively parallel, and are, in both, the vaniſhing lines of the ſolid angle of the cube.

On one ſide is a cube E, projected as in the former, but removed out of its place of projection, that the lines might not be confounded with thoſe of the ſcheme; the reader is to refer it to g, within, which point (correſponding with g, on the figure) the whole is ſuppoſed to be performed.

Here is a circumſtance determined which before was not ſuppoſed to be required, *viz.* that it ſhould touch the picture in the point g, the body of the figure being behind the picture; to effect which, from the point D, on the line C, D, raiſe a perpendicular D, G, equal to one ſide, or leg of the cube: draw G, F, parallel to C, P, and conſequently to the picture. In projecting the cube E, after having drawn g, *b*, and g, a, *(i. e.)* ſuppoſe from g, in the original ſcheme, draw g, *f*, parallel, and equal, to G, F, (which was made parallel to C, P,) then draw *f*, C, tending to C, *(i. e.)* to the ſame vaniſhing point, as F, C, and repreſenting a, parallel to it; draw alſo g, P, cutting *f*, C, in h, then the line g, h, will repreſent G, D, and be (perſpectively) equal to it, and g, will touch the picture. The reſt is performed as has been

ſhewn

ſhewn before. All this operation is ſuppoſed within the ſcheme or diagram (as is ſaid above) beginning at g, and then tranſpoſed to E, only to avoid confuſion of lines in the great ſcheme. The other cube K, is ſuppoſed to interſect the picture in the lines 5, 6,—6, 7, and 7, 8, the reſt being ſuppoſed behind; to repreſent which, another perpendicular H, M, is drawn on C, D, F, ſo much before the line G, F, as the cube is ſuppoſed to be before the picture, the reſt behind; and the ſame method is uſed as for the other E, only the triangle D, G, F, is here repreſented by *d*, *g*, *f*, within the cube; and, in order to make it advance before the picture, in the proportion required, a line g, t, equal to G, H, is ſet off from g, parallel to the vaniſhing line *a*, *b*; and the diſtance C, D, ſet off from C, to q: then q, t, is drawn, cutting c, g, in r; and r, P, cutting C, *d*, *f*, in 5, determines one line of the advanced part of this cube, from which the reſt is finiſhed; and when completed, the lines forming the triangular interſection, are reſpectively parallel to the three ſeveral vaniſhing lines; the uppermoſt paſſes through g, determining the other two. This alſo is performed within the ſcheme, the point r, there, anſwering to that on the cube, and the whole being tranſpoſed to K.

It appears, by theſe projections, that if the meaſures, and forms of objects, are known, they may be repreſented without geometrical plans, or elevations, which ſaves much time and trouble. And if it be required to aſſign the geometrical ſize, and ſituation of any figure already projected; as, for inſtance, the cube E; firſt draw through *f*, a line u, w, parallel to the vaniſhing line *a*, *b*, which line is therefore the interſection of the original plane with the picture (or what is called the ground line;) for it was before mentioned, that *g*, *f*, touches the picture; continue the lines i, h, and *l*, h, till they cut u, w, in n, and o; continue alſo m, *l*, and m, i, to u, and w: then having meaſured the angle d', a, *b*, in the large ſcheme, make u, o, L, equal to it, for a, is the vaniſhing point of h, *l*; draw w, I, parallel to o, L: in like manner meaſure the angle d', *b*, *a*, and make w, n, I, equal to it; draw u, L, parallel to n, I, which will complete the figure, or plan, L, I, in its geometrical ſituation, and

 pro-

proportion.—Or, to avoid the trouble of meafuring, and transferring the feveral angles, continue d', C, upwards, till c, *D*⁴, is equal to C, d', (which was made equal to C, D,) and make o, L, and w, I, parallel to *D*⁴, *a*; and u, L,—n, I, parallel to D⁴, *b*, which will anfwer the fame purpofe.

The like operation is repeated for the cube K, on the other fide, tranfpofed from r, (within the fcheme;) to which r, on the cube, correfponds, only this cube advancing, in part, before the picture, (as appears by the ground-line v, w,) is larger on that account; and, for the fame reafon, the original geometrical fquare, or plan, is neceffarily cut by the ground-line; in confequence of which the points n, o, are, in the interfection of the original fquare, with the reprefentation. The reft needs no explanation, as the two figures are intirely fimilar.—If this large fcheme appears, at firft fight, overcharged with lines, the reader, who has underftood the preceding rules, will readily perceive that very few of them (only) are neceffary to the projection of the objects reprefented; and that the others are added, partly to exhibit different manners of projecting the fame objects, but principally to fhew the correfpondence, and relation that feveral fyftems of lines have with each other, which, thus, are more evident than if drawn in feparate diagrams, and more effectually illuftrate the nature and ufe of vanifhing lines.

N. B. The whole profile of this fituation of the cube K, is geometrically erected on the line C, D, M, which is taken from d', where the original plan is defcribed, in the pofition feen by the fpectator, and reprefented in the perfpective, where C, 5, anfwers to C, d', in the geometrical plan, and $\frac{1}{2}$ 5, to $\frac{1}{2}$ d', &c. The lines croffing from the angles (in the geometrical plan) are parallel to the vanifhing line *a*, b, and confequently to the interfection; and N, M, anfwers to *N*, *M*, the fection or profile of the plan.

Fig. 47. In this fcheme the vanifhing line *a*, *b*, is ftill more oblique, and croffes that of the horizon, in order to fhew that even in fuch fituation, the manner of finding a plan on the horizontal plane is the fame

Plate XVIII.

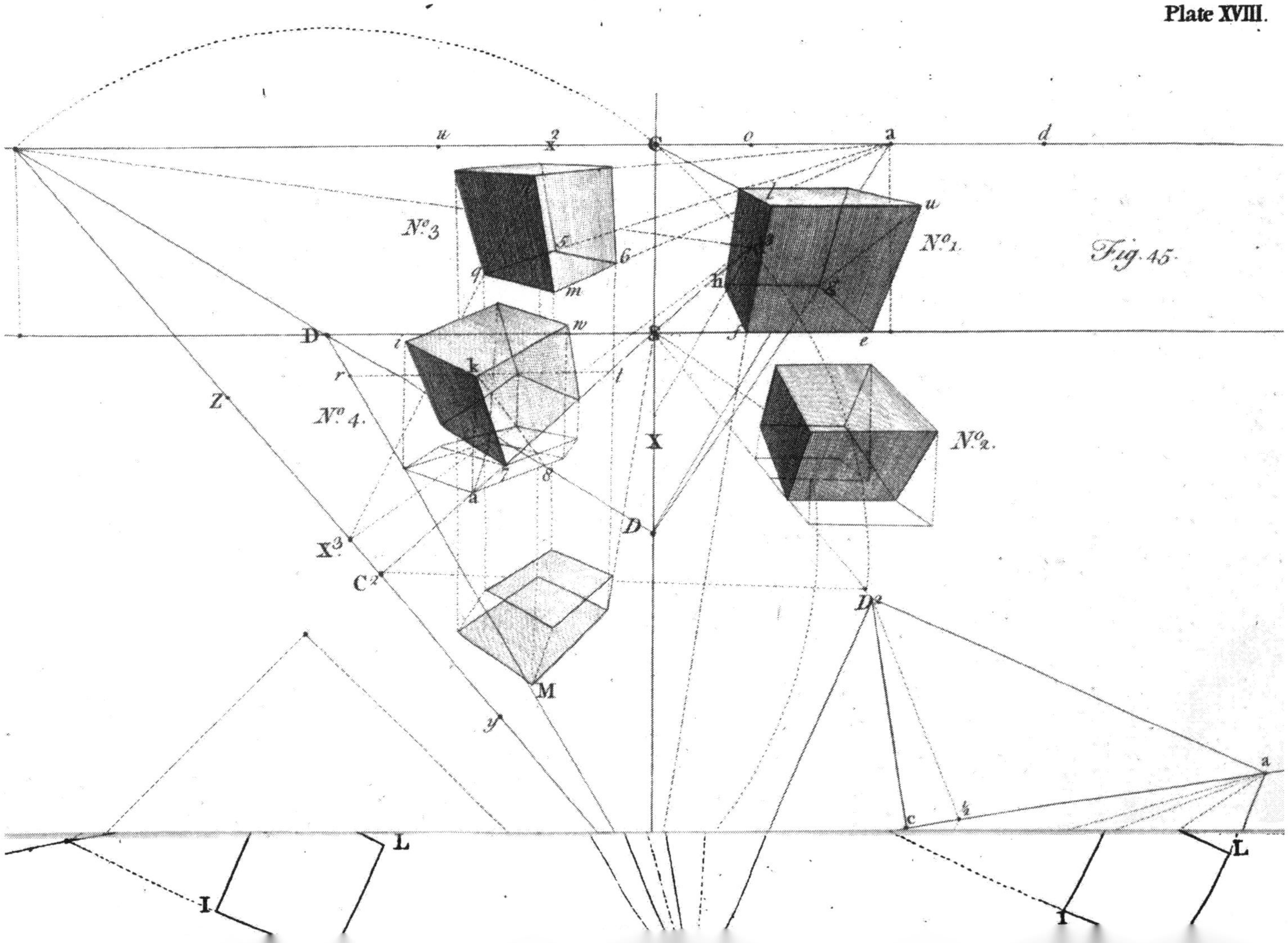

u
2
x
C
o
a
d
N°3
N°1
Fig. 45
q
m
6
h
g
u
D
w
i
k
r
l
e
Z
N° 4.
X
N°2.
a
D
X3
C2
D2
M
y
a
c
L
I
L
I

ſame as before exhibited, notwithſtanding a ſeeming difficulty ariſing from the vaniſhing point *a*, being below the horizon.—The cube A, being projected, as has been before taught, in order to find its plan perpendicularly on the plane of the horizon, firſt transfer the three vaniſhing points *a*, *b*, and P, perpendicularly to the horizontal line, viz. *b*, downwards; *a*, and P, upwards, to b, a, and p; then draw, from the point I, which touches the ground, to a, and to b; drop a perpendicular from II, to 2, and raiſe one from III, to 3; then draw from 2, to a, and from 3, to b, which will complete the plan of the lower ſquare or face I, II, III, IV; for the interſection of 2, a, and 3, b, will mark the point 4, perpendicularly, under IV; now draw from p, through I, and drop a perpendicular from V, interſecting p, I, in 5, and draw 5, a,—5, b; drop a perpendicular from VI, to 5, a, cutting it in 6; and from VIII, to 5, b, cutting it in 8; draw from 8, to a, and from 6, to b, which will complete the plan of the upper face V, VI, VII, VIII; for the point 7, will be found in the interſection of 8, a, and 6, b, perpendicularly under VII; after which, joining I, 5, which is the plan or ſeat of the line I, V, and 7, 4, the ſeat of VII, IV, the ichnography of the whole figure is determined on the plane of the horizon, and it will be found, on inſpection, that every line, and, conſequently, every face, is planned, which is eaſily examined by the correſponding figures.

The figure B, is not a cube, but a right angled ſolid, or parallelopiped, four of whoſe faces are parallelograms, as in the geometrical D, i, g, h, on the line C, D, and whoſe upper and lower faces are ſquares, as appears by the diagonal drawn from x[1], which is a biſection of the right angle *a*, D, *b*, and whoſe ſides are equal to h, i; but the depth of the whole figure is only equal to h, *g*; and, in order to determine that depth, either the angle h, D, *g*, may be transferred to the vaniſhing line of one of the faces, as here to *a*, P, by making a, d[1], *f*, equal to it, (d[1], c[1], being the diſtance of that vaniſhing line,) and drawing *f*, *h*, cutting m, P, in n; and then n, *l*, will be a diagonal, repreſenting D, h, by means of which the figure may be completed.—Or otherwiſe, thus: drawing, *l*, o,

 parallel

parallel to *a*, P, and equal to g, h; and transferring the diſtance P, d', to e, on the vaniſhing line P, *a*; and drawing e, o, cutting *l*, p, in q, the length *l*, q, is determined, by which the reſt may be finiſhed.

There is another kind of plan which may be projected on the plane of the horizon, by lines perpendicular to the oblique plane, on which the object is ſuppoſed to ſtand; for this the reader is referred back to Fig. 46, at the cube E, where the vaniſhing points uſed are S, and t, on the horizontal line in the large ſcheme, in which the vaniſhing points *a*, and *b*, are transferred to that line, by *a*, P, and *b*, P, repreſenting perpendiculars to the vaniſhing line *a*, *b*, of the original oblique plane. Now at the cube E, draw h, s, and h, t, then i, P, and *l*, P, interſecting them, in 5, and 6; draw 5, t, and 6, s, which completes this plan; for as it is formed by the continuation of the ſides of the figure which are perpendicular to the plane on which it ſtands, the plan of one face is (neceſſarily) that of the whole cube; the point h, being ſuppoſed to touch the horizontal plane.

As cubes, and cubical forms, are apprehended to be more uſeful than any others, as approaching nearer to thoſe of buildings, and moſt common objects, they have therefore been conſidered in many various ſituations: the plans projected after the figures themſelves, if not always neceſſary, are ſometimes ſo, as was before obſerved, and were exhibited on account of difficulties that had been ſuppoſed relating to ſuch projections. Thus having ſufficiently treated of the cube, and there being no more than five regular bodies, or ſolids, it might be deemed an omiſſion wholly to neglect the other four; wherefore here are given repreſentations of them all, by the vaniſhing lines of their faces, and, of ſeveral, by means of the ichnography, and orthography, alſo, to ſhew the different ways of proceeding. On the ſide of Fig. 48. is a geometrical deſcription of the ſeveral angles, as well of the ſection as faces, of a tetraedron, which muſt be underſtood before a perſpective repreſentation can be made.—G, H, I, is an equilateral triangle (whoſe angles are each 60 degrees) the baſe of a tetraedron.—I, N, K, is the ſection ſuppoſed to be raiſed up, perpendicularly, on the line I, K; in

Plate XXI.

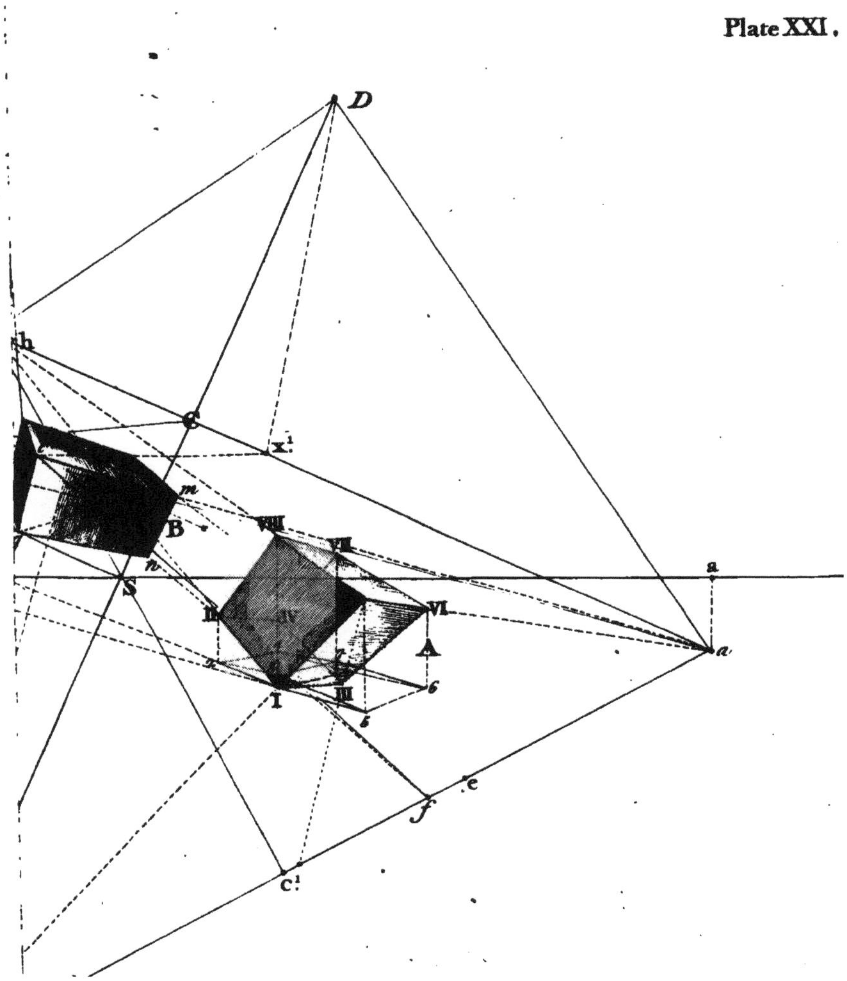

in which situation the angle I, K, N, represents the inclination of two of the planes or faces; the other two, *viz.* I, N, K, and K, I, N, represent the angle made by one side with a plane or face; I, K, is the diameter; and O, N, the axis.

N. B. By referring to this, occasionally, the reasons of the following operations will be better understood.

Fig. 48. No. 1. The tetraedron A, B, F, E, is thus projected. First draw, at pleasure, the vanishing line *a*, S, *c*; from S, raise a perpendicular to D, the distance given; let the side B, A, be also given, which continue to its vanishing point b; draw D, b: Then make an angle of 60 degrees on each side D, b, to *a*, and *c*; draw B, *c*, and *a*, A, cutting B, *c*, in F; then the base, or one face, is finished on the plane of *a*, S, *c*.—Now find the vanishing line, *c*, h, *f*, of planes, inclining to the face A, B, F, in the angle of inclination of two of the faces; that is, in the angle I, K, N; on the side B, F; that is, on its vanishing point *c*; and in it find the vanishing points e, and *f*, (*c*, being already found) and then drawing e, B, and *f*, F, the point E, is determined by their intersection; wherefore joining E, A, the tetraedron is completed.

N. B. The angle of inclination of two planes is always measured, as hath been already said, on a plane perpendicular to both of them; that is, perpendicular to their common intersection. Now D, *c*, (if turned forwards with D, S, till D, S, is perpendicular to the picture) is that intersection; therefore draw D, *g*, at right angles to D, *c*, and from *g*, erect a perpendicular (to a, S, *c*,) as *g*, h, which will be the vanishing line of planes, perpendicular to D, *c*, the common intersection; and D, *g*, being the distance of that perpendicular vanishing line, set it off on either side of *g*, as at *d*; there make the angle of inclination, *g*, *d*, *b*; then draw *c*, h, which will be the vanishing line of the face B, F, E: Find the distance of this vanishing line (*i. e.*) draw from S, a perpendicular to *c*, h, cutting it in C, which is its center; set off S, D, to d, parallel to *c*, h, then d, C, will be the distance diftance of that vanifhing line, which transfer to C, *D*, perpendicular on it; draw *c*, *D*, and make *c*, *D*, e, and e, *D*, *f*, both 60 degrees. If any difficulty remain concerning the diftance of the vanifhing line *c*, h, *f*, let it be conceived that d, and D, are both brought forward, fo as to be perpendicular to the picture over S, then they will coincide, and be the place of the eye; whence it will be evident, that d, C, muft be the diftance of the vanifhing line *c*, h, *f*.

The vanifhing line of a plane, perpendicular to another plane, is determined, by finding *only* the vanifhing point of lines perpendicular to fuch given vanifhing line, becaufe any line, perpendicular to a plane, makes an angle of 90 degrees with that plane every way: whereas a line, cutting a plane in any other angle, (for inftance 30) makes that angle but one way on that plane, wherefore it is neceffary, in order to find a plane at 30 degrees, to take another method: and, for the fame reafon, a plane paffing through a line perpendicular to another plane, will continue always perpendicular, though turned round fuch line every way. But if a plane were to be turned round a line making an angle of 30, &c. the angle would vary continually, fo as to make every other angle between 30, and its complement 150, (*i. e.* to 180, or two right angles;) for this reafon, it becomes neceffary, in order to find the vanifhing line of a plane interfecting another plane at 30, (or any other angle except 90,) to find, firft, the vanifhing line of a plane, perpendicular to the interfection of the two planes, whofe inclination is fought, on which to meafure that angle of inclination, otherwife it cannot be truely found.

Fig. 48. No. 2. *N. B.* In this fcheme, B, C, G, is the vanifhing line of the plane perpendicular to E, which is the vanifhing point of the interfection of the planes B, E, and E, C, inclined to each other in 30 degrees; B, A, C, the geometrical angle of 30 degrees; G, A, (equal to G, D,) being the diftance of the vanifhing line B, C, G; fo that if D, S, be raifed up perpendicularly over S, and the

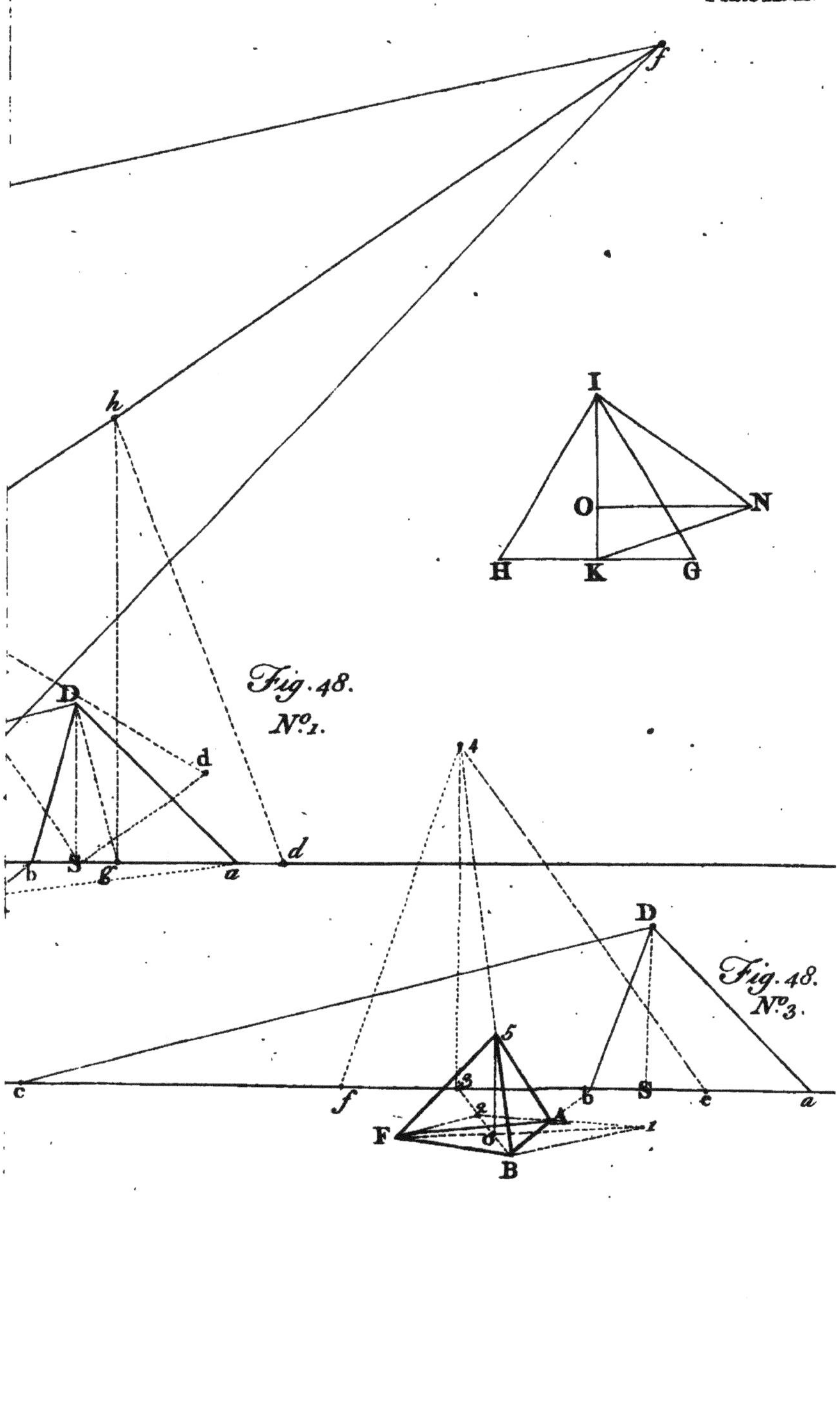

Fig. 48. N°. 1.

Fig. 48. N°. 3.

the arc A, D, together with it; and also if the triangle B, A, C, be raised on the line B, C; the point A, will move along the arc A, D, till A, coincide with D, which is the true situation; then will B, A, C, be a plane perpendicular to D, E, the intersection of the two planes B, E, and C, E.

No. 7. of Fig. 45.—S, is the center of the picture; S, D, the distance; the line A, S, D, is a vanishing line of planes perpendicular to the picture; and E, D², another vanishing line, parallel to A, S, D; but of planes inclining to the planes, whose vanishing line is A, S, D, in the angle S, D, C.—F, D², is the horizontal line.

It is required to find the angle of inclination, of the plane of the horizon, with the planes whose vanishing line is E, D², and the difference of the angles of inclination, between that of A, S, D, to E, D², and that of F, D², to the same E, D².

Set off the distance of the picture S, D, to D³, perpendicular to the horizontal line; draw D², D³, and D³, F, perpendicular to it; at F, raise the perpendicular F, E, cutting D², E, in E; then E, F, will be the vanishing line of planes, perpendicular to both the planes of E, D², and F, D²; from F, set off F, D³, (the distance of the vanishing line E, F,) to d, on the horizontal line. Now draw d, E, and E, d, F, will be *geometrically* the angle of inclination sought; (*i. e.*) of the plane of the horizon, with the planes whose vanishing line is D², E, *which was the first thing required.*

And this angle E, d, F, is larger than S, D, C, by 5 degrees, *which was the second thing required.*

N. B. The angle of inclination of the planes of A, S, D, and F, D², is A, S, F, or D, S, d, the real geometrical angle, made by their intersection, on the picture; because they both pass through S, and are therefore both perpendicular to the picture.

The representation, Fig. 48, No. 1, was formed entirely by vanishing lines; but the principles are so general, that many other methods may

may be uſed, ſome of which are ſtill ſhorter in particular caſes; as an inſtance, here is added one other projection of the ſame object, with one vaniſhing line only.

Fig. 48. No. 3. After having found the face *A*, *B*, *F*, No. 2, as before at No. 1, draw B, *a*, and c, A, meeting in 1, and F, b, and A, c, meeting in 2; draw 1, F, and B, 2, 3, whoſe interſection o, will be the center of the face A, B, F; erect a perpendicular at o, and, at 3, raiſe the perpendicular 3, 4; ſet off 3, D, (the diſtance of the vaniſhing point 3,) of either ſide, on the vaniſhing line *a*, S, c, as at e; draw e, 4, making the angle 3, e, 4, equal to O, I, N, and cutting the perpendicular 3, 4, in 4, which will be the vaniſhing point of the ſide B, 5; and the line 4, B, will cut the perpendicular o, 5, in the apex; from whence draw to A, and to F, by which the whole is completed.

N. B. *e*, 4, *f*, repreſents the ſection I, N, K, in the geometrical.

Fig. 49. For the octaedron, make an equilateral triangle R, F, G; draw its diameter F, L; on R, G, deſcribe a ſquare; draw the diagonal R, H, and from H, and R, with the radius F, L, deſcribe two arches interſecting each other in I; then the angle R, I, H, will be the angle made by two planes, or faces of the octaedron on the inſide; and the angle K, I, H, will be the angle on the outſide, or (properly) the angle of inclination, and to be uſed in projecting this figure; for R, H, is the axis of the ſolid, and R, I,—H, I, the diameters of two faces meeting in I.

Fig. 49. No. 1. To project the octaedron, perſpectively, *a*, S, c, is the given vaniſhing line of the plane on which it reſts; A, B, a given ſide of the figure, continued to its vaniſhing point *a*; make S, D, equal to the diſtance given; draw the lines *a*, D, and D, b, making with *a*, D, an angle of 60 degrees; and D, c, making the ſame angle with D, b; then draw A, c, and B, b, cutting A, c, in E, which finiſhes the face on which the ſolid reſts; then find the vaniſhing line of one other face, (which will be all that is neceſſary;) and, in order to it, find k, the vaniſhing point of lines perpendicular to the lines whose vanishing point is *a*; (*i. e.*) draw D, k, perpendicular to *a*, D, cutting *a*, S, c, in k; draw k, *l*, perpendicular to *a*, S, c; find its distance k, m, by setting off K, D, to m; from m, draw a line downwards to *l*, making an angle k, m, *l*, equal to K, I, H, (in the geometrical) with the line *a*, S, c; *which line l*, m, *if continued upwards, would make an angle with the same line a*, S, c, *equal to the inner angle of the inclination of two faces*; then draw *l*, *a*, which is the vanishing line sought; find its distance C, *D*, (*i. e.*) draw S, C; *D*, perpendicular to *l*, *a*; set off the distance S, D, to d, parallel to *l*, *a*; then set off the distance d, C, from C, to *D*:—*l*, *a*, thus found, is the vanishing line of the face A, B, h, and its opposite *g*, E, i. Now find the vanishing points, as directed above in the last figure; then draw e, A, and B, *f*, cutting it in h; then h, b, and h, c, and e, E, cutting h, c, in i; draw i, *a*, cutting h, b, in *g*; draw *g*, A,—*g*, E, and i, B, which will complete the whole.

Fig. 49. No. 2. Is a representation of the same figure standing on one of its points, or solid angles, with very few lines. For this projection, first draw any one given side 1, 3, to its vanishing point *a*; find b, the vanishing point of lines perpendicular to those, whose vanishing point is *a*, and draw 1, b; then draw 3, b; bisect the angle *a*, D, b, to o; draw o, 1, cutting 3, b, in 4; draw *a*, 4, cutting 1, b, in 2, which finishes the square 1, 2, 3, 4; at o, drop a perpendicular; set off the distance o, D, to e; thence draw e, p, making with o, e, an angle of 45; and, having found the center of the square 1, 2, 3, 4, and drawn a perpendicular through it, draw p, 1, cutting that perpendicular below in 6, and p, 4, cutting it above in 5; from these two extreme points of the axis, draw to 1, 2, 3, 4, which will complete the whole. For 1, 5, 4, 6, represents a square (as well as 1, 2, 3, 4;) and o, e, p, being half a square, the angles are rightly found.

Though the octaedron may be projected in this position with so few lines, yet as projections, by means of the ichnography and orthography, are proper in many cases, the manner of constructing and using them is here explained in the same example.

Suppose then, No. 3, the side 1, 3, only given; draw from its vanishing point *a*, any line, where there is convenient space, as *a*, 7, 8; and from b, the vanishing point of lines perpendicular to those whose vanishing point is *a*, draw through 3, and 1, of the line given, cutting the line *a*, 7, 8, in 7, and 8; then, through *a*, draw *f*, *g*, perpendicular to *a*, S, b; set off the distance *a*, D, to e, and draw e, *f*, upwards, making (with e, *a*,) half the angle R, I, H, (in the geometrical) and e, *g*, making the same with e, *a*, downwards, so that the angle *f*, e, *g*, be equal to the whole inner angle R, I, H. Now draw *f*, 8, and *g*, 7, meeting in 9; and *f*, 7, and *g*, S, meting in 10; which will form the perspective of the profile, or orthography. The plan or ichnography is so easy to be understood by inspection, being only the representation of a square, that it needs no description in words.

Now perpendiculars, from the corresponding points of ichnography and orthography, will meet in the several points which form the figure; and, by joining those points, the figure is completed; (*e. g.*) drawing from the point 8, to b, and raising perpendiculars from 1, and 2, of the plan, meeting 1, b, in 1, and 2, the points 1, and 2, in the figure itself, are found; and so of 3, 4; and by raising a perpendicular from the center of the plan, and cutting it by lines (tending to b,) from 9, and 10, of the profile, the points 5, and 6, in the figure, will be found also, by which it is completed.

> *N. B.* From ichnography, the perpendiculars are geometrically such; but from orthography, perspectively such.

This manner of projecting the orthography, is one of the great advantages of the new principles; for, according to the old, the geometrical orthography of this figure would not have been so simple; nor, indeed, would it have been any regular figure; and in architecture (where many members are to be represented) the orthographic projections for oblique situations are so confused, as to be scarce intelligible, and give no idea of the thing intended to be represented; for proof of which the reader is referred to *Pozzo's* second Volume.—The geometrical orthography is drawn above, by which it is evident that

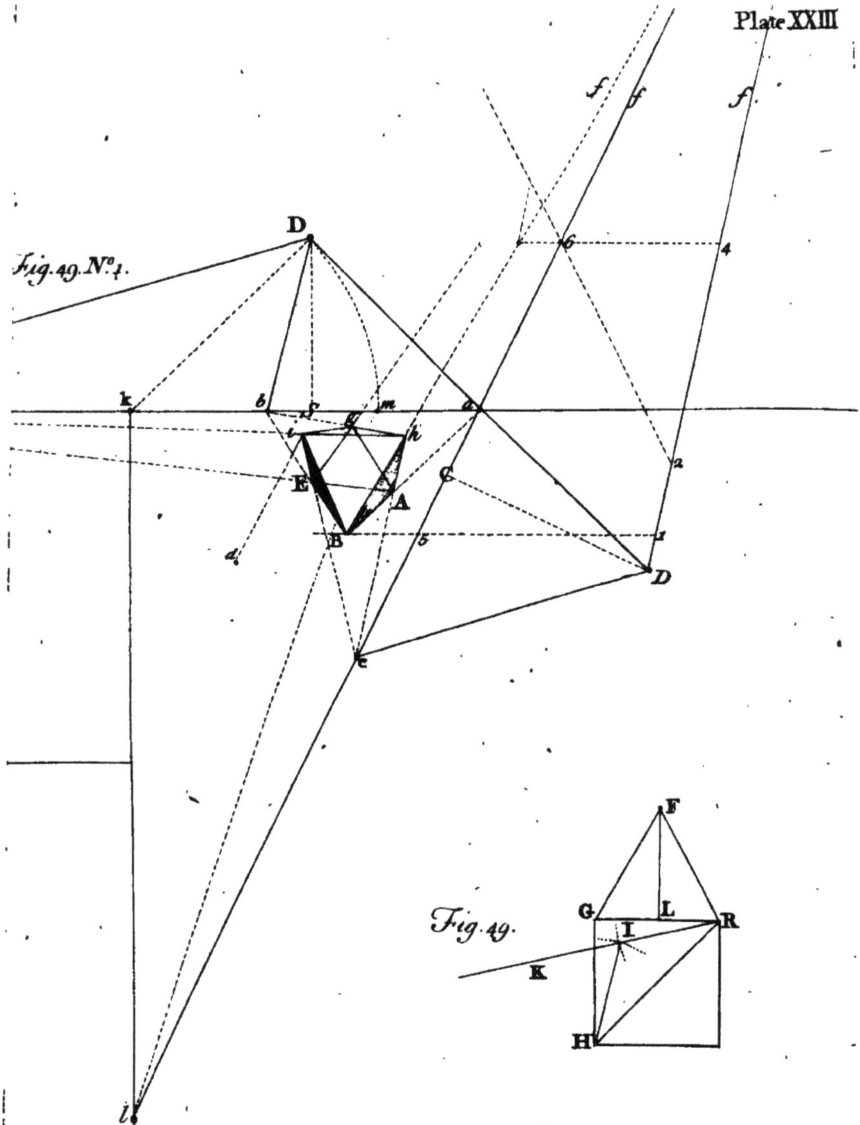

Fig. 49. No. 1.

Fig. 49.

the profile, here made use of, is the same kind of figure, having the same lines and angles perspectively.

And, on these principles, the orthography may, in all possible situations, be such plain, simple, and regular draughts, as an architect would make, for an elevation, with no other change than what the perspective necessarily produces, which never exhibits the figure of any object, otherwise than as seen in nature, supposing always the same situation of object, and spectator, as required in the picture.

To shew what expedients this general method affords, and how extensive the principles are, there is added another orthography of this figure, which represents a perfect square, with the two diagonals. In some cases this orthography, and in some the other, may be most convenient, according to the distances of the vanishing points. To project the figure by this orthography, let a diagonal 4, 1, (No. 4.) be given, whose vanishing point is o. Draw any where from o, at a convenient distance, for the orthography, another line o, 4, 1; find h, the vanishing point of lines perpendicular to those, whose vanishing point is o; draw h, 4, 4, and h, 1, 1, this determines the diagonal of the orthography; then find the vanishing point of lines, making 45 degrees with this diagonal; *(i. e.)* find the center c, of p, q, the vanishing line of the orthography, and its distance c, D^s; draw D^s, o, and then make an angle of 45 above, and below the line o, D^s, to q, and r; for o, is the vanishing point of the diagonal, and o, D^s, the distance of that vanishing point; and from these two points q, and r, finish the orthography (as was done from *f*, and *g*, in the last figure); then draw from *a*, to 1, and from b, through 4, of the first given diagonal, which will determine the side 3, 1, in its place; then draw from 3, and from 1, to p, and another line, *a*, 3, 1, below for the ichnography, which complete, by drawing 3, b, and 1, b, and h, 3, cutting 1, b, in 2, and *a*, 2, cutting 3, b, in 4. Now through this ichnography, drawing from p, perspective perpendiculars, these will determine all the points, as the geometrical perpendiculars did in the former figure. Lastly, lines from h, to the orthography, and from p, through the ichnography, will cut each other, respectively, in the corresponding points, to complete the figure.

This is again represented, under all the same circumstances, with a little difference in the position, only, at No. 5; in which h, o, b, is the vanishing line of the plane 1, 2, 3, 4,—o, p, of the plane 1, 5, 4, 6, and p, h, of the plane 3, 2, 6, 5, which are perpendicular to each other; as are the planes that form the solid angle of a cube.

These are on an oblique plane (the center of the picture being S,) which is the reason that the perpendiculars to the square 1, 2, 3, 4, tend to p; whereas in that, at No. 3, those perpendiculars were parallel to each other, the figure there being on the horizontal plane; but if in that the octaedron had been seen in front, so that the lines 1, 2, and 3, 4, had been parallel to the horizontal line *a*, b, the perpendiculars from the orthography would also have been all parallel to that line, and to each other.——The orthography of No. 3, is a section through the axis, parallel to one side 2, 1, or 4, 3; that of the last, No. 4, through the axis, and diagonal; so that here both plan and profile are squares.

> *N. B.* Though No. 4. might have been projected, in its situation, without either orthography, or ichnography (by means of the several vanishing points) yet as, in more complicated objects, this method is very expedient, it was thought proper to shew it, first, in so simple a figure, that it might be the more easily comprehended.

Fig. 50. For the representation of a dodecaedron, by vanishing lines only. Having the center of the picture S, and distance S, D, given, draw at pleasure the vanishing line of the plane of one face; and having found the center, and distance of that vanishing line, erect the distance perpendicularly to that line from that center, and there find the several vanishing points of the face proposed: this is the general method.——Here the face *a*, *b*, *c*, *d*, *e*, is chosen, which being supposed to lie on the horizontal plane, the vanishing line passes through S, and the distance of the picture S, D, is (in this case) the distance of the vanishing line; draw at pleasure *b*, *c*, for one side of the face proposed, which if it be not parallel to the vanishing line, continue till it cuts that line, and from such

Plate

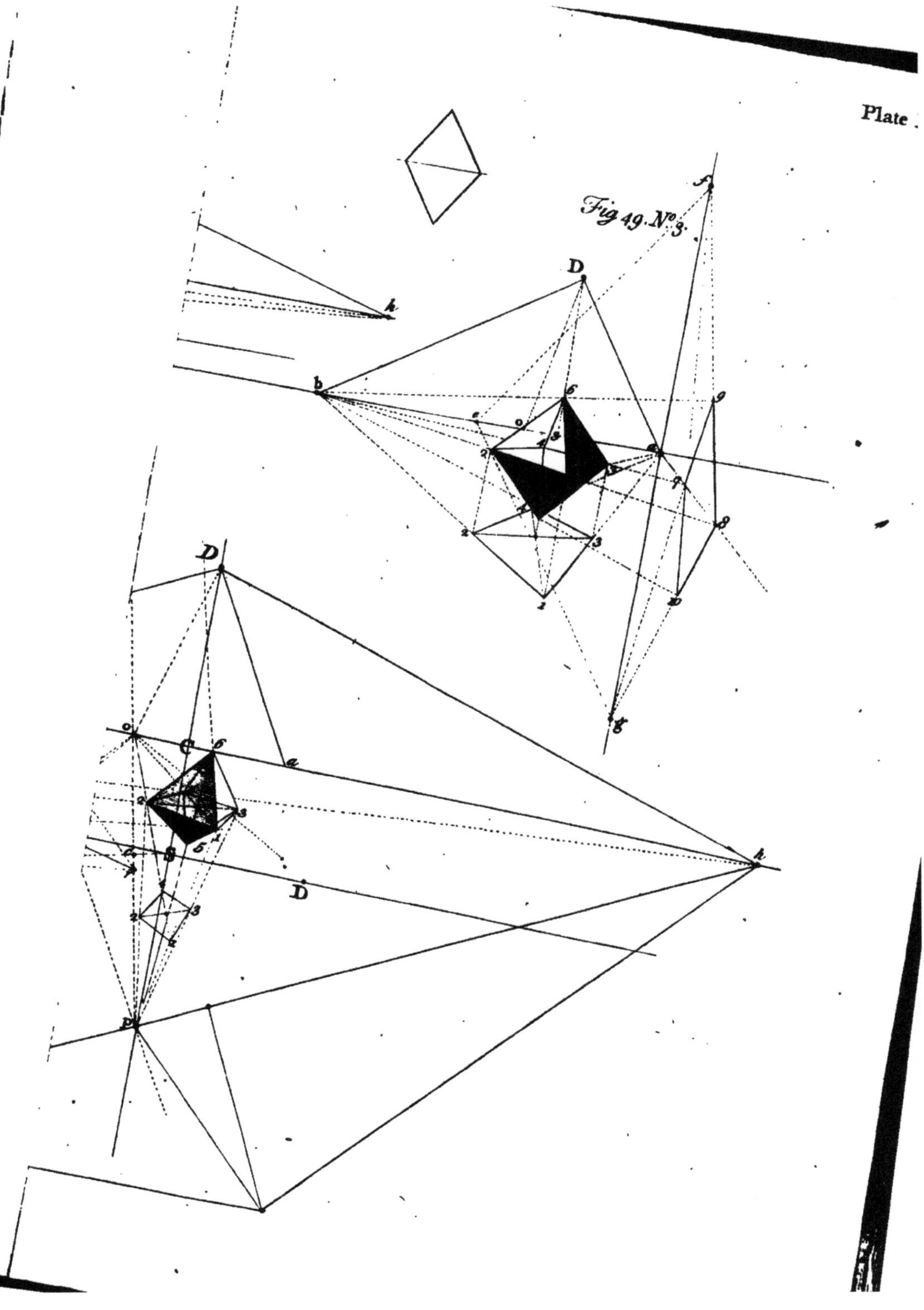

Fig. 49. No. 3.

ſuch interſection draw to D, and thence find the vaniſhing points; but as *b, c*, here, is parallel to the vaniſhing line, draw through D, another parallel, and make the ſeveral angles neceſſary to produce the vaniſhing points; *(i. e.)* deſcribe a pentagon at D, in the poſition required, and divide it into triangles; continue DE, DC, DB, and DA, to the vaniſhing line, cutting it in 1, 2, 3, and 4, which are all the vaniſhing points neceſſary: then draw 2, *b*, for D, C, 2, is parallel to B, A; and draw 3, *c*, for D, B, 3, is parallel to E, C: then draw 1, *c*, cutting 2, *b*, in *a*, for D, E, 1, is parallel to C, A; and draw 4, *b*, cutting 3, *c*, in *e*, for DA, 4, is parallel to BE: laſtly, draw 1, *e*, and 4, *a*, meeting in *d*, which finiſhes the face *b, c, e, d, a*.

For the next face, find the vaniſhing line of planes inclined to that of the face already deſcribed in the ſame angle as the faces of a dodecaedron are to each other, *(i. e.)* 63 deg. 30 min. externally (the angle within being 116 deg. 30 min. the complement of 63 deg. 30 min. to two right angles*. Now draw D, x, perpendicular to 4, D; from x, drop a perpendicular (to the vaniſhing line 4, S, 1, before found); ſet off the diſtance x, D, to d; draw d, p, making with x, d, an angle of 63 deg. 30 min. and cutting x, P, in P, which line will conſequently form an angle of 116 deg. 30 min. with the horizontal line, if continued upwards; then draw 4, P, which is the vaniſhing line ſought; wherefore find its center C^3, by drawing through S, perpendicular to 4, P; find its diſtance C^3, D^3, (by taking the diſtance S, D, in the compaſſes); then ſetting one foot in C^3, and the other at Y, in the ſame line, and from Y, to S, will be the diſtance, which tranfer to C^3, D^3); draw 4, D^3, and find the ſeveral vaniſhing points on this vaniſhing line, as on 4, S, 1, by making the ſame angles at D^3, as at D, *(i. e.)* of 36

Fig. 50. No. 2. * The angle of inclination of two faces of the dodecaedron is found, by making a regular pentagon, and drawing any diagonal, as *a, a*; then biſecting that diagonal in A, and raiſing a perpendicular A, B, to the oppoſite ſide, biſecting that ſide in B; and then with the diſtance A, B, as radius, deſcribing the arcs *a, b*, and *a, b*, meeting in *b*, and producing *a, b*, to E, the external angle E, *b, a*, is the angle of inclination ſought.

For if on the real ſolid any two parallel diagonals are drawn on two adjoining faces, and theſe diagonals are biſected, and perpendiculars drawn from each point of biſection to the ſide of contact, theſe perpendiculars will form the inner angle of 116 deg. 30 min. (very nearly): and the external angle of 63 deg. 30. min. is the angle of inclination.

degrees

degrees each, and proceed as before, for the first face; that is, taking *a*, *d*, here, for the given side, because 4, is its vanishing point, in the plane of 4, C[3], P, as well as in that of 4, 8, 1, the point 4, being the intersection of the vanishing lines of those two planes; draw 6, *d*, and 7, *a*; then 5, *a*, cutting 6, *d*, in *f*, and 4, *f*, cutting 7, *a*, in *g*; but 8, being too far distant to come within the picture, (instead of drawing 8, *f*, and 5, *g*, meeting in *h*, as in the first face) draw 5, *g*, and 6, *a*, cutting it in *h*: lastly, join *h*, *f*, which finishes this face.

Now draw a line through 2, 7, which will be the vanishing line of the face *a*, *b*, *g*, *i*, *s*, for 2, is the vanishing point of *a*, *b*, and 7, of *g*, *a*, both of these being sides of this face, (and two points in any right line being given, the line is thereby given); and having found the center C, and distance *D*[a], of that vanishing line, with its vanishing points 9, and 10, by the same operation as the last, draw *g*, 10, and 7, *b*, cutting it in *i*; draw *i*, 9, and *g*, 2, cutting it in *s*; lastly, join *s*, *b*, which finishes this face.

If it had been necessary to have found this vanishing line (for want of a second point) the same method must have been used as for the other, excepting that the perpendicular must have been drawn upwards, and the angle taken on the upper side of the vanishing line, 4, S, 1, and from thence a line must have been drawn cutting the said perpendicular, because this vanishing line (by the situation of its original plane) must necessarily make its acute angle, or angle of inclination, above the horizontal line.

Now draw 10, 3, 5, which will be the vanishing line of the face *g*, *h*, *i*, *k*, *l*, for 5, is the vanishing point of *g*, *h*, and 10, of *g*, *i*, and find the other vanishing point 11, of that vanishing line (for 3, through which it passes, was before found); draw 11, *i*; then draw 11, *g*, and 5, 1, cutting it in *l*, and *l*, 3, cutting 11, *i*, in K; lastly, join *l*, *h*, which finishes this face.

Thus having got two lines, *i*, *k*, and *i*, *s*, (of the next face *i*, *k*, *m*, *t*, *s*,) whose vanishing points are 11, and 9, draw through those two points the vanishing line of this face, which will also pass through 1, and 6, the remaining vanishing points; draw *k*, 1; then draw *k*, 9, and *i*, 1, meeting in *t*; draw 6, *t*, cutting *k*, 1, in *m*; lastly, join *s*, *t*, which finishes this face.

The

The uppermost face *k*, *l*, *m*, *n*, *o*, being parallel to *a*, *b*, *c*, *d*, *e*, has, of consequence, the same vanishing line, of which face the lines *k*, *l*, and *k*, *m*, being already drawn, draw 4, *m*, and *l*, 1, cutting it in *n*, and draw *s*, *n*; lastly, draw *l*, *o*, parallel to *b*, *c*, which finishes this face.

The remaining four faces are opposite, and parallel to four, on the other side, and are therefore drawn by means of their respective vanishing lines; the face *d*, *e*, *f*, *r*, *q*, is opposite and parallel to *i*, *k*, *m*, *t*, *s*; the face *c*, *e*, *q*, *n*, *w*, is opposite and parallel to *g*, *h*, *i*, *k*, *l*; the face *r*, *q*, *w*, *n*, *o*, is opposite and parallel to *a*, *b*, *s*, *i*, *g*; and the face *t*, *m*, *n*, *w*, *u*, is opposite and parallel to *a*, *d*, *f*, *h*, *g*: the same vanishing points, and the same manner of proceeding, determines all the points, and lines of these four, as of their opposites, though in contrary positions, and these compleat the dodecaedron.

There is one other dodecaedron on the side, which is projected by the same vanishing points.

Fig. 51. No. 1. In order to represent an icosaedron, the fifth and last of the regular solids, which is composed of 20 equilateral triangles, let one side 3, 4, be given, with its vanishing line *a*, *b*, *c*, and distance S, D. Continue the given side to its vanishing point *a*; draw *a*, D, and find the vanishing points *b* and *c*, by making *a*, D, *b*, and *b*, D, *c*, angles of 60 degrees; draw 3, *b*, and 4, *c*, cutting 3, *b*, in 2, which determines one face 4, 3, 2; then through *a*, find the vanishing line of planes, inclining to that of *a*, *b*, *c*, in the same angle as the faces of an icosaedron to each other (viz. 42 degrees) being the acute angle without, (the complement of 138, the obtuse angle within *,) by drawing D, *q*, perpendicular to *a*, D, and *q*, *p*, to *a*, *b*, *c*, which will be the vanish-

Fig. 51. No. 2. * The angle of inclination of two faces of the icosaedron is found, by making a regular pentagon, and on one side describing an equilateral triangle, and having drawn a diagonal of the pentagon, *a*, *a*, and the diameter of the triangle, as A, B; then taking A, B, for radius, and describing the arcs *a*, *b*, and *a*, *b*, meeting in *b*, and producing *a*, *b*, to E, the angle E, *b*, *a*, is the angle of inclination sought.

For, on the real solid, five equilateral triangles form a pyramid, whose base is a pentagon; therefore a diagonal of that pentagon will be the base of a triangle, whose legs (being the diameters of two of these equilateral triangles) will form the internal angle of 138 deg. (nearly): and the external angle of 42 deg. is the angle of inclination.

ing

ing line of planes perpendicular to the lines, whose vanishing point is *a*; then setting off the distance of that vanishing line (which is *q*, D,) to *r*, and from *r*, drawing *r*, *p*, making with *q*, *r*, an angle of 42, and then drawing *a*, *p*, that will be the vanishing line sought. To find the center C, and distance C, *D*[a], of this vanishing line, draw *a*, *D*[a], and find the other vanishing points of an equilateral triangle, as was done on the first vanishing line, *a*, *b*, *c*, viz. here, *n*, and *o*; now draw *n*, 4, and *o*, 3, cutting *n*, 4, in 5, which determines the face 3, 4, 5.

Then find, in the same manner, the vanishing line *c*, *k*, *i*, for the face 4, 2, 11, with this difference, that, as the former *a*, *n*, *o*, was taken below the first vanishing line *a*, *b*, *c*, because the face 3, 4, 5, comes forward, with respect to 3, 4, 2, this falls backward, with respect to the same face, and must therefore be drawn above *a*, *b*, *c*; and having found the vanishing points, as in the others, draw 2, *i*, and 4, *k*, cutting 2, *i*, in 11, which finishes this face.

Then through *b*, the vanishing point of the side 3, 2, find another vanishing line *e*, *b*, *f*, for the face 3, 2, 10, and in it the points *e*, and *f*, as in the former vanishing lines, and draw *e*, 2, and 3, *f*, cutting it in 10, which finishes the face 3, 2, 10, as the line D, a, (perpendicular to *b*, D,) goes beyond the picture, take S, d, a fourth of S, *D*, and draw a parallel to D, a, and proceed as if this 4th was the whole distance, till you find the vanishing line; then from *b* draw a parallel to the vanishing line, which parallel will be that sought. The perpendicular is taken downwards, viz. *a*, f.

Through *e*, the vanishing point of 2, 10; find another vanishing line; but as *e*, *b*, *f*, (in which is the point *e*,) does not pass through S, draw *e*, S, and proceed on it as before, on the vanishing line *a*, *b*, *c*, which will produce the vanishing line *e*, *g*, *b*, for the face 2, 10, 12, which is determined, by drawing 10, *g*, and 2, *b*, cutting 10, *g*, in 12; and now join 12, 11, which finishes another face, 2, 12, 11.

Then through *f*, the vanishing point of the side 3, 10, find one more vanishing line, *f*, *l*, *m*, for the face 3, 10, 1, by the same process, as the last; and, having found the vanishing points, draw *m*, 3, and *l*, 10, cutting *m*, 3, in 1, which finishes that face.

Then

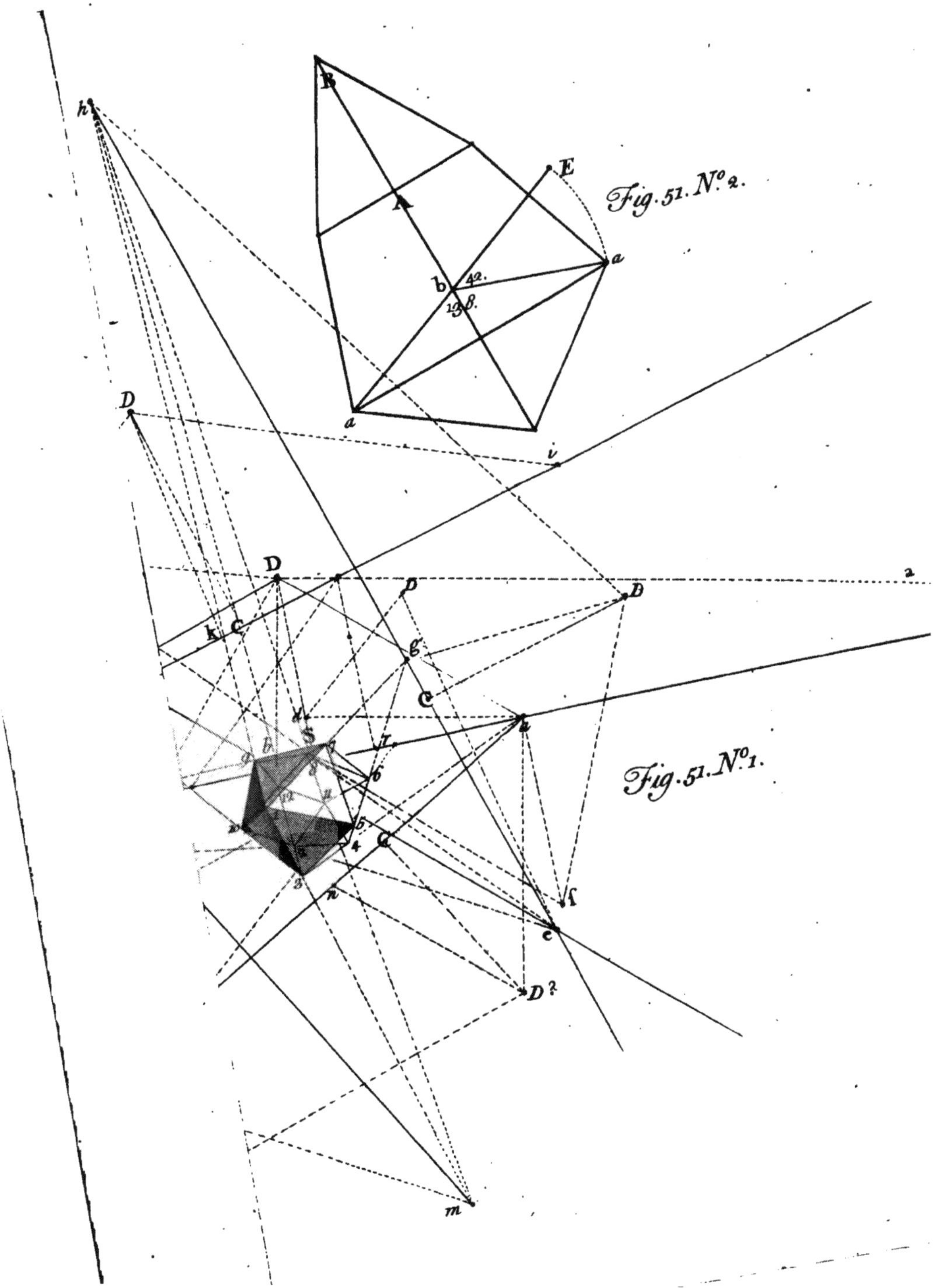

Fig. 51. No. 2.

Fig. 51. No. 1.

Then draw from *l*, through 11, for the side 11, 6, is parallel to 1, 10; draw 5, *g*, cutting 11, 6, in 6; then *e*, 6, and 5, *b*, cutting *e*, 6, in 7, which finishes the face 5, 6, 7, opposite, and parallel to 2, 10, 12; join 6, 4, this determines the face 4, 5, 6, (which, here, happens to fall in one line) and also the face 4, 6, 11.

Draw 6, *f*, and 7, *b*, cutting 6, *f*, in 8, which finishes the face 6, 7, 8, opposite and parallel to 2, 3, 10.

Draw *a*, 8, and 7, *c*, cutting *a*, 8, in 9, which determines the upper face opposite and parallel to 2, 3, 4; join 9, 10,—9, 1,—9, 12,—8, 11, and 8, 12,—5, 1, and 7, 1, which finishes the forwardest face, 1, 5, 7, and completes the whole figure.

2, 3, 4, and 7, 8, 9, being opposite and parallel, their vanishing line is the same, viz. *a*, *b*, *c*.

3, 4, 5, and 8, 9, 12, being opposite and parallel, their common vanishing line is *a*, *n*, *o*.

2, 4, 11, and 1, 7, 9, being opposite and parallel, their common vanishing line is *c*, *k*, *i*.

2, 3, 10, and 6, 7, 8, being opposite and parallel, their common vanishing line is *e*, *b*, *f*.

2, 10, 12, and 5, 6, 7, being opposite and parallel, their common vanishing line is *e*, *g*, *b*.

3, 1, 10, and 6, 8, 11, being opposite and parallel, their common vanishing line is *f*, *l*, *m*.

Fig. I. Below is a representation of the same solid, projected without any other vanishing line than that of the horizon, and also without ichnography, or orthography, any farther than the geometrical draught of a decagon, or double pentagon A, and the axis of the solid marked *o*, 1, 2, 3, which axis is divided by taking *o*, 1, equal to a side of the decagon, 1, 2, equal to radius (or a side of the hexagon), and 2, 3, equal to *o*, 1, in which division the middle part 1, 2, with either end, will be in extreme and mean proportion. Prop. 9. Book 13. Euclid.

N. B. A line is said to be cut in extreme and mean proportion, when the whole is to the greater segment, as the greater segment is to the less. Def. 3. Book 6. Euclid.

First draw the axis perpendicular to the horizon, and mark the divisions; then through 1, and 2, draw transverse lines, *(i. e.)* parallel to the horizon, and on them mark the length *c, b,* on one side, and *c, a,* on the other, but contrariwise; then set off the distance on the horizontal line, from S, the center of it, to *d,* and from *d,* draw through each extremity of the transverse lines, cutting the axis, and the points in which that is cut will determine the depth of each pentagon; the pricked line passing through 2, is so divided. The side *b,* 2, towards *d,* being equal to *b, c,* in the plan, and the side 2, *a,* equal to *c, a,* and the line drawn through 1, contrariwise, *(i. e.) c, a,* towards *d,* and *c, b,* on the opposite side; draw *d, a,* cutting the axis in *g,* and *d, b,* cutting it in *k*; after which, find the vanishing points of the sides of the pentagon, 4, 5, 6, 7, by drawing from *D,* (below) *D,* 4,—*D,* 5, &c. making 4, *D,* 5, an angle of 36 degrees, and the same angle with 5, *D,* 6, and 6, *D,* 7, which are all the vanishing points necessary: then, parallel to the horizontal line, draw *b, i,* through *k*; the point in which *d, b,* intersects the axis, and draw 6, *g,* and 5, *g,* cutting *b, i,* in *b,* and *i*; then *b,* 5, and *i,* 6: lastly, 4, *g,* and 7, *g,* cutting *i,* 6, in *b,* and *b,* 5, in *a,* which finishes the lower pentagon. The upper pentagon is determined in the same manner, and by the same points, with this only difference, that the operation is reversed, in order to produce a contrary position. After which the whole icosaedron is completed, by joining the respective points of the two pentagons, and drawing from the same points to the two poles of the axis. All which may be performed with less trouble, and in less time, than is requisite to form the geometrical ichnography, and orthography. Here is added another on the side, projected by the same points, only instead of drawing *d, b,* cutting the axis (as in the former) a pricked line is drawn through the axis from S, which being cut, from *d,* (the distance) through *b,* finds *k,* the middle of *b, i,* and from *d,* to *a,* finds *g,* and so for the upper pentagon.

Fig. K. In order to represent this figure, by the same method, on an inclined plane. Draw the vanishing line of such plane C, E, and from S, draw S, D, parallel to it; join C, D, and make D, P, perpendicular to

Plate XXVII.

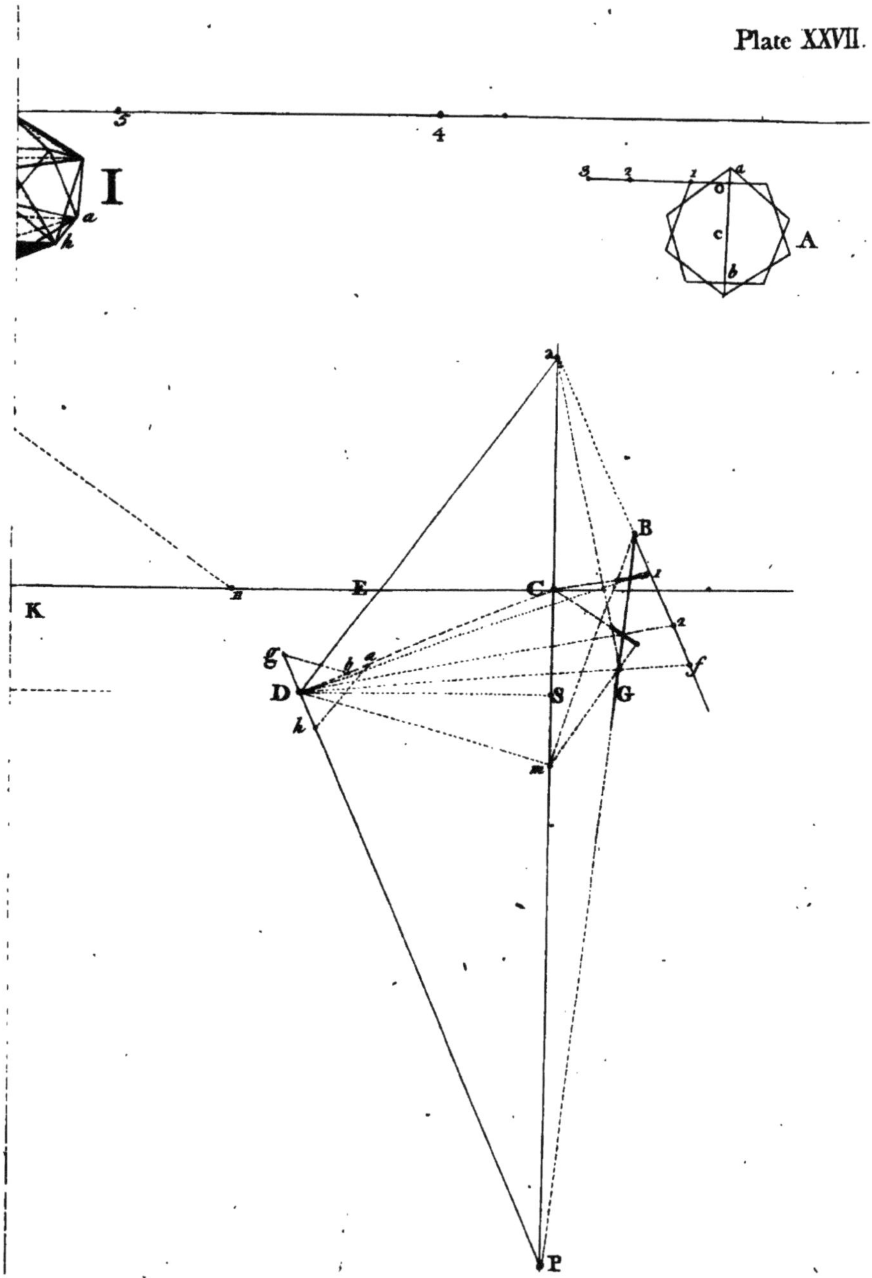

to it: draw at pleaſure P, G, B; draw B, *f*, parallel to D, P, and equal to *o*, 3, the axis at figure A, which divide in 1, and 2, according to the geometrical proportion; then from D, draw to thoſe diviſions, cutting B, G; theſe interſections determine the axis according to the perſpective proportion. Draw from C, lines through the two intermediate points of B, G; and, in order to find their reſpective lengths, ſet them off geometrically on C, D, from D, to *b*, and to *a*; that is, make D, *b*, equal to *c*, *b*, and D, *a*, equal to *c*, *a*; and on D, P, ſet off D, *b*, equal to *o*, 1; then drawing *b*, *a*, and D, a, parallel to it, a, will be a vaniſhing point (in the vaniſhing line P, S, C,) from which the axis, and tranſverſe line, will be divided in the proportion of D, *b*, to D, *a*; wherefore, by drawing a, G, and a, B, the two tranſverſe lines will be cut, the lower backwards, the upper forwards; in that proportion. D, *g*, is equal to *D*, *b*; ſo that drawing *g*, *b*, and D, *m*, parallel to it, *m*, will be the vaniſhing point dividing the ſame axis, and tranſverſe lines, in the proportion of D, *g*, to D, *b*; wherefore draw *m*, G, and *m*, B, which will cut the tranſverſe lines on the oppoſite ſides in this laſt proportion.

This is the preparatory work for the figure K, which is projected upon it, as on a ſkeleton, all the lines correſponding, as appears on inſpection; and all the reſt of the operation is the ſame as at figure I.

Fig. L. This method is an univerſal one; *(i. e.)* the ſolid in any ſituation may be projected by it, and is perhaps the ſhorteſt of all.—For let any face be given, 2, 3, 4, and through any angle of that face, find the axis of the ſolid; divide that axis, perſpectively, in the two points, ſerving for centers of the two pentagons; complete thoſe pentagons in the manner before taught, which, with the two poles of the axis, are all the points; and theſe being joined, the whole figure is formed.

It will be proper to draw (ſomewhere apart) the geometrical proportion of the axis, with its diviſions, and the angles made by the planes; *(e. g.)* draw *q*, *g*, for the axis; divide it in *y*, and *z*, the centers of the two pentagons; and through *z*, draw, at right angles, *k*, *z*; make *z*, *k*, equal to the ſhorter ſide of the diameter of a

 pentagon;

pentagon; draw *k*, *g*; then *z*, *k*, *g*, will be the angle made by the interſection of the plane of the lower pentagon, with a face of the ſolid, terminating at the lower pole *g*, and conſequently *z*, *g*, *k*, will be the angle made by the axis with that face, *g*, *k*.

Having given the face 2, 3, 4, with its vaniſhing line, diſtance, and points, find the vaniſhing line *b*, *p*, of planes perpendicular to *c*, the vaniſhing point of 4, 2, (one ſide of that face); and at *x*, the diſtance of this vaniſhing line *b*, *p*, draw *x*, *p*, making the angle *a*, *x*, *p*, equal to *z*, *k*, *g*; draw *c*, *p*, which will be the vaniſhing line of the planes of the lower and upper pentagon (2, 4, 5, 1, 10, being the lower) of which one ſide is 4, 2; and by means of that ſide, with the vaniſhing line *c*, *p*, that pentagon is finiſhed. Now find *b*, the vaniſhing point of lines perpendicular to the vaniſhing line *c*, *p*, and draw 3, *b*, which will be the indefinite axis of the icoſaedron; biſect the angle *e*, *d*, *f*, to *p* *; draw *p*, 1, cutting 4, 2, in *l*, and *l*, 1, will be the diameter of this pentagon, whoſe center is determined by the interſection of its diameter with the axis, and from that center to 3, will be the perſpective repreſentation of *z*, *g*; wherefore from 3, draw a line in any convenient direction, ſo as not to interfere with the figure, as 3, *o*, and parallel to it, *b*, *d*, equal to *b*, D², the diſtance of *b*; then draw from *d*, through the center, cutting 3, *o*, in *k*; this interſection will mark the place of the center of this lower pentagon, geometrically on 3, *o*, by which meaſure the reſt of the geometrical axis is divided, as appears above, at *q*, *g*, by means of parallels from *y*, *z*, and *g*. Now draw from the diviſions of 3, *o*, to *d*, cutting the axis in the upper center and pole; from *p*, draw through the upper center, and make that part of the upper diameter, from the center to 11, equal to the lower, from

* *N. B.* This biſection is made to find the vaniſhing point *p*, from which a line (drawn to 1,) will divide 4, 2, in half, and ſo become the diameter of the lower pentagon; for *e*, is the vaniſhing point of 4, 1, which is parallel to 2, 10; and *f*, of 2, 1, which is parallel to 4, 5. The ſame point *p*, might alſo have been found, by drawing *d*, *p*, perpendicular to *d*, *c*, for *c* is the vaniſhing point of the line 4, 2. Or as *p*, is in the plane of the vaniſhing line *e*, *f*, and alſo in that of *b*, *p*, it muſt be in their interſection, and therefore is found, as here, in the interſection of theſe two vaniſhing lines.

the

the center to 1, by drawing from 1, through the upper center to *b*, *p*, (the vanifhing line of the plane paffing through the axis,) cutting it in *i*; then drawing from *i*, to the lower center, cutting the upper diameter in 11, which will be the angle of the upper pentagon over the middle of the fide 4, 2, of the lower pentagon; and, in the fame manner, find the other part of the upper diameter; that is, from the upper center, through *l*, the middle of 4, 2, draw to the fame vanifhing line *b*, *p*, and from the point of interfection *, draw through the lower center, cutting the upper diameter in *r*, which will be the middle of 7, 9, the line of the upper pentagon, over the point 1, of the lower pentagon; draw from the vanifhing point *c*, through *r*, which will produce the line 9, 7, indefinitely; draw from *e*, through 11, cutting that line in 9, and from *f*, through the fame point 11, cutting it in 7, which determines the length of 7, 9; draw *g*, 11, and *e*, 7, which finds 6; then *f*, 9, and *c*, 6, cutting it in 12; draw 11, 12, which finifhes this upper pentagon. Now draw from 6, 7, 9, 11, and 12, to 8, the upper pole; then join the correfponding points of the two pentagons, which completes the icofaedron.

* *N. B.* The line here directed to be drawn, is fo nearly parallel to *b*, *p*, that the point of interfection falls at too great a diftance to be conveniently ufed; yet being the fame method by which the laft point 11, (of the fame diameter) was found, it was proper to direct it, as beft, when the points fall within reach.

But an expedient may be ufed to find *r*, the other extremity of this upper diameter. From *i*, (in the line *b*, *p*,) draw one line through the center of that diameter, indefinitely, and another through 11, (the extremity already found); and, at any convenient diftance, draw a line through them both, parallel to *b*, *p*, as L, *w*, I, *x*, cutting thefe lines in I, and *w*: now as *i*, 11, neceffarily paffes through the center of the lower pentagon, and *i*, 1, through one extremity of its diameter; draw alfo *i*, *l*, through the other extremity, cutting the fame line L, *w*, I, *x*, in L; by this means the proportion of the two parts of the diameter is found geometrically: therefore, in the line L, *w*, I, *x*, make I, *x*, equal to L, *w*, and draw *i*, *x*, which will cut the upper diameter in the point *r*.—*This is thus particularly explained for its general ufe.*

The

The FOURTH PART.

Fig. 52. No. 1. IN this part it is propofed to exhibit feveral expedients to facilitate the practice; and firft to divide a perfpective line in any proportion.

Let it be required to divide A, B, whofe vanifhing point is V, into four equal parts. Draw V, d, in any direction, and of any length, and A, *f*, parallel to it; draw d, B, cutting A, *f*, in *f*; divide A, *f*, into four equal parts, at *c*, *d*, and *e*; draw d, *c*,—d, *d*, and d, *e*, which will cut A, B, in C, D, and E, the points required.

If room be wanting, any nearer diftance will anfwer the fame purpofe, as *D*: in this cafe, draw *D*, B, cutting A, *f*, in 4; and divide A, 4, in the fame number of equal parts, at 1, 2, and 3; and draw *D*, 1,—*D*, 2, and *D*, 3, which will find the fame points.

Again, at No. 2, V, *D*, is drawn in another direction; for it may be in any, at pleafure, provided A, *f*, be drawn parallel to it; and here it is required to divide A, B, into two equal parts only; therefore bifect A, *f*, in *e*, and draw *D*, *e*, cutting A, B, in E, the point fought. Or, if it be more convenient, draw V, d, and A, f, parallel to it; bifect A, f, in 9, and draw d, 9, which will cut A, B, in the fame point E; for the truth of the operation depends on the parallelifm of the two lines, V, d, and A, f. And in all thefe cafes, the lines from *D*, or d, to the feveral divifions of A, *f*, or A, f, reprefent parallels, therefore the lines A, B, muft be divided as the originals.

If V, d, No. 1, be the true diftance of the vanifhing point V, and A, the interfection of the picture, by the original line; then A, *c*, *d*, *e*, *f*, are the true originals, or geometrical proportions; and therefore when it is required to find the original proportions of a perfpective line, already divided, the true diftance and interfection muft

2 be

Plate XXVIII.

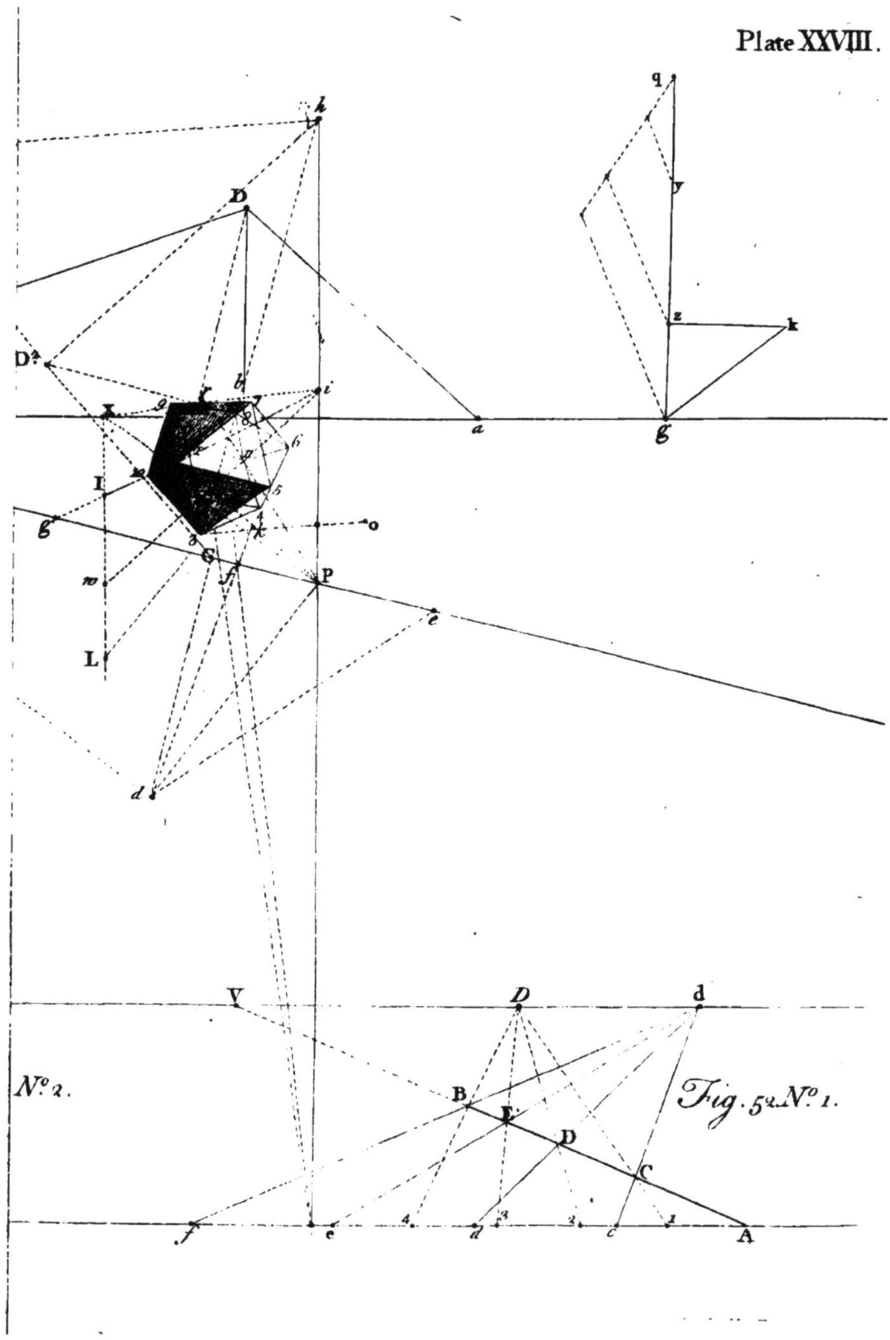

be taken.—But in order to find the perſpective diviſions on a line already projected, the above operations are equally true, whatever diſtance be taken; and although A, be not the interſection; for A, B, any part of a perſpective line, will be truly divided by this method.

At No. 3. it is required to make a ſegment on the perſpective line A, V, from the point C, towards V, equal to A, B, on the ſame line. Draw D, C, till it cuts A, *e*, in *c*; make *c*, *e*, equal to A, *b*, and draw *e*, D, cutting A, V, in E; then will C, E, be, perſpectively, equal to A, B.

Or, if it be required to make the perſpective of a part equal to *b*, A, (on the original line;) at the diſtance of *c*, from *b*, divide the original line A, *e*, in the manner required, and draw *c*, *D*, and *e*, *D*, which will determine the part C, E; and ſo of any other proportions.

Fig. 53. No. 1. Here is an original plan, in its geometrical proportion, placed obliquely below the ground line; it is required to project it in perſpective. Continue the ſeveral diviſions to that line, and having found the two vaniſhing points *a*, and *b*, draw from thoſe points to the ſeveral interſections, which will form the perſpective repreſentation; but as it often happens, that on one ſide there may not be room for many interſections, becauſe they run much wider than on the other ſide, after having drawn one only, as to *c*, and drawn from thence to *b*, which finds the point 1, take any other point between *b*, and S, as B, and draw from thence through 1, cutting the ground line in C, and make uſe of the diſtance *o*, C, (inſtead of *o*, *c*,) ſetting that off, from C, to *f*, and from *f*, to *g*, &c. as often as neceſſary; and drawing from *f*, to B, and from *g*, to B, &c. the ſame points 2, 3, 4, &c. will be found, as if there had been ſpace to repeat the diſtance *c*, *o*, as many times; then draw 1, *b*,—2, *b*,—3, *b*,—&c. which will complete the work.

Fig. 53. No. 2. The ſame thing is done without a geometrical plan: and here the meaſures of the original ſquares are ſet off equally on each ſide of *o*, as 1, 2, 3, 4, and the diſtances *b*, D, and *a*, D, brought

brought down to the vaniſhing line at 9, and *d*; and, after having drawn the two extreme lines *a*, *o*, and *b*, *o*, then drawing, reſpectively, 9, 1,—9, 2,—9, 3,—9, 4, and *d*, 1,—*d*, 2,—*d*, 3,—*d*, 4, the points of the extreme lines *b*, *o*, and *a*, *o*, are found; from which points, on one ſide, drawing to *a*, and, on the other, to *b*, the plan is completed. And if room were wanting for S, D, above, the points *b*, *a*, and 9, *d*, might be found by means of d, below, making S, d, equal to the diſtance S, D.

Fig. 54. If it be required to find a ſegment of F, *b*; from F, towards *b*, equal to A, B, of the line A, *a*, bring down *a*, D, the diſtance of the vaniſhing point *a*, to d; draw d, B, cutting the ground line in *e*; bring down alſo *b*, D, the diſtance of the vaniſhing point *b*, to *d*; draw *d*, F, cutting the ground line in *f*; make *f*, *g*, equal to A, *e*, and draw *d*, *g*, cutting F, *b*, in E; then will E, F, repreſent an original line, equal to the original of A, B, and therefore will be equal, perſpectively, to A, B, which is all that is neceſſary to find the length F, E, perſpectively, equal to A, B. But as it is indifferent whether the ground line A, *g*, be uſed for this purpoſe, or any other parallel, and as ſome other is often more convenient, take any line parallel to the vaniſhing line, as B, 6, and draw d, A, cutting it in 4, and *d*, F, cutting it in 6; then make 6, 5, equal to 4, B, and draw *d*, 5, which will cut F, *b*, in E. Or take any other parallel, as 1, F; make F, 3, equal to 1, 2, and draw *d*, 3, which finds the ſame point E: for d, A, *e*, and *d*, *f*, *g*, are equal triangles, being between the ſame parallels, and having equal baſes; [Euclid, Book 3. Prop. 38] and B, 6, or 1, F, being parallel to the ſame vaniſhing line *a*, *d*, will cut off equal triangles from *e*, d, A, and *g*, *d*, *f*; therefore, &c.

Fig. 55. Another way of dividing perſpective lines, is by marking the geometrical proportions on the rays, from D, as on D, *a*,—D, *b*, the rays of the vaniſhing points *a*, and *b*, of A, B, and A, G, F. Make D, 1, and D, 2, equal, and draw D, 6, parallel to 1, 2; then a line from 6, cutting A, *b*, and A, *a*, in any parts, will divide thoſe two lines equally, as 6, G, B, makes A, G, and A, B, perſpectively, equal.

If

Plate XXV.

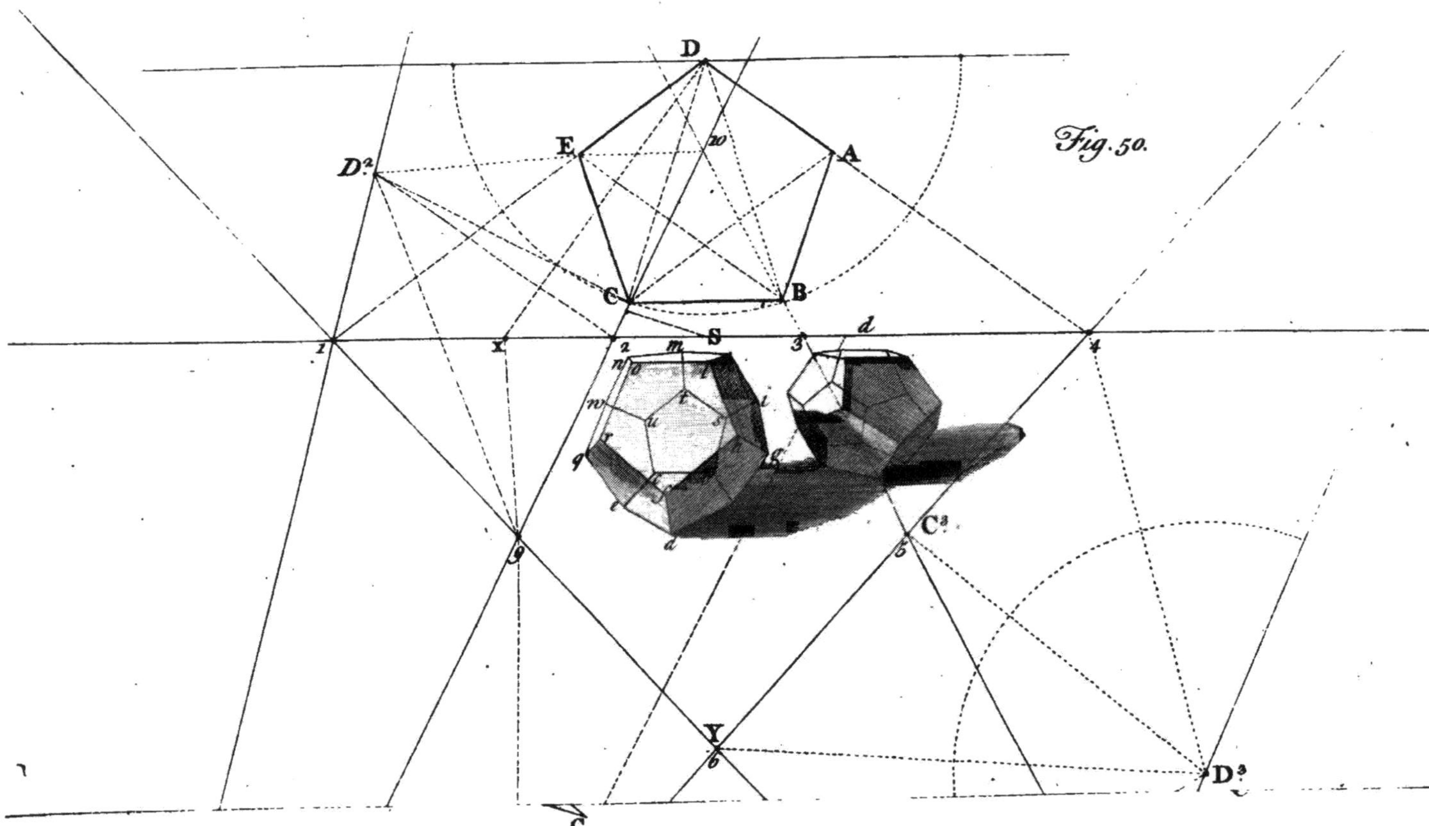

Fig. 50.

Plate XXIX.

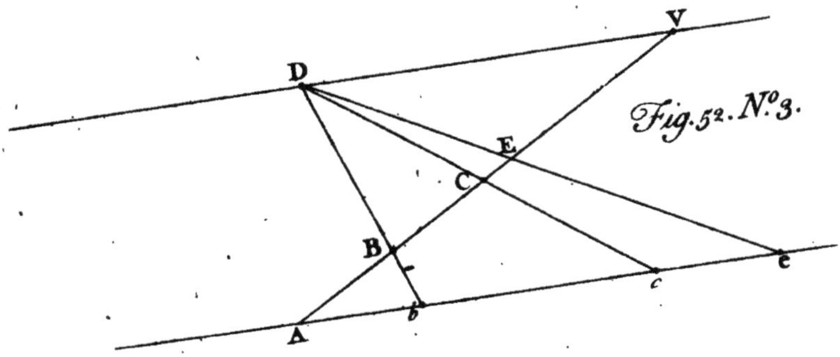

Fig. 52. No. 3.

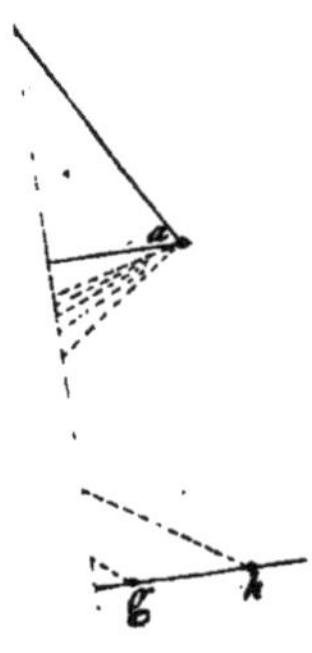

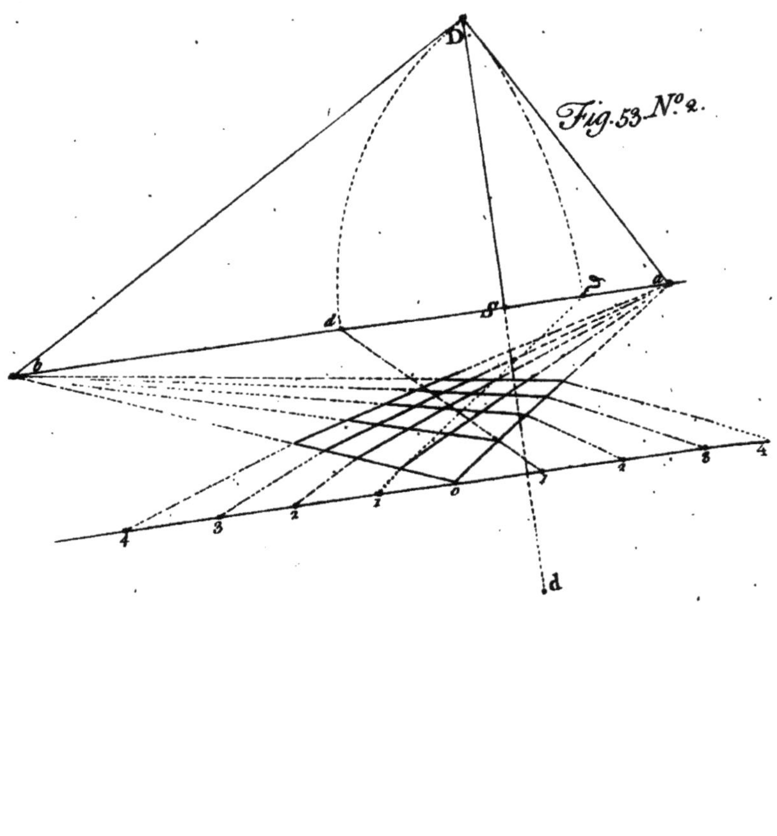

Fig. 53. No. 2.

If any other proportion be required, mark it on the ray of the line; for instance, D, 3, is equal to D, 1, and ½. Draw D, 5, parallel to 1, 3; and draw 5, B, cutting A, *b*, in F; then A, F, is in the same proportion to A, B, as D, 3, is to D, 1.

A, *c*, is another perspective line; D, *c*, its ray; and *c*, its vanishing point; and 1, 4, divides D, *a*, and D, *c*, unequally; and D, 6, being parallel to 1, 4, the line 6, E, B, divides A, *c*, and A, *a*, in E, and B, perspectively, in the same proportion; A, E, being to A, B, perspectively, as D, 4, to D, 1, geometrically.

Fig. 55. No. 2. This method may also be used in cases like that of 54. Let E, F, be a perspective line, whose vanishing point is *a*, it is required to make A, B, (of another line) equal to E, F. Draw from A, to *a*, the vanishing point of E, F; and draw A, E, cutting the vanishing line in *e*; draw *e*, F, cutting A, *a*, in C; then A, E, F, C, will represent a parallelogram, whose opposite sides being parallel and equal, A, C, must be equal to E, F. Now make D, 1, and D, 2, equal; and draw D, *f*, parallel to 1, 2; draw *f*, C, cutting A, *b*, in B; then will A, B, be equal to A, C, (as by the last Figure;) but A, C, is equal to E, F; therefore A, B, is also equal to E, F; which was to be done.

Fig. 55. No. 3. B, A, is given, it is required on E, A, to make A, C, equal to B, A. Draw 4, 1, making D, 4 and D, 1, equal; draw D, 5, parallel to 4, 1; then draw 5, B, cutting E, A, in C, and C, A, will be equal to B, A; which was to be done.

But if 5, goes beyond the picture, divide D, 4, in half, at 2; and draw D, 3, parallel to 2, 1; then (having divided A, B, perspectively, in half at 6,) draw 3, 6, which will cut E, A, in the same point C.

N. B. The manner of dividing a perspective line in half, is described at Fig. 52, No. 2.

Fig. 55. No. 4. Let the same things be given as before; but the distance D, being beyond the picture, take a fourth (or any) part of the

the diſtance at *D*; then take a fourth of S, V, at E, and draw *D*, E, which will be parallel to V, D, which tends to the true diſtance; therefore the angle at *D*, will be the ſame as at D.—Draw *c*, *d*, making *D*, *c*, and *D*, *d*, in any proportion required, and *D*, *e*, parallel to *c*, *d*; ſet off S, *e*, four times to F, and draw F, B, cutting S, A, in C: then will A, C, be to A, B, as *D*, *d*, is to *D*, *c*, (*i. e.*) in the proportion required.

N. B. Any line drawn from F, will cut the ſame lines in the ſame proportions, as F, *f*, *b*; for A, *b*, is to A, *f*, as A, B, is to A, C; (*i. e.*) as *D*, *c*, is to D, *d*.

Fig. 56. As this is the place allotted for expedients, the reader is referred back to Fig. 45, where the manner of finding, on the horizontal plane, the plans, or ichnographies, of cubes projected on oblique planes, is deſcribed. The letters, conſtantly uſed, ſhew the ſituation in general; but here is a difficulty peculiar to this poſition, which is, that the ſide a, *b*, is exactly in front, and, for that reaſon, it is impoſſible to find the ſeat, or ichnography of the point a, without ſome expedient; therefore draw a, *a*, and b, *b*, both parallel to the horizontal line; draw at pleaſure from S, (which is the vaniſhing point P, brought up to the horizontal line), cutting b, *b*, in *b*; draw P, *b*, cutting a, *a*, in *a*; draw *a*, C, perpendicular to the horizontal line, cutting S, *b*, in C; draw C, A, parallel to *b*, b; then A, will be the point ſought, viz. the ſeat of a, on the horizontal plane, by which the ſeat, or plan of the upper ſquare is found on that plane.

Fig. 57. No. 1. At Fig. 31, are ſeveral lines tending to a point beyond the limits of the picture, and there, as well as elſewhere, the reader is referred to this place for expedients in ſuch caſes; which frequently happen, eſpecially when the diſtance of the picture is conſiderable. The preſent figure ſhews the manner of drawing lines to an inacceſſible point. Suppoſe A, B, and C, D, two lines, tending to ſuch point, beyond the picture; it is required to draw from *g*, a line, tending to the ſame point. Draw N, O, through *g*, in any direction, and B, D, parallel to it, at any convenient diſtance, within the picture; at D, with the compaſſes, ſet off the length of N, O, as D, E;

ſo

Plate XXX.

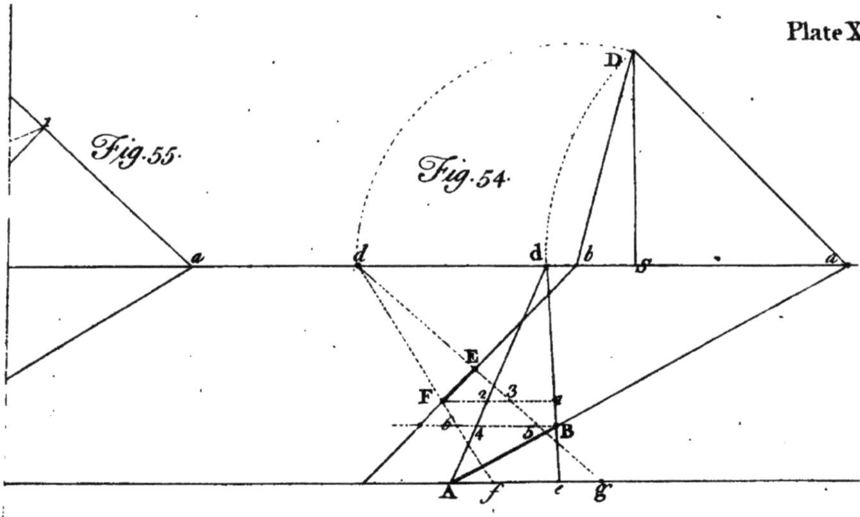

Fig. 55.

Fig. 54.

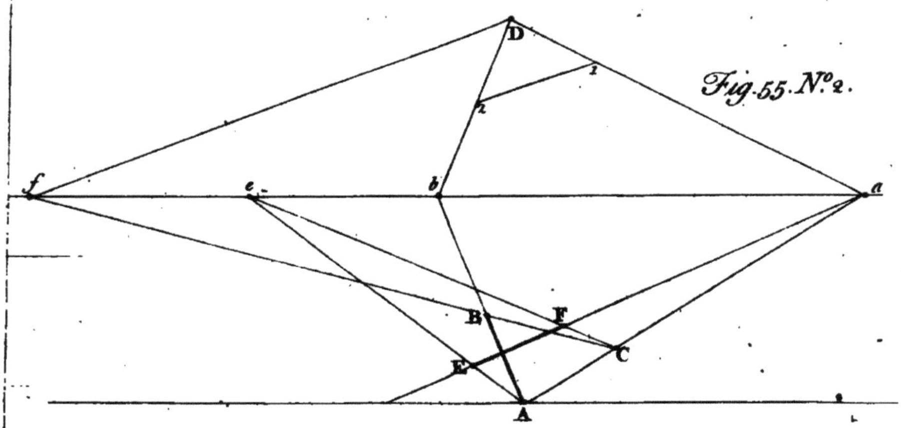

Fig. 55. No. 2.

so that E, intersects the line A, B; divide D, E, in F, making D, F, equal to O, *g*; draw F, *f*, parallel to A, B, cutting B, D, in *f*; then draw *g*, *f*, which will tend to the same point with A, B, and C, D; for B, D, is divided in *f*, in the same proportion as D, E, is divided in F, (*i. e.*) as N, O, in *g*, (Prop. 2. Book 6. Eucl.) Let there be another point, from which it is also required to draw to the same inaccessible point, whether between the lines A, B, and C, D, or without, as here at *h*; which, if it be so situated, as that a line N, O, may conveniently be drawn to it through *g*; then draw N, *g*, O, *h*, and take the distance O, *h*, and add it to the line E, D, from D, to I; and draw I, *i*, parallel to *f*, F, cutting B, D, in *i*, and drawing *h*, *i*, it will tend to the same point; for the triangle D, I, *i*, is similar to D, F, *f*; and therefore D, *i*, is to D, I, as D, *f*, to D, F; and, consequently, D, *i*, to O, *h*, as D, *f*, to O, *g*.

Let it also be required to draw from *k*, to the same point. Draw 1, 2, through *k*, parallel to B, D; set off 1, 2, from *f*, to 3; divide *f*, 3, in 4, as 1, 2, in *k*; draw 4, 5, parallel to A, B; and then drawing *k*, 5, it will tend to the same point.—Here *g*, *f*, is used instead of C, D, as more convenient; for any two lines tending to the same point, will answer the purpose.

Fig. 57. No. 2. Another method is proposed: let A, B, and C, D, be two lines tending to a point, beyond the picture; now, in order to draw from *e*, to the same point, draw any line through *e*, cutting these two lines in A, and C; and at any convenient distance B, D, parallel to A, C, draw A, D, and (parallel to D, C,) draw B, *b*, cutting A, D, in *b*; then draw *b*, *d*, parallel to B, D, and consequently equal to it; draw *e*, D, cutting *b*, *d*, in F, which divides *b*, *d*, in the same proportion as A, C, is divided by *e*; wherefore set off *d*, F, to D, *f*, or (which is the same thing) draw F, *f*, parallel to *d*, D, and drawing *e*, *f*, it will tend to the point required.

By the same process, *m*, *p*, is found, tending to the same point, viz. draw *m*, *n*, parallel to A, C; draw *n*, D, cutting B, *b*, in *s*;

draw *s*, *t*, parallel to B, D; draw *m*, D, cutting it in *t*; then set off *s*, *t*, from B, to *p*; and drawing *m*, *p*, it will tend to the same point.—The only requisite is to find the same proportions on the line B, D, as on A, C, or on B, *p*, as on *n*, *m*.

Fig. 57. No. 3. Now, on these principles, suppose S, *f*, the horizontal line, (or the vanishing line of any other plane,) S, D, the distance, D, *b*, a parallel to an original line, tending to a vanishing point beyond the picture; it is required to draw from *a*, to the same vanishing point.—Draw *a*, *d*, and *b*, *e*, both parallel to S, D; continue *b*, D, till it cuts *a*, *d*, in *d*; draw *b*, *g*, parallel to S, *f*; draw *d*, *g*, cutting S, *f*, in *i*; draw *a*, *i*, cutting D, S, (continued) in *h*; set off *g*, *h*, from *b*, to *e*, (or S, *h*, from *f*, to *e*,) or draw *h*, *e*, parallel to S, *f*; then drawing *a*, *e*, it will tend to the vanishing point required.—It is evident, that *b*, *f*, might have been set off from S, to *g*, instead of drawing the parallel *b*, *g*; or that a parallel to S, *f*, from *h*, would have determined *e*, as well as setting off S, *h*, at *f*, *e*, &c.

Fig. 57. No. 4. Let *a*, *b*, and C, *d*, be two lines, tending to a vanishing point; if there are any number to be drawn to the same point in the same line, as 1, 2, and 3, draw a, *c*, parallel to *a*, C, at any convenient distance; then draw from C, 1, 2, and 3, parallels to a, *a*, cutting a, *c*; then from *c*, and the other intersections of a, *c*, draw to O, any point in *a*, *b*, and through 7, the intersection of *c*, O, with C, *d*, draw 7, 8, another parallel to a, *c*; then from 1, 2, and 3, draw through the respective intersections of the line 7, 8, viz. 1, 4,—2, 5, and 3, 6, which will be the lines required, all tending to the same vanishing point.

Fig. 58. No. 1. Suppose A, B, a perspective line, to be divided in any proportion, but its vanishing point to be beyond the picture; continue D, S, to A, B, cutting it in *e*; draw at pleasure *e*, *i*; set off B, *g*, from *e*, to *h*; draw S, *h*, and D, *i*, parallel to it; set off *h*, *i*, from *g*, to *l*, upwards; draw D, *l*, and A, M, parallel to it. (By this means, *e*, *i*, will be divided proportionally to D, *e*, (*i. e.*) *e*, *h*, to *e*, S, as *h*, *i*, to S, D; and g, *l*, will be to *g*, B, as

Plate XX

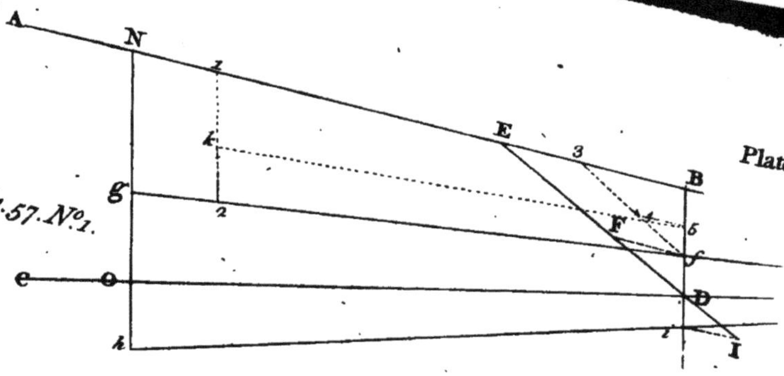

Fig. 57. No. 1.

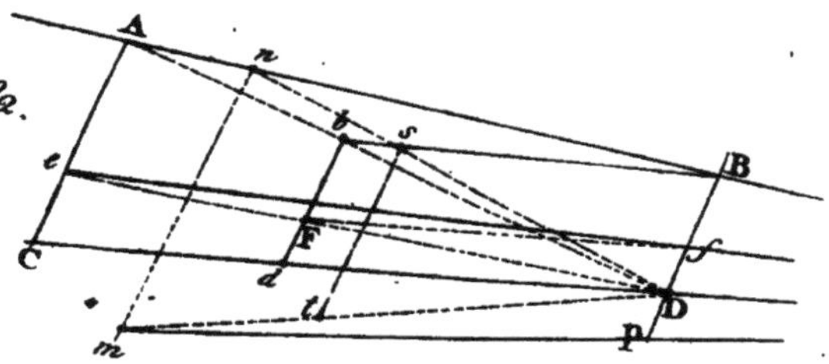

Fig. 57. No. 2.

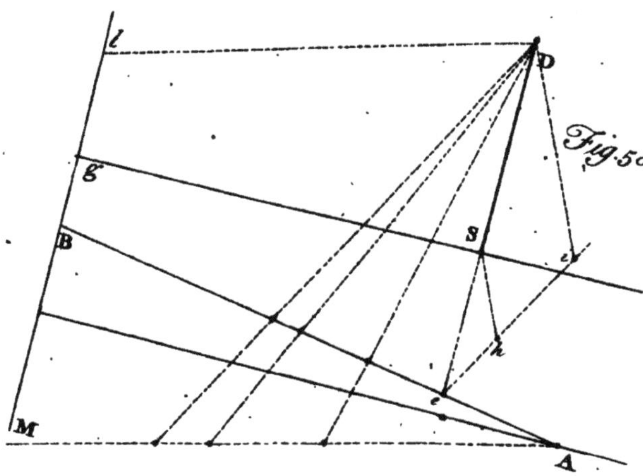

Fig. 58. No. 1.

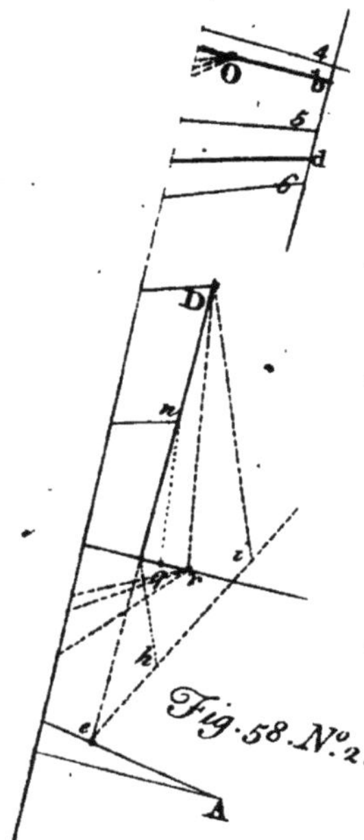

Fig. 58. No. 2.

as S, D, to S, *e*, which is the proportion wanted.) Now A, M, will be the original of A, B; therefore, on it, make the geometrical divisions required; draw from these divisions to D, which will cut A, B, perspectively.

N. B. If D, *l*, had been already drawn (as well as A, B,) then only draw A, M, parallel to it, and proceed as above.

Fig. 58. No. 2. After *e*, *i*, is divided, if room be deficient below for A, M, draw *n*, *p*, (from *p*, the extremity of the picture) parallel to D, *l*, and bring down *n*, to *q*; *(i. e.)* make *p*, *q*, equal to *p*, *n*; then draw from D, parallel to *n*, *q*, which finds *r*, the distance of the vanishing point of A, B; then make the geometrical division on A, *c*, as *a*, *b*, *c*, from which points draw to *r*, and the lines *a*, *r*, *b*, *r*, and *c*, *r*, will cut A, B, in the same points.

Fig. 59. No. 1. Let E, F, be given, and the direction of E, G, drawn at pleasure, in order to form either a cube, or any other cubical figure, of known measures, (the horizontal line, with its distance, being always supposed to be given, or known). Continue the side E, G, till it meets the horizontal line in *a*, which will be its vanishing point; draw *a*, D, and D, *b*, perpendicular to it, cutting the horizontal line in *b*; draw E, *b*; then E, *g*, parallel to D, *a*, and E, *h*, parallel to D, *b*; and make these two lines of the geometrical lengths required (as here they are both equal to E, F): draw *g*, D, cutting E, *a*, in G, and *h*, D, cutting E, *b*, in H; by which operation those lengths are determined: draw G, *b*, and H, *a*, which finish the lower square or plan: raise perpendiculars at G, and H, and the remaining angle; and draw F, *a*,—F, *b*, cutting the perpendiculars at G, and H, in I, and K: lastly, draw I, *b*, and K, *a*, which completes the cube.

Fig. 59. No. 2. If room be wanting, below, for the lines E, *g*, and E, *h*, they may be drawn parallel to the horizontal line, as in this scheme; but then the distance *b*, D, must be brought down to d, and drawing d, *g*, will find the same point G, in the line E, *b*, as by the above operation; and the distance *a*, D, must also be brought down to *d*, from whence, drawing to *b*, the point H, will be found. The rest is as No 1.

Fig.

Fig. 59. No. 3. Is an expedient, in cafe the point *a*, is beyond the picture. Continue the line G, E, whofe direction is given as before, indefinitely towards *D*; and fet off the diftance of the picture S, D, from S, to *D*, the point where that diftance cuts G, E, continued. From O, in the horizontal line, at the extremity of the picture, draw a parallel to G, E, *D*, cutting S, *D*, in d; tranfpofe S, d, to *d*, on the line S, D; draw *d*, O, and D, *a*, parallel to it, which will tend to the true vanifhing point *a*, beyond the picture. Now proceed, as at No. 1, or No. 2; and having drawn E, *b*, and found the points G, and H, and drawn G, *b*, bifect the angle *a*, D, *b*, to *c*; draw *c*, E, cutting G, *b*, in L; draw L, H; then raife the feveral perpendiculars at G, L, and H; draw F, *b*, cutting H, K, in K; and *c*, F, cutting L, M, in M; draw *b*, M, cutting G, I, in I; join F, I, and M, K, which completes the whole. If a parallel to S, *D*, be drawn from O, cutting the line D, E, G, in a, then O, a, will be equal to O, *a*, (fo that if *a*, O, and a, O, were both raifed up perpendicular to the picture, and alfo D, S, and *D*, S, on S; then *a*, would coincide with a, and D, with *D*:) by which means the lines O, d, and O, *d*, may both be fpared.

The fame figure is repeated feveral times, on purpofe to fhew by what various means the fame effect may be produced; but if the lines of the three operations were crowded together in one fcheme, they could fcarce be feparated by the eye or underftanding, fo as to difcover what was peculiarly, and diftinctly effential to each.

If they appear to be fomewhat intricate, it muft be confidered, that they are to be ufed on extraordinary occafions only, and may be always avoided, if the artift chufes rather to take fufficient room on another fcale, than confine himfelf to the fpace which happens to be left in his picture.

Fig. 60. Let A, C, be a perfpective line; it is required to find the geometrical length of a part, as A, B. If its diftance C, D, be within the picture, and room to fet it off on the vanifhing line, tranfpofe that diftance from C, D, to E; draw E, B, cutting the ground

Plate XXXII.

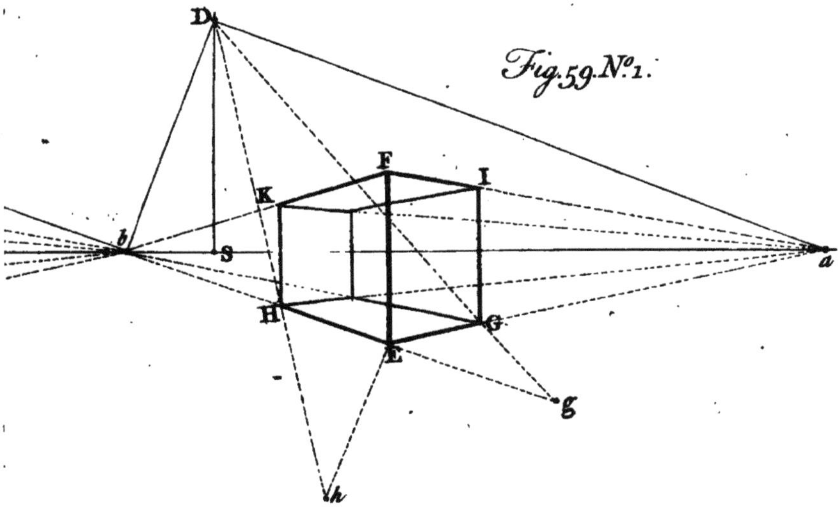

Fig. 59. No. 1.

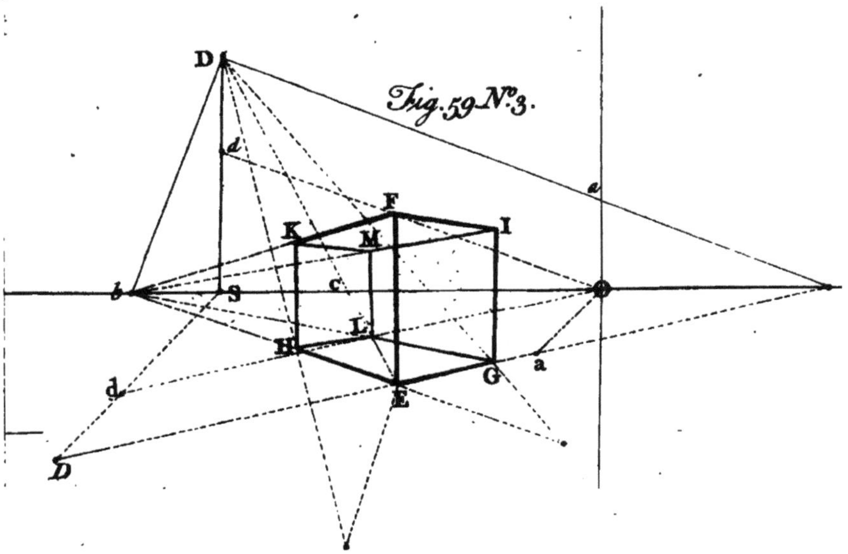

Fig. 59. No. 3.

ground line in F; then A, F, is the geometrical length ſought.—But if D be out of the picture, take any portion of S, D, as here S, *d*, a fourth, and S, *c*, a fourth of S, C; draw *c*, *d*, which will be a fourth of C, D; tranſpoſe *c*, *d*, from C, to *e*, and draw *e*, B, cutting A, F, in *f*; then A, *f*, will be a fourth of A, F, the geometrical length ſought.—It is evident, that the ſame expedient will ſerve to find any proportion of A, C; for ſuppoſe it had been required to cut off the geometrical length A, F, thereon, this is only reverſing the operation, (*i. e.*) drawing E, F, cutting A, C, in B; or, if room be wanting, drawing *e*, *f*, which finds the ſame point B.

Fig. 61. No. 1. In order to find the vaniſhing line of a plane making a given angle with another vaniſhing line; it has been taught to find, firſt, the vaniſhing line of planes at right angles with both, on which to meaſure the angle of inclination. Now ſuppoſe Q, S, B, the vaniſhing line given; it is required to find the vaniſhing line of planes, making a certain angle therewith, and paſſing through B, their common interſection. To this end, find Q, the vaniſhing point of lines perpendicular to B; draw Q, P, perpendicular to Q, B, which will be the vaniſhing line, perpendicular to both planes; ſet off its diſtance to *d*; draw *d*, P, making Q, *d*, P, the angle of inclination; and, laſtly, draw B, P, which will be the vaniſhing line ſought. But if room be wanting, above, for the diſtance S, D, divide S, B, in half, at *b*, and take S, *D*, half of S, D, and find *q*, the vaniſhing point of perpendiculars to *b*; draw *q*, *p*, perpendicular to *q*, B; ſet off the diſtance of *q*, to *r*; and draw *r*, *p*, making *q*, *r*, *p*, the angle of inclination: draw *b*, *p*, which would be the vaniſhing line ſought, if half the diſtance was the true diſtance. Now, therefore, from B, draw a parallel to *b*, *p*, which parallel will be the vaniſhing line ſought.

Fig. 61. No. 2. Let it be required to draw a line through B, S, at the point A, in any angle, perſpectively, as (*e. g.*) 45 degrees; this is done by making the ſame angle at D, drawing D, *d*, and then *d*, A, which is the line ſought. But if room be wanting, take S, *d*, the half of the true diſtance (or any leſs proportion, as may be neceſſary;) make

make the ſame angle at *d*; draw *d*, *D*; then divide S, A, in half, at *a*; draw *D*, *a*; and, laſtly, draw through A, a, parallel to *D*, *a*, which will be the line required.

Fig. 62. When the parallel D, C, of any line *b*, *a*, runs out of the picture, before it reaches the vaniſhing line, any other line, within the picture, will anſwer the purpoſe, as D, *c*, by drawing from *a*, *b*, and *f*, parallels to it, cutting the ground line in *e*, *g*, and *h*, from which, ſeverally, drawing to *c*, the perſpective points of *a*, *b*, and *f*, are found in the poſition required.

Fig. 63. No. 1. The center and diſtance of the picture being given, let B, A, be an original line, in any direction (*e. g.*) inclined to the picture in the angle B, A, *B*; and, cutting it in A, (A, *B*, being its ſeat, or orthographic projection on the picture) it is required to find the perſpective length of A, B. Draw S, V, parallel to that ſeat, and S, D, perpendicular to it, and equal to the diſtance; draw D, V, parallel to the original A, B; draw A, V; then V, is the vaniſhing point, and A, V, the indefinite perſpective repreſentation. And the length of A, B, is determined, by drawing B, D, cutting A, V, in *b*. Or ſetting off the diſtance V, D, to *d*, and A, B, to *B*, and drawing *B*, *d*, finds the ſame point *b*.

This is the moſt general ſcheme for the purpoſe, becauſe the angle of incidence is, at once, referred to the picture, without regard to any other plane, and ſo the original line may have any inclination, without making the leaſt difference in the operation, on account of the poſition of the picture.

But another example or two, with additional circumſtances, may farther illuſtrate this kind of operation.

Fig. 63. No. 2. A, B, is an original line; A, *a*, its ſeat on the picture; A, *b*, the perſpective of A, B, found as in the former; B, *a*, (parallel to S, D,) its ſeat on the ground; *a*, *b*, the perſpective of that ſeat, found by drawing *a*, S; for if D, S, be turned forward on the point S, and B, *a*, turned backward on the point *a*, till both are perpendicular to the picture, it is evident that *b*, will be the perſpective of B, and, conſequently, *a*, *b*, of *a*, B.

Plate XXXIII.

Fig. 61 No. 1.

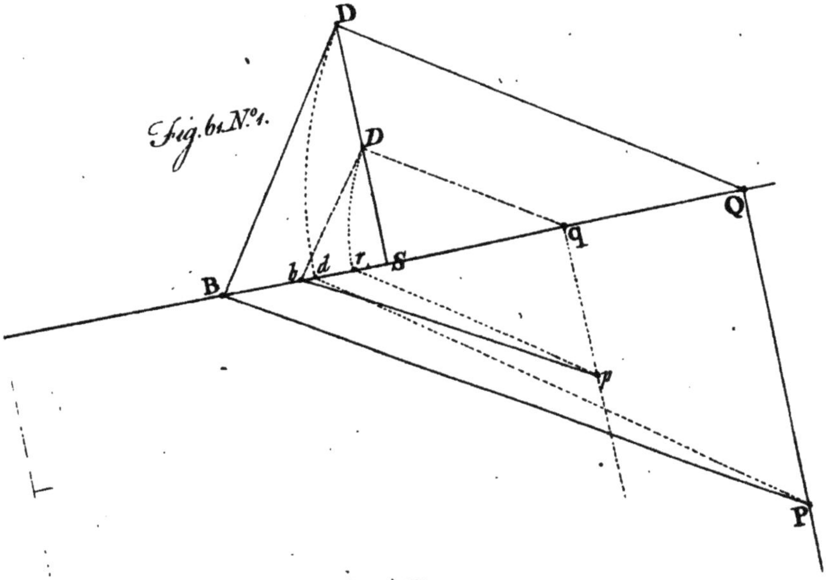

Fig 63 No. 1

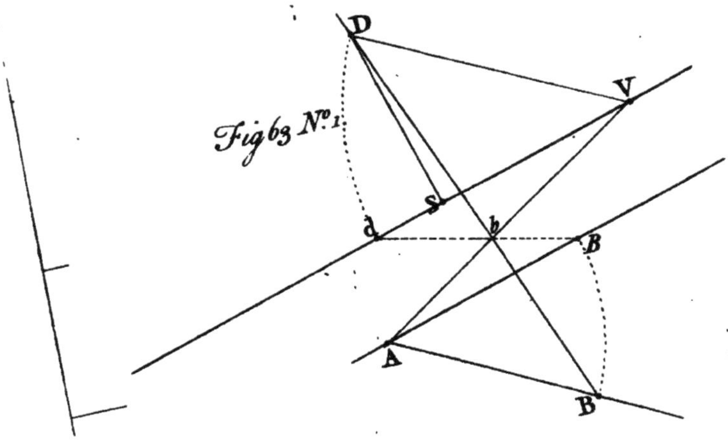

Fig. 63. No. 3. A, B, is an original line; A, its interſection with the picture; A, *a*, its ſeat on the picture; V, its vaniſhing point, found as at No. 1; and A, *b*, its perſpective, which is all that is neceſſary: but beſides, let it be required to find its ſeat on the ground, in the direction of the original line; *(i. e.)* ſuppoſing a plane paſſing through it, and its ſeat on the picture. Draw B, *a*, parallel to S, D, which will be that ſeat; for, turning the triangle S, D, V, forwards on S, V, and the triangle A, B, *a*, backwards on A, *a*, till both are perpendicular to the picture, the plane A, B, *a*, will cut the picture in the line A, *a*, and the ground, in the line B, *a*.

And to explain it ſtill farther, *a*, B, is turned round on *a*, to *a*, *B*, ſuppoſed perpendicular to the picture, and lying on the horizon; A, a, drawn on the picture perpendicular to the horizon; and to theſe is alſo joined the line *B*, a, which is the true geometrical ſeat of the original A, B, (perpendicularly) on the ground; as *B*, *a*, is its ſeat in the direction of the original line, a, and *a*, being their interſections with the picture. The perſpective of *a*, B, is *a*, *b*, for S, muſt be its vaniſhing point by conſtruction, D, S, being parallel to B, *a*. And the perſpective of a, *B*, is a, *b*, drawn to *v*, its vaniſhing point, which is found by drawing a perpendicular from V, to the horizontal line: for the geometrical line a, *B*, being on the ground, perpendicularly under the original line A, B, its vaniſhing point muſt neceſſarily be on the horizontal line, perpendicular to V, the vaniſhing point of A, B; wherefore a, *b*, drawn towards *v*, is the perſpective of a, *B*. To make this (if poſſible) more clear, S, *d*, is drawn perpendicular to the horizon, and equal to S, D, (the diſtance); and *d*, *v*, drawn parallel to a, *B*, which finds the ſame vaniſhing point *v*.

Theſe circumſtances are thus minutely explained on this, and other occaſions, that the univerſality of the principles may appear in their application to the various caſes that occur, or may be required.

Fig. 64. Let A, B, be given as the ſide of a ſquare to be projected, ſpace being deficient every way; draw A, S, and B, S; and from any convenient portion of A, S, or B, S, (as here a 4th,) draw *b*, *f*, parallel to A, B; then take the fame portion of the diftance, (*i. e.*) a 4th, as S, D; draw *f*, D, and D, *g*, at right angles to it; draw *g*, *b*, and fo finifh the fmall fquare, *a*, *b*, *e*, *c*, by the ufual method:—then the large fquare is completed, by drawing parallels to the fides of the former, as B, E, parallel to *b*, *e*; A, C, parallel to *a*, *c*; B, C, parallel to *o*, *c*, *b*, for the diagonal; and laftly, C, E, parallel to *c*, *e*.

Or, inftead of B, C, parallel to *b*, *c*,—S, *c*, continued, will find the point C; or S, *e*, continued, will find the point E; either of which is fufficient for the purpofe.

This may not be an improper place to decide a queftion much debated, viz. Whether the reprefentation of a long wall, on a picture parallel to it, fhould be made of the fame height, at the utmoft extent, as directly oppofite to the eye, fince it appears of lefs height the farther it is extended? To which queftion, the anfwer is, that the wall fhould be drawn of equal height, how far foever extended; becaufe the reprefentation will appear as much lefs, in proportion, at the extent, as the original appears.

Fig. 65. Let A, B,—C, E, be the original wall; D, the eye of the fpectator; and, confequently, A, D,—B, D,—C, D, and E, D, vifual rays; and *a*, *b*, *c*, *e*, the reprefentation on a parallel plane; the triangles A, D, B, and *a*, D, *b*, are fimilar, as are the triangles C, D, E, and *c*, D, *e*; and the lines A, C,—B, E, and *a*, *c*,—*b*, *e*, are all parallel, as are alfo *a*, *b*, and A, B, and *c*, *e*, to C, E: therefore *c*, *e*, muft be equal to *a*, *b*, *which was to be proved*; and in like manner, and for the fame reafons, 2, *b*, and *e*, 4, are equal, being the reprefentations of the equal lines 1, B, and E, 3, made equal to A, B, and C, E. See Euclid, Book I. Prop. 37, 38, 39, &c.

Of the fame nature is that other queftion, Whether, in reprefenting a row of columns, ftanding on a line parallel to the picture, thofe, which are more diftant from the center of fuch picture, fhould be made equal to, or lefs, or bigger than the nearer? It is allowed they appear lefs; but the anfwer to this queftion is, that they ought (in this fituation of the

picture)

Pl.XXXIIII.

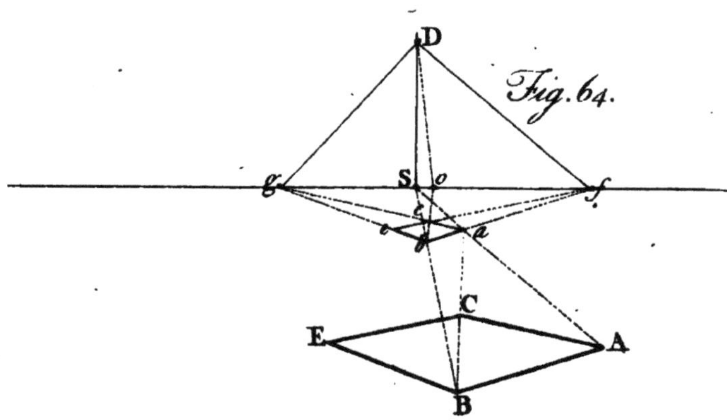

Fig. 64.

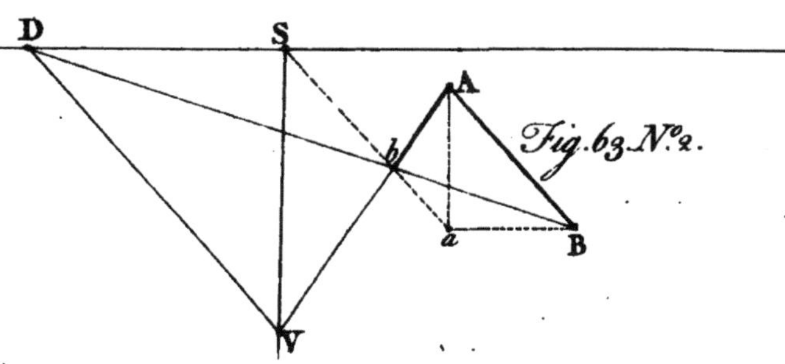

Fig. 63. No. 2.

...g. 63. No. 3.

picture) to be made bigger; and, though so painted, will really appear as much less, in the painting, as they appear in nature.

g. 66. Let A, B, and C, be the plans of three columns, either square or round; and first suppose them square; it is evident, that the representation of them will take up the space marked by the visual rays, from the extreme angles to D, the spectator's eye, on the parallel picture, whose section is S, *k*; *(i. e.)* the representation of A, will fill the space S, *f*; that of B, will fill the space *g*, *h*; and that of C, the space *i*, *k*.

If the columns are round, the several spaces, which are filled by their representations, will be determined by the pricked rays, cutting the line S, *k*, which spaces are marked by small arches.

But if the picture be placed on the line S, 2, the representations of the round columns will be equal to each other, or nearly so. And if on the line S, 3, or any other between 2, and D, (the end S, remaining unmoved) the representations of the more distant columns will then, indeed, be in less spaces of the picture, by certain proportions, according to their several distances.—But on all these pictures, they will be truly represented, and will equally exhibit the images of the originals to the eye of the spectator at D, who will necessarily form the same ideas of the proportions, and distances of the objects, from any one of these pictures, as from any other of them; which may all be considered as transparent planes, or as one such plane, moveable on a hinge at S, from *k*, to 2, or 3; which plane no more hinders the spectator from discerning the original objects, than the common medium of air; and as all the visual rays are necessarily right lines, the picture, or medium, makes no alteration in their directions, which are continued, without interruption, from the several parts of the originals, to D, through any one of these transparent planes, and whichsoever be chosen, the representations can be determined by nothing but the intersections of those visual rays with such plane, and cannot possibly be false, if these intersections are truly found.

N. B. The rays for the round columns are determined, by making tangents to the several circles from D; and the points, in which they touch, are found, by bisecting the line from D, to the center of each circle, as D, 5, for the circle C; and with the length 4—5, as radius, making an arc through the center, cutting the circumference in the points sought.

If the circles were nearer each other, and D at a greater distance, the difference would be proportionally less, and at a sufficient distance, not at all offensive; as indeed nothing, that is truly represented, can be; but even at this, or any distance, the rule (being demonstrably just) cannot vary, and therefore must be universal.

Fig. 67. No. 1. The usual points and lines being given, it is required to represent a door open at any angle. Let *l*, *c*, be the side given, on which it is supposed to turn; S, *b*, the side of the room on the floor; make S, D, *a*, equal to the angle required; draw *a*, *c*, cutting the ground line in *i*; then *i*, *c*, *b*, will represent the same angle: and, for the breadth of the door, draw *i*, *g*, parallel to D, *a*, and D, *c*, cutting it in *g*; from *g*, to *k*, set off the geometrical breadth, and draw D, *k*, cutting *c*, *i*, in *e*; then will *c*, *e*, be the perspective breadth sought, equal to *g*, *k*.—Now, for the thickness, draw D, *b*, perpendicular to *a*, D; and draw *b*, *e*, to *b*, which will be the direction of the edge; draw *b*, *k*, *f*, which will be parallel to D, *b*; and make *k*, *f*, of the thickness required; draw *f*, D, which will determine the thickness, perspectively; or, instead of drawing *b*, *k*, and D, *f*, continue *g*, *k*, to *i*, on the ground line, and a parallel from *f*, to the same; and, from those intersections, draw to *a*, which will give the thickness of the door; draw *e*, *m*, parallel to *c*, *l*, and *a*, *l*, cutting it in *m*; and draw *b*, *m*, which finishes the door. Or, as

Fig. 67. No. 2. Instead of drawing *i*, *g*, and *b*, *k*, below the ground line (in order to determine the breadth and thickness of the door) bring down the distance *a*, D, to d, and draw d, *c*, cutting the ground line in *g*; and make *g*, *k*, equal (geometrically) to the breadth; draw d, *k*, cutting *a*, *c*, in *e*, which finds the perspective breadth: then, for the thickness of the edge, bring down, in like manner,

Pl.XX

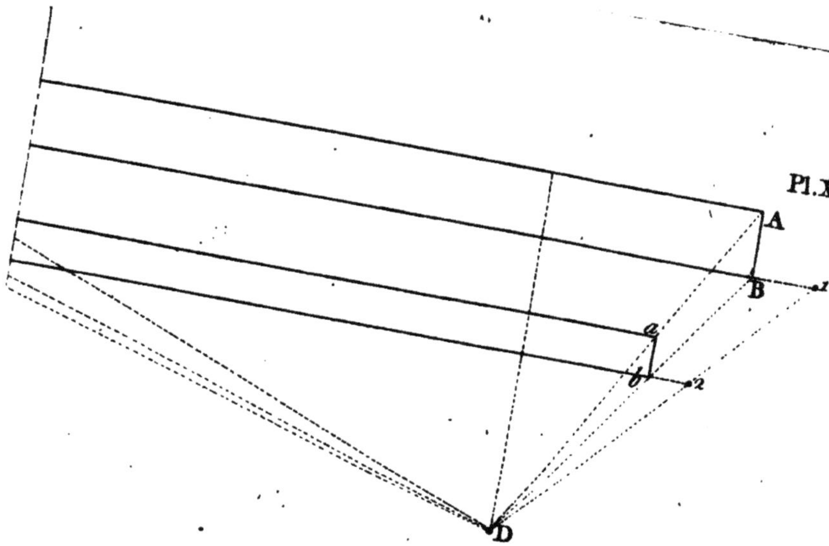

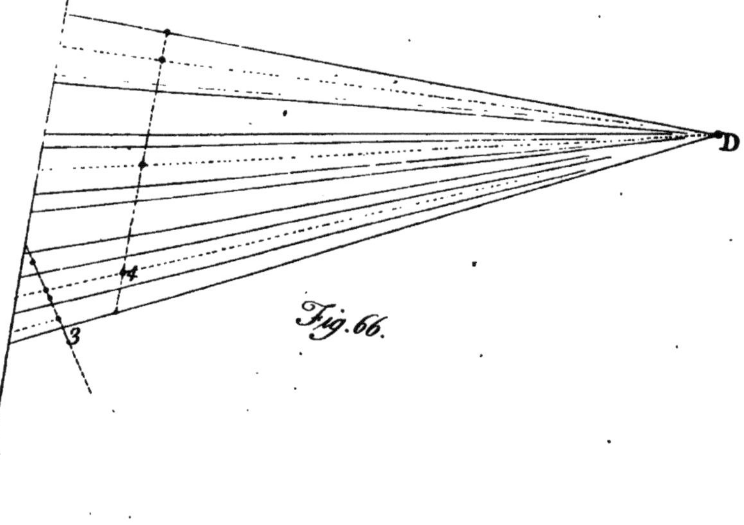

Fig.66.

manner, *b*, D, to *d*, and draw *d*, *e*, cutting the ground line in *o*; make *o*, *f*, equal to the thickneſs, and draw *f*, *d*; all the reſt is as the former.

N. B. If the door be ſhut, the point *e*, (at No. 1.) will touch E; and *m*, will touch M. Or again,

Fig. 67. No. 3. For the breadth, draw the pricked line *c*, 4, parallel to the horizontal line, and equal to one third of *c*, *l*, the heighth (which is here the geometrical breadth,) and D, 1, parallel to it, of any length; draw 1, 2, cutting D, 1, and D, *a*, equally, in 1, and 2, and D, 3, parallel to 1, 2; and draw 3, 4, which will cut *a*, *c*, in *e*; then *e*, *c*, will be the perſpective breadth. This method has been before explained at Fig. 55, No. 1, and 2, and is, in many caſes, very expedient. The thickneſs is found as in the two former, and the perſpective direction is determined by the lines *b*, *e*, and *b*, *m*.

N. B. The point *e*, which determines the breadth of the door, may be any where in the pricked ſemicircle, if the angle of the aperture be not particularly required.

Fig. 68. Having a ſquare *e*, *b*, *g*, *f*, given, to make, on it, an octagon, draw *a*, *b*, through the center, perſpectively parallel to the ſides *e*, *g*, and *b*, *f*; (*i. e.*) from their vaniſhing point; and *c*, *d*, alſo, through the center, at right angles to *a*, *b*, perſpectively; then draw D, Æ, making an angle of 67½ degrees with S, D, (which is the geometrical angle that *e*, *a*, makes with *a*, *b*,); and, then, from Æ, draw to *e*, cutting *a*, *b*, in *a*, which is one of the angles; and from the ſame point Æ, through *b*, cutting *d*, *c*, in *c*, another angle; and again to *g*, cutting *c*, *d*, in *d*; and alſo through *f*, cutting *a*, *b*, in *b*, which determines the laſt angle; *e*, *a*,—*c*, *b*,—*g*, *d*,—and *b*, *f*, being all parallel; and, laſtly, join *c*, *e*,—*c*, *g*,—*g*, *b*,—*f*, *d*,—*d*, *b*, and *b*, *a*, which completes the octagon.

This is done in leſs time than deſcribed, for all the four points wanting, are found without once moving the end of the ruler from Æ.

If the picture will not admit the length S, Æ, then, inſtead of the angle S, D, Æ, of 67½, make S, D, B, an angle of 22½, which

which (being the complement of $67\frac{1}{2}$ to 90) is the geometrical angle that *e*, *a*, makes with *e*, *b*; and from B, draw through *e*, which will cut *c*, *d*, in *c*; and from the ſame point B, to *f*, cutting *c*, *d*, in *d*; and through *b*, cutting *a*, *b*, in *b*; and, laſtly, through *a*, to *g*, cutting *a*, *b*, in *a*; by which means all the ſame points are found, and the octagon completed, by joining the reſt.

The other octagon (of pricked lines) is formed by the ſame vaniſhing points.

Fig. 69. No. 1. In order to repreſent a cornice, firſt draw the geometrical elevation only, as here for the Doric, in pricked lines; then draw lines from S, through every angle of the projection, as 1, 2, 3, &c. and draw from D, through A, meeting the line S, 1, in *a*; and ſo on, from D, through every interſection of the line A, B, as D, 4, meeting the line S, 2, in *o*, and D, 5, meeting the line S, 3, in *p*, &c. by which operation the whole corniee is completed without any geometrical plan.

The reaſon of this proceeding will appear on inſpection of the ſquare 6, *a*, 1, A, which is the ſquare of the whole projection, and of which A, *a*, is the diagonal, iſſuing from the corner, or angle of the wall.

And when it is neceſſary to determine an outer angle at the extremity, make there a ſquare correſponding to the above, as 11, 7, 8, 9, which is eaſily done, by means of the lines already found; and to determine the mouldings of this angle, perpendiculars muſt be raiſed from thoſe of the firſt, already completed, to the diagonal A, *a*; and from the ſeveral interſections, lines drawn to S, will cut the diagonal 11, 8, of this ſquare; from which interſections, dropping perpendiculars, theſe, meeting the ſeveral members, will determine the mouldings of this laſt angle. For inſtance, from the point *p*, raiſe a perpendicular to *q*, in the diagonal A, *a*; and from *q*, draw to S, cutting the diagonal 11, 8, in *r*; from *r*, drop a perpendicular, meeting the ray *p*, S, in *t*; which is the point ſought; and ſo of the reſt.

N. B. The

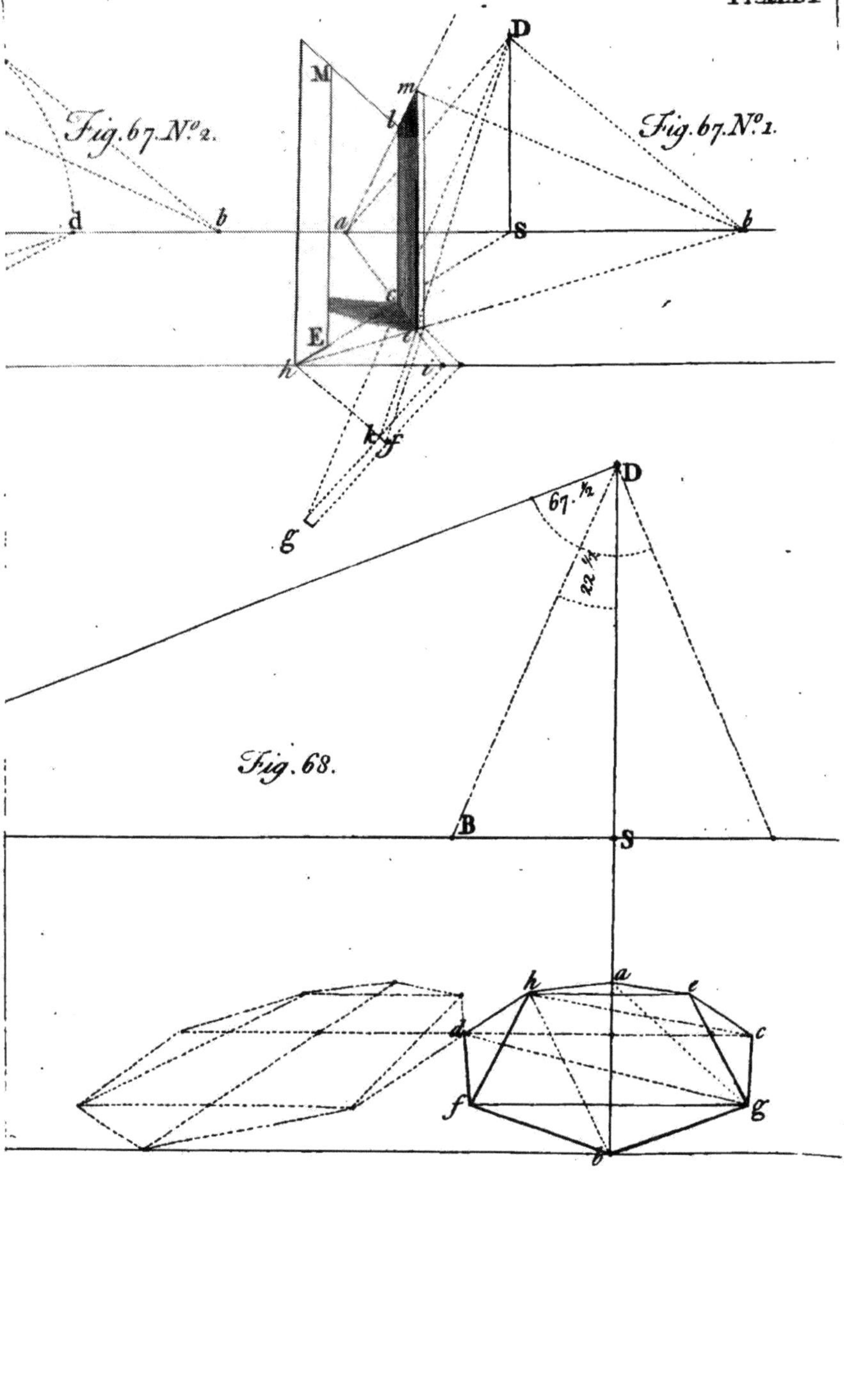

Fig. 67. No. 2.

Fig. 67. No. 1.

Fig. 68.

N. B. The ſecond diagonal 11, 8, is that iſſuing from the corner of the wall, in this place; and is parallel (in the geometrical) to 6, 1, in the former ſquare; and the reaſon for uſing theſe different diagonals, is that A, *a*, projects obliquely forwards, and 11, 8, projects at right angles to it, or obliquely backwards.

Fig. 69. No. 2. The operation is, here, for an inner angle, exactly the ſame as in the former, for an outer angle, to the determination of the outlines of the mouldings incluſive; after which, the difference is, that from *a*, and the reſt of the projections (in the former) the line *a*, 6, with thoſe under it, are parallels; whereas, in this latter, they are all rays from S; and the line *a*, 8, with thoſe under it, in the former are rays, but in this latter are parallels.

Fig. 69. No. 3. Omitting the geometrical elevation, only knowing the meaſures; let it be required to project the cornice (for inſtance, of the Ionic order) immediately on a given part of the picture, without raiſing it higher (as in the former example). Draw A, B, for the uppermoſt line; and from B, to A, (the geometrical projection of the whole cornice) ſet off the ſeveral parts of that projection; draw from B, to *d*, the diſtance, brought down to the horizontal line, and from A, to C, the center, cutting B, *d*, in *a*; then *a*, B, will be the perſpective diagonal of the cornice. Now draw from all the diviſions between A, and B, to C, cutting the diagonal *a*, B; and, from all theſe interſections, drop perpendiculars, and another perpendicular alſo from B; and, on this laſt, mark the ſeveral geometrical heights of the members; and from theſe points, draw to *d*, cutting all the perpendiculars, and their reſpective interſections will determine the perſpective projections of all the members, by which the cornice will be completed; *(e. g.) e*, C, cuts the diagonal in *f*, and *e*, *d*, cuts the perpendicular *f*, E, in E, which determines the projection of that member, and ſo of the reſt.—The points of the projection being thus found, may ſerve either for an outer angle, (as here,) or for an inner angle, (as in the laſt example,) the perſpective extremities remaining the ſame. And if an inner angle be required from any other point in B, C, as G, draw G, *d*, cutting A, C, in *k*; then G, *k*, will be (perſpectively) parallel to B, *a*, and, conſequently, will repreſent the diagonal, by which ſuch inner angle may be completed, as the outer was by means of B, *a*.

Fig. 69. No. 4. When it is required to project a cornice (as here of the Corinthian order) not parallel to the picture, from a point given, as B; draw firſt the geometrical diagonal of the projection B, A, parallel to the horizontal line, and mark on it the angular projections of the ſeveral members; and having biſected the right angle d, D, *d*, and continued the line of biſection to *o*, in the horizontal line, and brought down the diſtance *o*, D, from D, to *D*½, draw B, *o*, and A, *D*½, cutting it in *a*; then B, *a*, will be the perſpective diagonal. Now draw from all the diviſions of A, B, to *D*½, cutting B, *a*, in the ſeveral perſpective points of the diagonal, from which drop perpendiculars, as alſo one from B; and, on this laſt, mark the geometrical heights of the ſeveral members; and, from all theſe points, draw to *o*, cutting their correſpondent perpendiculars, which interſections will determine the angular points of the cornice; and drawing lines from every one of theſe angular points, to the vaniſhing points d, and *d*, the cornice is, thus far, completed.

And, for the inner angle H, draw H, *o*, and *a*, *d*, cutting it in *b*, which gives this diagonal; and divide it, by drawing from the ſeveral diviſions on B, *a*, to *d*; then dropping perpendiculars, from the points thus found, in H, *b*, they will meet their reſpective correſponding lines (already drawn) from the perſpective angular points of the outer angle B, to *d*, and theſe laſt interſections will determine this inner angle.

The ſame operation determines the outer angle G, with theſe only differences, that the diagonal of this laſt is not parallel, but perpendicular to the two former, *(as was particularly explained at the N. B. of No. 1, with reſpect to that Doric cornice)*; and the lines run to the oppoſite vaniſhing point d.

N. B. *The manner of finding the ſhadows of theſe cornices is explained in the* SUPPLEMENT.

Fig.

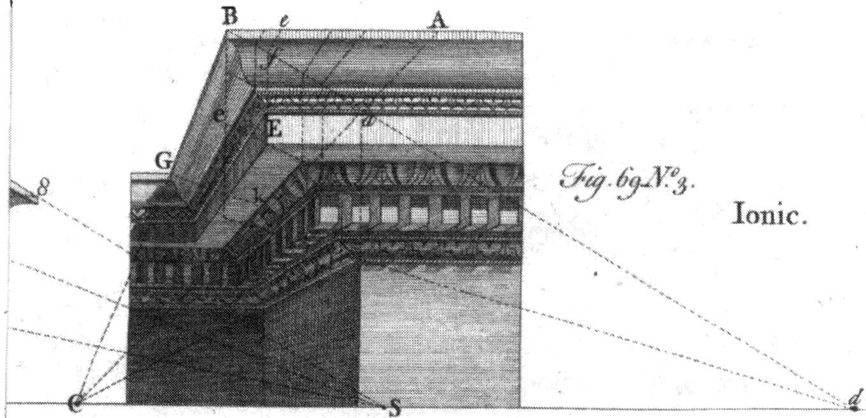

Fig. 69. No. 3.

Ionic.

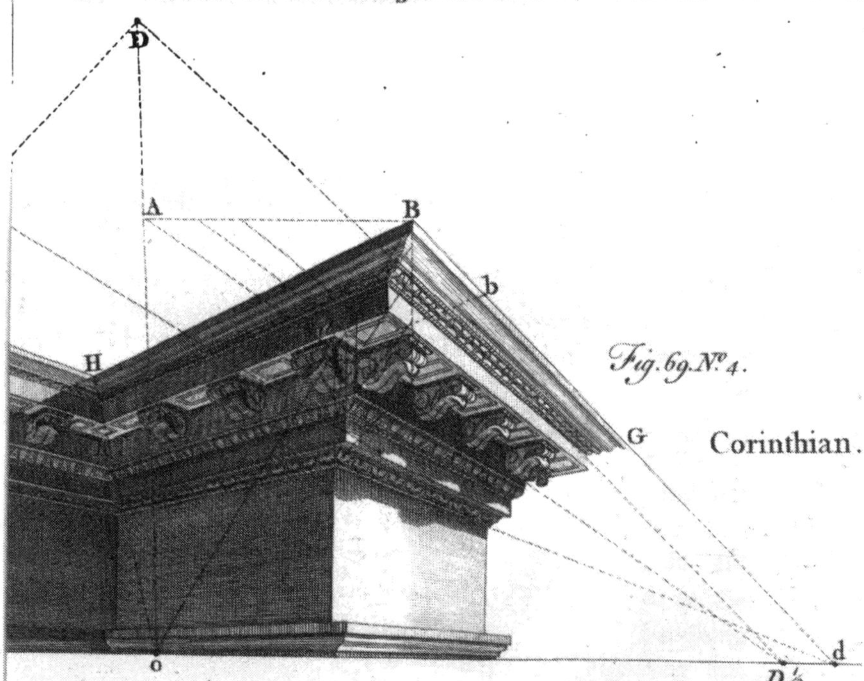

Fig. 69. No. 4.

Corinthian.

Fig. 69. No. 5. In this, and the following figures, the ſkeleton, or caſe only, of the whole cornice, is projected in ſtraight lines, that the reaſon of the operation may appear more ſimply and clearly, unembarraſſed with that number of points, and lines, which are neceſſary in determining minutely each member.

The center and diſtance being given, as uſual, draw firſt the ſquare A, B, E, F, for the breadth of the ſolid; then draw A, C, and D, E, cutting it in G; draw G, H, parallel to A, E, and draw E, C, cutting it in H, which will give the cubical perſpective of the ſolid; produce B, A, to I, making A, I, equal to A, E, for the projection of the whole cornice, (which, in four of the orders, is equal to the height, according to moſt architects; *(i. e.)* in all but the Doric); draw C, I, and 3, E, cutting it in K; and 1, H, cutting the ſame line C, I, in L; then draw 2, F; and laſtly draw K, M, (parallel to A, B,) cutting 2, F, in M, which completes the figure.

N. B. A, E, is the height of the cornice; and A, K, is the diagonal of its projection.

Beſides that the pricked lines, within, ſhew the conformity of this operation to the former figures, let it be conſidered that the triangle K, A, E, repreſents the angular projection of the whole cornice; for 3, 4, is the vaniſhing line of the plane of that triangle, and 3, the vaniſhing point of K, E; as the triangle L, H, G, repreſents another projection of the cornice (the plane of which is perpendicular to K, A, E,) whoſe vaniſhing line is therefore 1, 2, and the vaniſhing point of H, L, is 1. The other angles are determined in the ſame manner; for 1, 2, is alſo the vaniſhing line of the triangle M, B, F, it being in the ſame plane as L, G, H, and 2, the vaniſhing point of F, M; ſo is alſo 4, 3, the vaniſhing line of P, N, O, this triangle being in the ſame plane with K, A, E; and 4, is the vaniſhing point of O, P.

1, C, 3, is alſo the vaniſhing line of the plane K, L, H, E; for 1, 3, and C, are all vaniſhing points in this line: 2, 3, is the vaniſhing line of the plane K, E, F, M; and 1, 4, is the vaniſhing line of the plane L, H, P, O; and 4, C, 2, is the vaniſhing line

N of

of the plane M, P, F, O; for 4, 2, and C, are all in this line, &c.

Fig. 69. No. 6. If the cornice be Doric, as that projects more, in proportion to its height, than the other orders, all the difference is in taking A, *e*, instead of A, E, with its correspondent measures, &c. which will necessarily give 3, 2, in this scheme, for a vanishing line, instead of 3, 2, (at No. 5.) and 1, 4, instead of 1, 4; the rest of the operation being the same as above.

N. B. In this figure, the plane M, *p*, *f*, *o*, happens to fall in the vanishing line 4, C, 2.

Fig. 69. No. 7. This figure (which is seen by the angle) cannot need much explanation, after what has been already said; the lines *e*, *f*, and *g*, *h*, being (with *e*, *g*, and *f*, *h*,) in a plane parallel to the picture, have no vanishing points; *a*, *b*, has *o*, for its vanishing point; and *i*, *k*, has *p*: for as this vanishing line *o*, *p*, passes through the center of the picture, the distances C, *o*, and C, *p*, are to C, *d*, (the distance of this vanishing line) as the side of a square to its diagonal; by which means the height and projection of the cornice keep their proportions, the angular projection being to the height, as the diagonal of a square to its side, in the four orders, which have their heights and projections equal. Hence it is evident, on inspection, that the perspective angle *b*, *a*, *q*, (or C, *a*, *o*,) represents the geometrical angle C, *d*, *o*, as *s*, *k*, *i*, (or C, *k*, *p*,) does C, *d*, *p*.

Fig. 69. No. 8. This figure differs from the last, only, in its being obliquely situated to the plane of the picture in every respect, the last having the lines *e*, *g*, and *f*, *h*, parallel to it.

The scheme sufficiently shews the operation, on the principles so often explained; the letters *a*, *e*, *g*, and *k*, mark the angles of the cornice, as in the former; and *o*, is the vanishing point of *a*, *b*, found by making *o*, $\frac{1}{2}$, as the side of a square, to $\frac{1}{2}$, *y*, the diagonal, (which $\frac{1}{2}$, *y*, is equal to $\frac{1}{2}$, D, the bisection of the angle E, D, F,) for this is the proportion of *q*, *b*, to *q*, *a*. E, *o*, is the vanishing line of the plane *a*, *e*, *f*, *b*; and F, *o*, the vanishing line of the plane *a*, *g*, *h*, *b*.

4 The

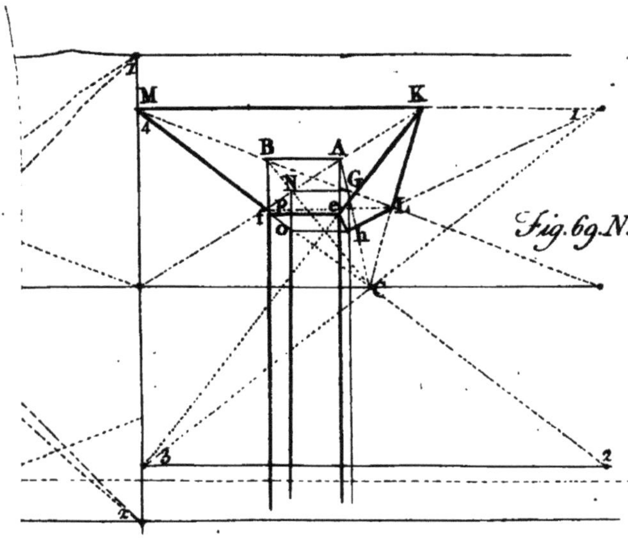

Fig. 69 No. 6.

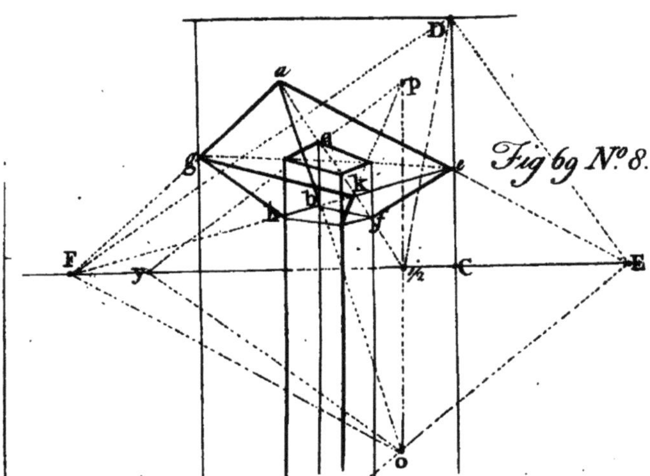

Fig. 69 No. 8.

The FIFTH PART.

OF SHADOWS.

THAT part of perſpective, which relates to the projection of ſhadows, is leſs neceſſary, than any of the preceding parts, and is wholly omitted by *Pozzo*, in his treatiſes on the ſubject, though one of the greateſt maſters in the executive part, and who ſeems to have done every thing elſe by rule.

However, it was thought proper to give a few examples, not only of caſes that moſt commonly occur, in the courſe of practice, but alſo of ſome others leſs uſual, and more difficult, to ſhew the application of theſe principles to this purpoſe, as well as to correct the miſtakes of ſome writers on the ſubject.

Fig. 70. No. 1. In this ſcheme, the light is ſuppoſed to come from the ſun, which being conſidered as at an infinite diſtance, the rays are treated as parallel; but it does not follow, that therefore the ſhadows muſt be repreſented parallel, except in one caſe, (and that very rare,) which is, when the rays are parallel to the picture; an inſtance or two of which ſhall be firſt given.

The rays of light are here ſuppoſed to come from the ſun, and are not only parallel among themſelves, but alſo to the picture, and therefore the moſt ſimple, and moſt eaſy to project. Any one ray, as *f*, *g*, being drawn in the direction required, all the reſt muſt be parallel to it. Draw from F, the bottom of the line *f*, F, a parallel to the horizontal line, meeting *f*, *g*, in *g*, which determines that ſhadow; for *g*, is the ſhadow of *f*, on the ground, and F, *g*, of the perpendicular line F, *f*; and ſo for each perpendicular line, as, for *h*, *i*, draw *h*, H, parallel to *f*, *g*; and *i*, H, parallel to the horizontal line, meeting in H; and *k*, K, parallel to *f*, *g*; and, laſtly, *l*, K, parallel to the horizontal line, meeting in K; and the ſame operation for the open door, which completes the whole.

N. B. If one only of the points *g*, or H, had been found, the other would be determined, by drawing through that, already found, to S, the vaniſhing point of *i*, F, which is perſpectively parallel to H, *g*, &c.—for H, *g*, the ſhadow of *b*, *f*, is parallel to it in the original, and therefore both run to the ſame vaniſhing point S.

Fig. 70. No. 2. This figure, though two walls only, is exhibited, to ſhew the manner of determining the ſhadow on a plane ſtanding obliquely to the horizontal line. Having drawn B, E, parallel to A, *b*, the direction of the rays, as in the former, and G, E, parallel to the horizontal line, meeting it in E, G, E, will be the ſhadow of G, B; but as it is interrupted by the wall C, L, raiſe a perpendicular at L, (where G, E, cuts the bottom of that wall) and draw A, C, cutting it in *e*; then C, *e*, will be the ſhadow of the line B, C, on the plane C, L; for, all the rays are parallel to A, *b*, and *b*, is the vaniſhing point of B, C, therefore A, *b*, is the vaniſhing line of the plane made by the rays which paſs through the line B, C; and (*a*, A, being the vaniſhing line of the wall C, L,) A, is the vaniſhing point of the common interſection of the two planes, whoſe vaniſhing lines are *b*, A, and *a*, A; therefore A, is the vaniſhing point of the ſhadow C, *e*, of the line B, C, on the wall C, L.

If the reader finds any difficulty in conceiving this, let him imagine the wall C, L, continued to its vaniſhing line *a*, A, and the plane of rays to its vaniſhing line *b*, A, theſe planes will then interſect at A; and as both planes paſs through the eye, ſo alſo muſt their interſection, which will be a line from the eye terminating in A.—It cannot be forgot, that all lines, drawn from the ſame vaniſhing point, are, perſpectively, parallels; (*i. e.* repreſent lines geometrically parallel;) wherefore if D, were brought forwards on S, perpendicular to the picture, it would repreſent the eye, and D, A, the interſection ſought. Now A, C, *e*, repreſents a parallel to D, A, in this ſituation of D.

The point *e*, however, might have been determined by the line B, E, interſecting the perpendicular from L, in this particular caſe, as the wall breaks the ſhadow G, E, in L; but, otherwiſe, the general rule is as above.

Fig.

Fig. 70. No. 3. Is the ſame ſubject, with this only difference, that the wall C, L, is ſhorter, on which account, the ſhadow G, E, of B, G, is thrown, wholly, on this ſide of it, ſo that the line G, L, E, cannot interſect the bottom; which diſpoſition is choſen, on purpoſe to ſhew the uſe of the vaniſhing point A, in determining the direction of the ſhadow on the wall C, L, as explained above.

Though this alſo might have been found, by continuing the line N, L, till it cuts G, E, in L, and there raiſing a perpendicular, meeting the ray B, E, in *e*, and then drawing C, *e*.—But inſtead of all this work for the direction of one line, nothing more is neceſſary, than drawing from A, through C, as has been explained.

If the line *a*, N, L, be continued, and the ray A, *c*, till they meet in *E*; and the parallel *E*, *G*, be drawn, and alſo the line *b*, N, G, till it meets *E*, *G*, in *G*; and the perpendicular *G*, *B*, be raiſed, and *b*, *c*, *B*, continued, till it meets *B*; and the ray *B*, *E*, be drawn parallel to A, *b*; then the ſhadows (repreſented by *c*, *e*, and G, E,) brought down to *G*, *E*, will unite in *E*, and, by that means, illuſtrate the whole operation,

Fig. 71. No. 1. Here, though the ſhadows are geometrically parallel among themſelves, they are, nevertheleſs, oblique with reſpect to the picture (as is generally the caſe); and, for this reaſon, the ſhadows will all tend to the ſame vaniſhing point in the horizontal line.

U, is the vaniſhing point of the rays of light, found by drawing from the eye, to the picture, in the direction choſen, or given, for that purpoſe. To conceive this, ſuppoſe *D*, S, raiſed up, on S, till perpendicular to the picture: in that ſituation, *D*, U, is the parallel of the rays, cutting the picture in U, which is therefore the vaniſhing point of them.

And raiſing a perpendicular from U, to the horizontal line, cutting it in V, that will be the vaniſhing point of all the ſhadows, caſt on the plane of the horizon, by all objects perpendicular to that plane; ſo that the ſhadow of any point is found, by drawing firſt from ſuch point to U; and then from the ſeat of the ſame point to V: *for inſtance*, from the point b, (of the object A,) draw to U; and again from B, the

the ſeat of b, draw to V, cutting b, *V*, in *b*; this will be the ſhadow of b, on the ground, and B, *b*, will be the ſhadow of the whole line b, B: in like manner, drawing *c*, U, and C, V, cutting it in *e*, that is the ſhadow of *c*; and thus is alſo found *f*, the ſhadow of f: after which, by joining all theſe points, is completed the whole ſhadow of the object A, on the ground.

For the ſhadow of the octaedron, the ſeveral points of it marked 1, 2, 3, 4, are all found in the ſame manner, viz. by drawing from the ſeveral angles to U, and from their ſeats reſpectively to V, each angle, ſeat, and ſhadow, being marked by the ſame character; for inſtance, 2, the angle on the body of the octaedron; 2, its ſeat perpendicularly under it; and 2, its ſhadow; and ſo of the reſt. Thus alſo may be found the ſhadow of any object not perpendicular, by finding the perpendicular ſeats of the principal points, and uſing ſuch ſeats, and points, as perpendicular lines; (*e. g.*) having found *g*, the ſeat of E, draw E, U, and *g*, V, interſecting in *h*, that will be the ſhadow of E; and drawing *h*, G, is determined the whole ſhadow, on the ground, of the pole G, E.

But for thoſe ſhadows, which fall on planes not horizontal, ſome other expedients are to be uſed, as that of A, on the parallelopiped H. Having firſt found the ſhadow on the horizontal plane, raiſe two perpendiculars where that ſhadow touches the edge, (as at *i*, and *k*,) to *l*, and *m*; and ſince the upper ſide is parallel to the horizon, draw from *l*, and *m*, to the ſame vaniſhing point V, which determines it: ſo alſo is found the ſhadow of the cube on the bottom of the parallelopiped A, firſt drawing a perpendicular from *n*, upwards (where the ſhadow on the ground cuts the line *n*, B,) and determining the top of that perpendicular *w*, by the line *o*, U; then for the point *p*, continue V, *ſ*, backwards, till it cuts *q*, S, in *r*; at *r*, raiſe a perpendicular to *t*; draw *t*, U, which finds the point *p*; and, laſtly, draw *p*, *w*, which finiſhes that ſhadow. Or if B, *n*, be continued backwards, till it meets *q*, S, as in *x*, and a perpendicular be there raiſed, cutting the line *o*, S, in *y*, a line drawn from *y*, to *w*, will find the ſhadow *p*, *w*.

N. B. This

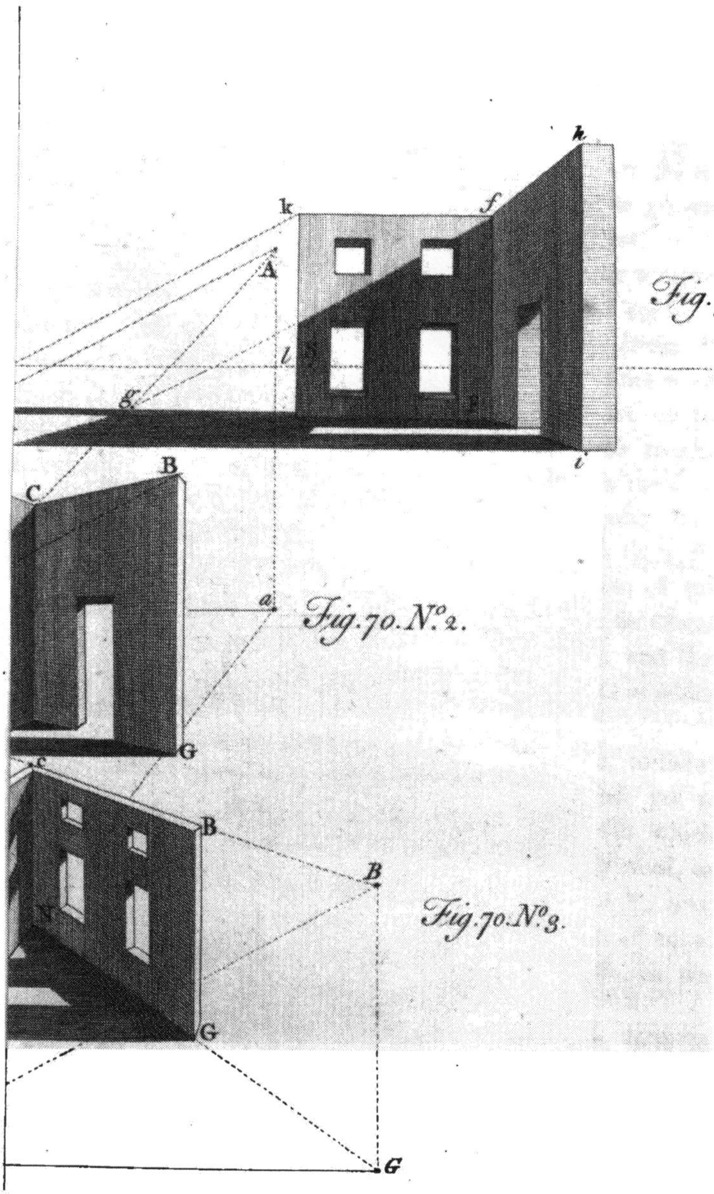

Fig. 70. N.° 1.

Fig. 70. N.° 2.

Fig. 70. N.° 3.

N. B. This line *y*, *p*, *w*, runs not to any vaniſhing point, becauſe it is parallel to the picture.

The ſhadow, on the ground, of the plank, that reſts upon the cube, is found by dropping a perpendicular from the point, where it touches the edge, to the ground; and drawing from the top to U, and from the bottom to V, is found one point on the ground, which is ſufficient. For, drawing from N, through that point, to the horizontal line, is found the vaniſhing point M, of the ſhadow on the ground; to which vaniſhing point, draw from the other corner of the plank, which reſts on the ground, and one line more (from the top of the plank to U,) completes this ſhadow, ſuppoſing the whole of it on the ground: that part of it, on the upper face of the cube, is found, by drawing from the points, where the plank touches it, to the ſame vaniſhing point M; and that other part, on the front of the cube, by continuing the line, of the bottom of the cube, from *q*, through the ſhadow on the ground to *z*; then drawing from the points in which the plank touches to *z*, and †. The reaſon of this operation is obvious; for, ſuppoſing the front of the cube to extend beyond *z*, the ſhadow of the ground would there meet it, and that part of the ſhadow, on this face, muſt be between the points in which the plank touches the cube, and the ground at †, *z*.

Here are added four perpendicular poſts, on the ſame line, to ſhew, that though the ſhadows of them are geometrically parallel, yet as they are not caſt in a direction parallel to the picture, (in which caſe they would be parallel, and equal, in perſpective,) they muſt, in this direction of the light, have all the ſame vaniſhing point V, and, therefore, cannot be parallel in their repreſentations, nor of equal lengths, though they are all of the ſame height, or depth, on the picture, from the front line on which the poſts ſtand.

The error of making the ſhadows parallel, in this caſe, is to be obſerved in the Jeſuit's Perſpective. The author might poſſibly be miſled, by conſidering, that as the ſun is ſo large a body, and ſo diſtant, the rays of light from thence deſcend in parallel lines, or (which is the ſame thing) in lines not to be diſtinguiſhed from parallel;

parallel; but he ſhould alſo have conſidered, that all parallel lines, not parallel to the picture, will, on the picture, have a common vaniſhing point, to which they mutually tend, as the preſent caſe requires, and which makes ſo great a difference in the repreſentation. For all lines, in perſpective, are ſuppoſed to paſs through the eye of the ſpectator, and to meet the plane of the picture ſomewhere (except thoſe which are parallel to that plane); and the point wherein any line, ſo paſſing through the eye, interſects the plane of the picture, will be the vaniſhing point of all other lines parallel to that line.

This is the very conſtruction of a vaniſhing point, on which almoſt the whole practice of perſpective depends.

N. B. In the Jeſuit's Perſpective, the 3d edition, tranſlated by *Chambers*, 1743, page 132, the ſecond example is falſe, as the extreme lines of the ſhadow (though caſt forwards) are made geometrically parallel, which ſhould run to a vaniſhing point in the horizontal line, and would then repreſent parallels; and, in the text, the reader is inſtructed in this falſe method. Page 133, falſe, inaſmuch as all the lines, at the feet of objects, *(i. e.)* the direction of the ſhadow which ought to run to a vaniſhing point to repreſent parallels, are made geometrically parallel to H, K, L, and the reader is inſtructed ſo to make them. Page 134, is right, where the ſun is directly behind; and he is right alſo, where the ſun is ſuppoſed to caſt the ſhadows parallel to the picture; but he is falſe in every oblique direction, which directions are much more frequent than any others. Theſe errors are plainly owing to his not underſtanding (or not conſidering) the neceſſity, and uſe of vaniſhing points; perhaps he was ſenſible of the difficulty of oblique directions, which ſeems to be the reaſon that, for five pages together, all the ſhadows are caſt in the ſame direction, *(i. e.)* all of them parallel to the picture; ſo that they afford no variety, except of the objects; that is, no variety of inſtruction, or any caſes that

need

need it. His ſhadows, from artificial lights, are true; but no difficult or intricate caſes are given, either of objects placed obliquely, or ſhadows thrown on planes oblique to each other; but all on planes parallel, or at right angles to each other.

And moſt of the miſtakes into which many painters, and writers on this ſubject, have fallen, (who perhaps may not have been altogether deficient in ſcience) are owing to the attention to objects, as they appear generally in nature, without referring their appearances to the eye of a ſpectator fixed to a point, or without ſufficiently conſidering what kind of images ſuch appearances, in nature, muſt neceſſarily form, on a tranſparent plane, between the eye and object, in every different direction.

It was ſaid above, that by drawing a perpendicular from U, to V, this laſt would be the vaniſhing point of the ſhadows of all lines perpendicular to the horizontal plane; and alſo, that the ſhadows of any other lines (not perpendicular) might be determined, by finding the ſeats of any points on the ground, and drawing from ſuch points to U, and from their ſeats to V; and thus was found *b*, the ſhadow of E, and the whole ſhadow of the octaedron, and other objects.

But to ſhew the extenſive uſe of vaniſhing points, here is added another method for oblique lines: 7, 8, is a poſt inclined to the horizon, but parallel to the picture. Draw from U, a parallel to 7, 8, cutting the horizontal line in *u*, which will be the vaniſhing point of the ſhadow of 7, 8, on the ground; draw 8, U, and 7, *u*, cutting it in 9; then 7, 9, is that ſhadow, without farther operation: and if there were many lines in the ſame direction, that is, parallel to 7, 8, it might be worth while to find their common vaniſhing point *u*, to which all their ſhadows would tend; but, otherwiſe, it may be determined by the vaniſhing point V; for dropping a perpendicular from 8, to 10, this will be its ſeat; wherefore, having drawn 8, U, as before, draw 10, V, which finds the ſame point 9; then drawing 7, 9, that will find the ſame ſhadow.

The reader will obſerve, that the poſt 7, 8, though not perpendicular to the horizontal plane, is, however, parallel to the picture;

O and

and in case of any obliquity in an object, if still parallel to the picture, a line, as U, *u*, drawn parallel to such obliquity, will always truly find *u*, the vanishing point of the shadow. For the triangles *u*, 9, U, and 8, 9, 7, are similar, as well as the triangles V, 9, U, and 8, 9, 10; and the line 8, 9, U, is common to both pair of triangles; therefore it must be divided in the same point 9, by either of the correspondent lines 7, *u*, or 10, V.

But when the original is not only oblique to the horizon, but also to the picture (as the post 11, 12); then the vanishing point of such oblique line must be found by means of a scheme like that at Fig. 63, which (if understood) will render this intelligible. Or the vanishing point of 11, 12, for instance, which is such an oblique line, and whose seat is 13, 12, may be found, by continuing the line 13, 12, to its vanishing point S; thence dropping a perpendicular; and, lastly, continuing the projected line 11, 12, till it cuts that perpendicular in Θ, which is the vanishing point sought. This post leans forwards, in an angle of 65, marked at D; *(i. e.)* the angle S, D, Θ, and whose vanishing point being Θ, below; thence draw through U, till it cuts the horizontal line, which intersection will be the vanishing point of the shadow; and having drawn 11, U, (as in all the former cases) draw from 12, to that vanishing point, cutting 11, U, in 14, and then 12, 14, will be the shadow sought. To shew that this shadow is truly found, draw from 13, the seat of 11, to V, which will cut 11, *V*, in the same point 14, and is a proof.

> *N. B.* When the vanishing point is first given, then the seat is found by drawing a perpendicular from Θ, to the horizontal line, cutting it, as in S; then drawing S, 12, and a perpendicular from 11, cutting it in 13.

And this will be general, for any line, viz. to draw from its vanishing point, through the vanishing point of the ray of light, to the vanishing line of the plane on which the shadow is to be projected, whether it be the horizontal plane, or any other; and this intersection, with the vanishing line of the plane on which the shadow is cast, will be the vanishing point of the shadow. For (in this scheme) imagine the plane D, S, Θ, raiſed on S, Θ, till D, S, be perpendicular to the picture; then a line D, U, determines the vaniſhing point of the rays; and, conſequently, a line through Θ, and U, to the vaniſhing line of the horizon, will give the vaniſhing line of the plane of rays paſſing over the whole line Θ, 12, 11, and therefore, alſo, the vaniſhing point of the ſhadow 12, 14. *See this farther explained in the* SUPPLEMENT.

Fig. 71. No. 2. Is a cube on an inclined plane; *a*, S, *b*, is the vaniſhing line of that plane, W, is the vaniſhing point of the lines 1, 2,—3, 4,—5, 6, and 7, 8; wherefore, having given U^2, for the vaniſhing point of the rays, draw from W, through U^2, to V^2, (in the vaniſhing line *a*, S, *b*;) and then, drawing from 3, 5, and 7, to U^2, and from 4, 6, and 8, to V^2, the ſhadows of 3, 5, and 7, are determined, which are all the points neceſſary for completing the whole ſhadow.

Fig. 71. No. 3. In this ſcheme the object is (as the laſt) on an inclined plane, and the ſun obliquely behind the object; on which account U, the vaniſhing point of the rays, will be above V, the vaniſhing point of the ſhadows; for it is to be always remembered, that every vaniſhing point is formed by a line paſſing through the eye parallel to the original; and whereſoever ſuch line cuts the plane of the picture, that interſection is the point ſought. Now if the ſun be beyond the object, a parallel to its rays will, neceſſarily, cut the picture ſomewhere above; and as S, is the center of the picture, and S, D, its diſtance, imagine D, S, raiſed on S, perpendicular to the picture; in that ſituation, D, U, is the parallel to the rays (whoſe direction is ſuppoſed to be given); therefore U, is the vaniſhing point of thoſe rays; and as P, is the vaniſhing point (which will be perſpectively perpendicular to the vaniſhing line *a*, C, *b*, and) of 1, P, and all its parallels, draw U, P, cutting the line *a*, C, *b*, in V, and that will be the vaniſhing point of all the ſhadows; wherefore, drawing U, 1, U, 2, U, 3, and then from V, through the ſeat of each line, the points 1, 2, and 3, of the ſhadow, are found.

Fig. 71. No. 4. In order to ſhew the conformity of operation, here is added the ſame figure, with ſimilar circumſtances, on the plane of the horizon. U, V, is, in this scheme, therefore, *geometrically* perpendicular to the vanishing line *a*, S, *b*, and parallel to the lines 1, *p*,—2, *p*,—3, *p*, whose shadows are sought. The rest needs no explanation.

N. B. In this, and all the former, after having drawn U, 1, or any one of the rays, and V, P, interfecting it in 1, all the other points of the shadow may be found, by only drawing through the bottoms, or seats, of the remaining lines from V, and then drawing to the vanishing points *a*, and *b*, of the figure, which will find the points 2, and 3, as 1, *a*, finds 2, and 2, *b*, finds 3, &c.

Fig. 71. No. 5. Here is once more the same object, with the sun behind it; V, the vanishing point of the shadows coinciding with S; U, the vanishing point of the rays perpendicularly above it. Having drawn U, 1, and V, *o*, cutting it in 2, the rest is determined as in the *N. B.* of the last, viz. by means of the vanishing points *a*, and *b*; and as the cube is a little oblique before S, the ray U, 1, 2, determines the plane of 2, by which the whole is completed, as has been explained. But if the cube had been directly before S, it would have been very difficult; or if the object had been a single line, as 4, 7, it would have been impossible, without an expedient; because the ray U, 6, and the line of the shadow V, 7, coincide; in which case, draw V, 8, at pleasure, and from 7, draw a parallel to *a*, S, *b*, cutting it in 8; draw 8, 9, parallel to 7, 4, and equal to it; draw U, 9, cutting V, 8, in 3; lastly, draw 3, 6, parallel to 8, 7, which determines the point 6.

Fig. 72. No. 1. In this scheme, the light O, is supposed that of a candle, or other luminous point, whence it is diffused every way as from a center; its foot, on the ground, is F. In order to find the shadow of the door *b*, *e*, *h*, draw F, *b*, cutting S, H, in *g*; there raise a perpendicular, and draw O, *e*, cutting it in *c*; then *b*, *g*, will be the shadow on the ground, and *g*, *c*, on the side of the room; and to find the direction of *c*, f, as *a* is the vanishing point of the top and bottom of the door, draw *a*, *b*, H, cutting S, H,

Fig. 71. No. 1.

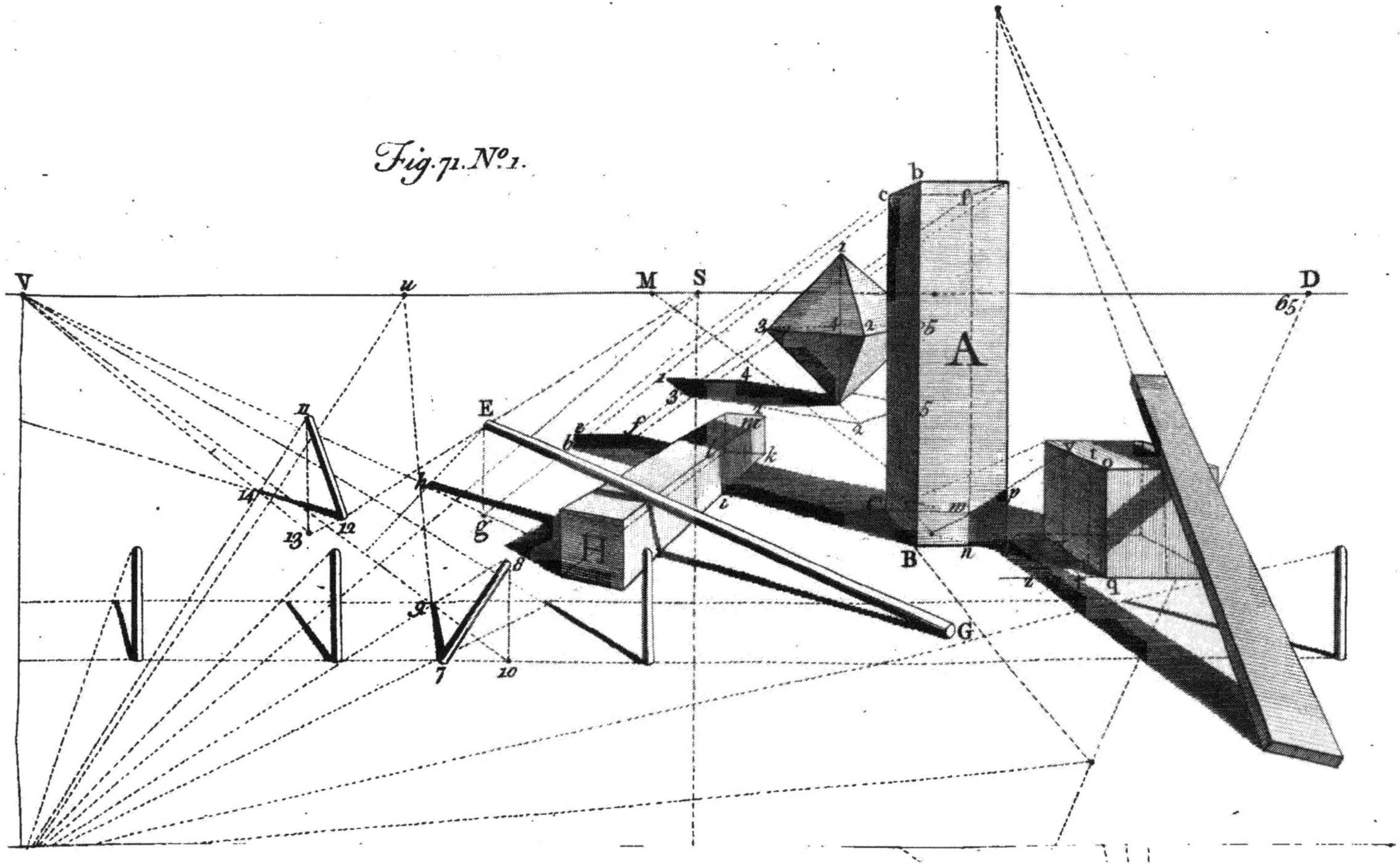

S, H, in H; and then H, will be the interſection of the plane of the door with the plane on which this part of the ſhadow is caſt; draw H, *i*, parallel to *b*, *e*, and *a*, *b*, *e*, cutting it in *i*, which will be the point wherein the line *a*, *b*, *e*, meets the ſame plane; wherefore draw *i*, *c*, which will be the direction, ſought, of the ſhadow *c*, *f*; laſtly, draw *f*, *b*, which completes the whole ſhadow.

It is evident, that if the plane of the door was continued, it would meet the ſide of the room in H, *i*; and the point *c*, having been found by the perpendicular *g*, *c*, the direction of the ſhadow, paſſing through *c*, muſt be *i*, *c*, *f*.

Or the ſhadow *b*, *f*, *c*, might be found by a method more geometrical, thus.

Fig. 72. No. 2. Having drawn F, *b*, *g*, (as before) and the perpendicular *g*, *c*; and alſo having drawn *a*, *b*, H, and the perpendicular H, *i*, and *a*, *b*, *e*, cutting it in *i*; and found the vaniſhing line *a*, *k*, of the plane of rays paſſing through the line *a*, *b*, *c*, *i*; from *k*, the interſection of this vaniſhing line with S, *k*, the vaniſhing line of the ſide of the room (on which part of the ſhadow is caſt) draw *k*, *i*, cutting *g*, *c*, in *c*, and the angle of the room in *f*; and draw *b*, *f*, which finiſhes the ſhadow.

N. B. The vaniſhing line *a*, *k*, is found, by drawing a line through *a*, parallel to Θ, *m*; for Θ, *m*, repreſents a ray parallel to the picture, found by drawing F, *l*, parallel to the horizontal line, and *l*, *m*, perpendicular to it, cutting *a*, *b*, *e*, in *m*; and then, drawing Θ, *m*.

Or (without uſing the vaniſhing line *a*, *k*,) draw Θ, *a*, and F, *a*, raiſing a perpendicular at the interſection of it, with the edge of the room, cutting Θ, *a*, in *o*, which will be the foot of the light on the ſide of the room; and Θ, *o*, will be perſpectively in the direction of (or parallel to) *e*, *b*; wherefore draw *o*, *b*, *f*, &c.

This is farther explained in the ſeveral manners following, becauſe many ſuch caſes happen, and the underſtanding this, fully, may be of great uſe. *a*, *b*, continued, cuts the ſide of the room in H, and a pera perpendicular being raiſed at H, and *a*, *b*, *e*, continued, they meet in *i*.—So that if the plane of the door was continued, H, *i*, would be the extreme edge, touching both that ſide, and the floor of the room, and could have no ſhadow, either on the ſide, or *below*; but, in that caſe, there would be a ſhadow *above*; becauſe *f*, is the angle of the room, and *b*, *f*, being in a plane parallel to the picture, and *f*, *i*, in a plane perpendicular to it, the whole ſhadow would be the triangle *b*, *f*, *i*; for Θ, F, *l*, *m*, is a plane parallel to the picture, and *m*, *e*, *b*, *a*, the edge of the top of the door, continued to the horizon at *a*; therefore Θ, *m*, (being parallel to the picture) may be conſidered as the interſection of the plane of rays, paſſing over the top of the door; and, conſequently, *a*, *k*, (parallel to it, paſſing through the eye, and cutting the picture) is the vaniſhing line of that plane; and, cutting S, *k*, the vaniſhing line of the ſide of the room, on which part of the ſhadow is caſt, *k*, will be the vaniſhing point of the interſection of thoſe two planes, viz. of the rays, and ſide of the room; wherefore, drawing *k*, *i*, this line determines the ſhadow *c*, *f*, and drawing *b*, *f*, the whole is determined.

Or drawing *b*, *f*, parallel to *a*, *k*, meeting the angle of the room, that will determine the point *f*, by which *f*, *c*, is found; for the plane of the rays is parallel to *a*, *k*, and *b*, *f*, is parallel to the picture, and is interſected by the plane which generates the vaniſhing line *a*, *k*; as *a*, *k*, is the vaniſhing line of the plane of rays paſſing through the line *a*, *b*, *e*, *i*; and *o*, *b*, *f*, being the interſection of that plane, with the plane on which that part of the ſhadow is caſt, *b*, *f*, muſt be parallel to *a*, *k*. Again, *o*, is the ſeat of the light on the plane of the ſhadow, and *b*, is the ſeat of *e*, *b*, on the ſame plane; therefore *b*, *f*, the ſhadow of *e*, *b*, muſt be the continuation of the line *o*, *b*; and that line is neceſſarily parallel to *a*, *k*, (by conſtruction) becauſe the plane of this part of the ſhadow is parallel to the picture; and the plane Θ, *m*, *i*, *k*, *a*, cuts both the plane of the picture in *a*, *k*, and that which receives the ſhadow in *o*, *b*, *f*, which two latter are parallel planes.

The other door *l*, *q*, *k*, in No. 1, is opened at right angles, and,

and, consequently, S, is the vanishing point of the top and bottom. Draw F, *k*, cutting the side of the room in *m*; raise a perpendicular *m*, *n*; draw O, *l*, cutting *m*, *n*, in *n*; then draw S, *n*, cutting the angle of the room in *p*; and join *p*, *q*, which finishes the shadow. Or *q*, *p*, might have been first found thus: Draw O, S, and, in that line, find *t*, by a perpendicular from the intersection of F, S, with the bottom of the room, which point *t*, is the seat of O, on the plane *p*, *q*, that is, the farther side of the room; and drawing *t*, *q*, *p*, that will be the direction of the shadow, on this plane; and draw S, *p*, and O, *l*, meeting in *n*.

The two square blocks, A, and B, against the wall, are introduced to shew the course of the shadows, which need little explanation; only it is to be observed, that *t*, being the foot of the light on the wall, is to be used, on that plane, as F, on the floor. Thus draw from *t*, through all the points which touch the wall, to the beginning of the cieling, and through those intersections (with the edge, or angle of the cieling) draw from S; then from O, draw through the projecting angles, of each block, lines meeting all those rays from S, and the several points of the shadow, on the cieling, are terminated.

The shadow of the hollow square C, is found in the same manner, only remembering, that as *t*, represents the foot (of the light) on the wall, and as the depth of the hollow is to be regarded in casting the shadow, so the foot must be as low as that depth, which is found by drawing from the top of one of the lines, viz. 1, to *t*, and a parallel to it from the bottom of the same line 2, cutting O, S, in V, which will be the foot of the light for this hollow; then drawing V, 2, and O, 1, meeting in 3, draw from 3, a line parallel to 1, *z*, which will give the indefinite shadow of 1, *z*, in the bottom; and draw from 1, meeting that line where it intersects the angle of the upper side; and one more line from O, through *z*, cutting the parallel from 3, which gives the determinate shadow of *z*, and completes the whole. Or the shadow of the line *z*, 1, (on the upper plane of the square hollow) may be found, by means of the foot of the light on that plane; thus. Continue the line from 1, parallel to the horizontal line, and continue the perpendicular from *t*, till that cuts it; then draw a line from S, through that interſection, and a perpendicular from O, cutting it; and from this laſt interſection (which is the foot of the light) through 1, draw the ſhadow ſought, and a line from O, through *z*, determines the length of it.

Then, for the ſhadow of the ladder, draw from its vaniſhing point 4, through O, and from S, through F, meeting in G; draw from G, through each foot of the ladder, to the interſection of the floor with the farther ſide of the room continued, cutting it in 5, and 6; then, where G, F, S, cuts the ſame line of interſection (as at 7,) raiſe a perpendicular, cutting G, O, 4, in A, and draw A, 5, and A, 6, which lines will cut the top of the ladder, and (having before drawn G, 5, and G, 6,) by theſe means the whole ſhadow is found from G, to 5, and 6, on the floor, and from A, to 5, and 6, on the wall, ſuppoſing no other object to intervene.

For G, O, 4, is the line in which all the plane of rays muſt paſs to the two ſides of the ladder G, 4, repreſenting a line parallel to them, paſſing through the light O, and touching the ground in G, and the wall in A.

But as G, 5, and G, 6, meet the other ſide of the room in 9, and 10, draw from theſe laſt points to 4, which will determine that part of the ſhadow, and would meet A, 6, and A, 5, in their interſections with the angle of the room, if there were no door, or if the door were ſhut.

Again, as the door will alſo receive part of the ſhadow, draw from 11, and 12, (where G, 5, and G, 6, meet *a*, H, the interſection of the plane of the door) to 13, and 14, where A, 6, and A, 5, interſect the edge of the door, which completes the whole ſhadow. Or the vaniſhing points of theſe two lines 11, 13, and 12, 14, may be found, by raiſing a perpendicular at *a*, which perpendicular will be the vaniſhing line of the plane of the door; and from *F*, and *G*, (both in the horizontal line) drawing *F*, 4, and *G*, 4, cutting that vaniſhing line, in their reſpective vaniſhing points *f*, and *g*; and then drawing *f*, 14, and *g*, 13, is found the ſhadow on the door.

N. B. *This is farther explained in the* SUPPLEMENT.

The

The ſhadow of the table on the ground is determined, by drawing lines from F, the foot of the light, through each angle of the table, on the ground; and then drawing from the light, itſelf, through all the upper angles, meeting thoſe lines from F, reſpectively. And for that part of the ſhadow on the door, continue the line of the bottom of the door *k*, *w*, till it meets F, *x*, as in *y*; at *y*, raiſe a perpendicular, cutting O, *x*, in L; draw L, S, which determines the ſhadow on the door, and completes the whole.

The ſhadows of the windows are found, in a like manner; for inſtance, the window E. Find the foot of the light on the plane E, which is to receive the ſhadow, thus: Draw a parallel from F, cutting the ſide of the room, 15, continuing the line F, 15, and find, there, the thickneſs or depth of the window 15, 16; draw O, 17, parallel to F, 16, and 16, 17, parallel to F, O; then 17, will be the foot of the light ſought: draw 17, 18, and O, 19, cutting it in 20; from 20, raiſe a perpendicular, cutting the inner lines of the window, which determines the ſhadow; and ſo of the reſt.—For the round window, the like method is uſed, the ſame point 17, being the foot of the light, for that whole plane; take two or three lines from the outer, to the inner circle, parallels to O, 17, and draw from 17, through the bottoms and from O, through the tops, and their ſeveral interſections will give the points of the ſhadows, &c. on the inner plane.

N. B. *At Fig.* 72, *No.* 3, *and* 4, *in the* SUPPLEMENT, *is the continuation, and concluſion of what relates to ſhadows.*

Of the images or reflections of objects in reflecting planes.

Fig. 73. IN this ſcheme are repreſented the reflections of ſeveral objects, in the water. Every object is ſeen as far, or deep within the reflecting plane, as it is placed without it. Thus, to find the reflection of the pile A, part of which is in the water, and the reſt above the ſurface of it, meaſure from the top to that ſurface, and ſet off the ſame meaſure downwards to *a*.

P But

But for the pile B, which inclines, the perpendicular height from the ſurface of the water muſt be taken. If it inclined ſo, as to continue ſtill parallel to the plane of the picture, then a perpendicular from the top would touch the water at 2, in which caſe, B, 2, would be the meaſure to be taken downwards, and then the reflection would be equal to the repreſentation of the object; and if it inclined inwards, ſo as that the top was perpendicularly over 1, then B, 1, would be that meaſure (ſhorter than the repreſentation of the object); if forwards, ſo as to be perpendicularly over 3, then B, 3, is the meaſure, which is the meaſure here taken, and 3, 3, is the perpendicular depth of the reflection, which therefore makes the reflection longer than the repreſentation of the object.

The principal difficulty, in moſt reflections, is to find the ſeat of the object on the ſurface of the reflecting plane; for when that is found, the reflection is made, by repeating that diſtance either geometrically, or perſpectively, as the caſe may require, in, or on the reflecting plane: the block C, hangs over the water, and projects from the wharf, touching the edge of it, at the point 4; therefore meaſure from 4, to the ſurface of the water 5; then draw from S, (the vaniſhing point of the four ſides of the block) through 5, and drop a perpendicular from its extreme angle, cutting S, 5, in 6, which is its ſeat on the ſurface of the water; and this meaſure repeated downwards, finds the reflection of that angle, by means of which the reſt is eaſily determined. Or having firſt found the reflection of the edge of the wharf, by repeating the perpendicular 4, 5, downwards, to 7, draw a line from S, through 7, and a perpendicular, from the corner of the block, cutting that line, will find the ſame corner, or angle ſought. The reflection C, is ſimilar to its original, and all the rays run to S, as in the original.

The reflection of the block E, is found in the ſame manner; the vaniſhing point of E, is F, but the vaniſhing point of its tranverſe ſides is beyond the picture, to which the correſponding ſides of the reflection, or image, is drawn, as well as thoſe of the block itſelf: the piece E, hangs over the piece C, but makes ſo ſmall an angle (with a per-

perpendicular from its interſection *e*,) that it becomes neceſſary to uſe an expedient; therefore draw (from *e*,) a line parallel to D, S, as *e*, *f*, and another from the edge, or corner, of the block, to *g*; draw F, *f*, *g*, and drop perpendiculars from *f*, and *g*; then meaſure from *f*, downwards, to the ſurface of the water *h*, and repeat that meaſure to *i*; draw F, *i*, cutting the perpendicular from *g*, in *k*, and transfer *i*, *k*, backwards, by parallel lines, perpendicularly under E, which will determine the reflection I, K, by which the reſt is completed; (*i. e.*) dropping perpendiculars from *e*, and the corner of E, the parallels from *i*, and *k*, will meet them in I, and K, and the line K, I, will terminate in F, the vaniſhing point of its original.

The reflection of G, is found on the ſame principles. In order to find its ſeat, draw from its lower angle a line parallel to D, S, and a ray from 11, the angle of the wharf, to S, cutting that parallel in 8; drop a perpendicular from 8, and cut it in 9, by another ray from the ſurface of the water, under 11; drop a perpendicular from the lower angle of G, and draw 9, 10, parallel alſo to S, D, cutting that perpendicular in 10, which will be the ſurface of the water; meaſure therefore from the top of G, to 10, and repeat that to 12, which will be the reflexion ſought.

Here is introduced a row of trees, to ſhew in what manner they are to be reflected, and how many of them would be ſeen. Continue the ray, or line, on which they ſtand, forwards to the margin, or edge, of the wharf; from thence take the diſtance to the ſurface of the water, and repeat it downwards by a perpendicular; and, from the lower extremity of that perpendicular, draw a line to S, and then to that line drop a perpendicular from the firſt tree; and from this laſt point of interſection, meaſure the tree downwards, and mark the top, and ſtem, of that inverted tree; thence draw lines to S, which lines will receive perpendiculars from each tree above, whoſe interſections will give the places of the reflected trees, reſpectively.

And it appears that no more than parts of the three forwardeſt trees will be viſible, in the water, by reflection.

Here, and every where, ſuch objects, and ſuch aſſemblage of objects, only are repreſented, as ſeem beſt calculated to exhibit examples for the inſtruction intended, and not any regular figures, or agreeable pictures.

Fig. 74. No. 1. The reflection, or image, of the figure A, ſuppoſed to ſtand before a looking-glaſs, is found on the ſame principles as reflections in the water, with this difference, in the proceſs, that the ſeat on the reflecting plane, and the image beyond, or within it, are both *perſpectively* found in this and every vertical ſituation, except when the object, and its reflected image, are in a line parallel to the picture; whereas in the horizontal, *(i. e.)* in water, they are only, and always found geometrically; therefore, having found the diſtance from A, the foot of the figure, to *a*, the plane of the looking-glaſs, on the viſual ray A, S, repeat the ſame diſtance, on the ſame ray, onwards, that is, within the glaſs, to a, which will determine the foot of the image; there raiſe a perpendicular, and draw another ray from the head of the figure to S, cutting that perpendicular, which interſection determines the height of the image; and in like manner any points of the original figure may be found, by drawing rays to S, from ſuch points through correſponding perpendiculars.

And in the ſame manner is found the image of the figure B, in the glaſs, before it; but this figure is again reflected in the glaſs, behind it (which is over the chimney,) by geometrical meaſures, taking firſt the diſtance to the plane of the glaſs from B, to *b*, and again the ſame diſtance to b, within the glaſs; which is an operation ſo fully explained in the preceding figures (reflected in water) as to need nothing more here: it will be obſerved, that, in this latter caſe, the image is always equal to its original, whatever be the diſtance; whereas, when perſpective meaſures are neceſſary, the images become leſs, in proportion to their diſtance.

As theſe repreſentations are made purely for inſtruction, it was neceſſary to place the figures where the images could be reflected without grouping, or giving them any relation to each other; and for the ſame reaſon here are two of the glaſſes inclining forwards, in order to

Plate. XLI.

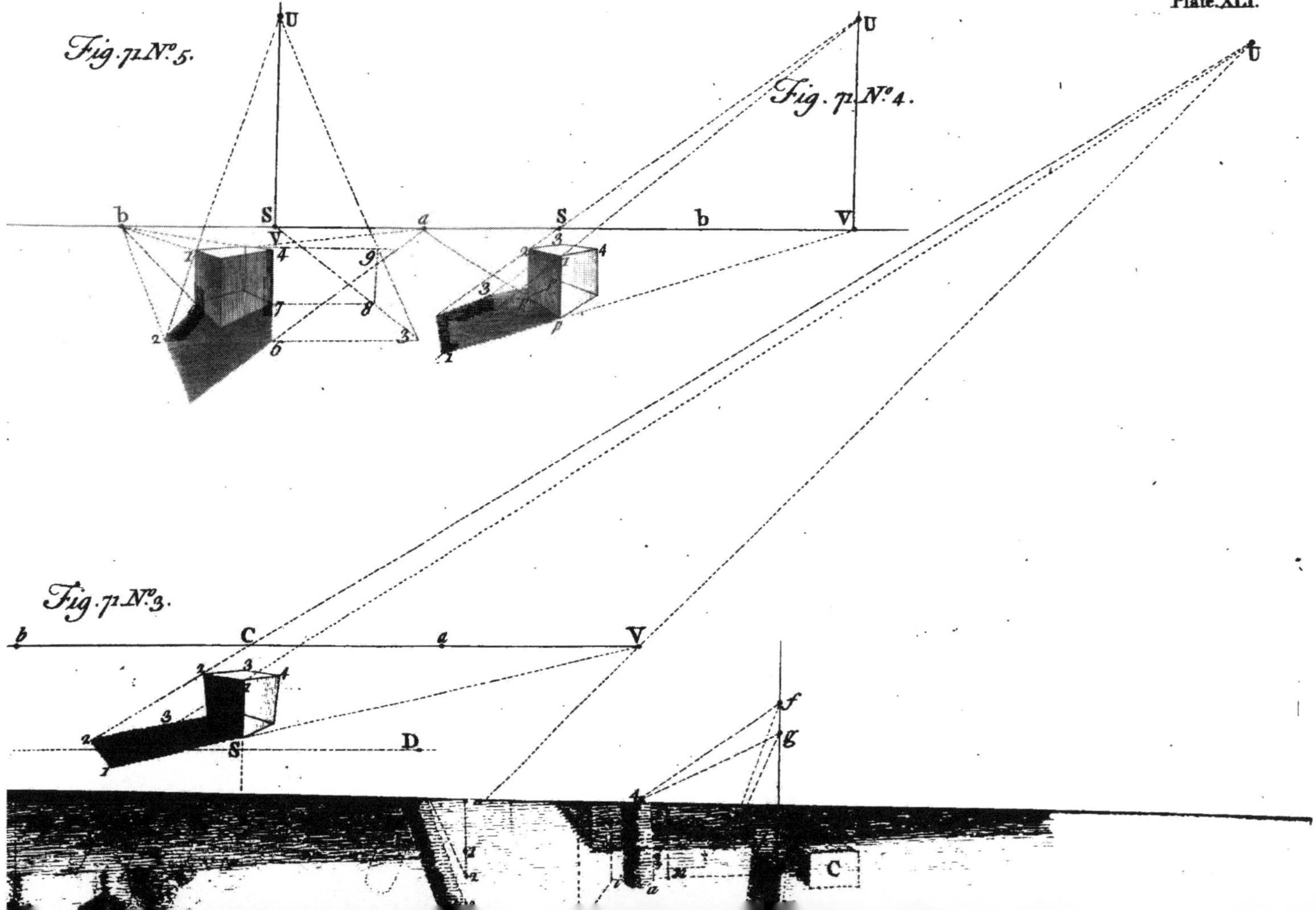

ſhew the manner of finding reflections, in ſuch ſituation; they both incline in an angle, of 18 degrees, with the ſide of the room; as that oppoſite to the figure F, whoſe image is found by the ſame general law, but the particular circumſtances require explanation; and firſt the vaniſhing line of the plane of the glaſs runs through E, below, which is the vaniſhing point of the ſides of it, and the bottom touches the wainſcot in the points *c*, and *d*. Wherefore, having drawn E, *c*, and E, *d*, and dropped a perpendicular from *c*, or *d*, to the floor, as here from *c*, to 5, draw S, 5, cutting E, *c*, in 6, through which a parallel to S, D, (as 6, *f*,) will be the bottom of the glaſs on the floor (ſuppoſed beyond the wainſcot). Now drawing F, S, cutting 6, *f*, in *f*, and drawing E, *f*, this line will give the indefinite ſeat of the axis of the figure on the glaſs, and G, being the vaniſhing point of perpendiculars to the plane of the glaſs, draw F, G, cutting E, *f*, in *g*, which is the ſeat of the foot of the figure; wherefore double, or repeat F, *g*, within the glaſs perſpectively (as has been frequently taught) to *h*, which will be the foot of the image, or reflection in the glaſs, and alſo drawing from the head of the figure to G, cutting E, *f*, *g*, in 7, that will be the ſeat of the head; this diſtance from the head to 7, being repeated perſpectively, finds the head of the image, which is now eaſily completed, as the others.

The axis of the image might be found, by continuing the axis of the original figure, perpendicularly from F, upwards, till it meets the axis of the ſeat E, *f*, *g*, 7, in H, and drawing H, I, which will be the axis of the image; for this point I, is the vaniſhing point of the image, found, by making E, D, I, an angle of 18 degrees.

If the reader finds any difficulty to conceive this operation, or the reaſon of it, he is referred to the ſcheme below,

Fig. 74. No. 2. which is a geometrical repreſentation of it, with the ſame characters. F, *o*, H, is the axis of the original figure; *f*, *g*, 7, H, the ſection of the glaſs with the ſame inclination as in the picture; *g*, 7, is therefore the ſeat on the glaſs, and *h*, *o*, the image, which laſt meets F, *o*, in H, as above. F, *f*, in the geometrical ſcheme, is the floor; *f*, *h*, the ſame reflected (the angle of reflection being equal to that of incidence);

cidence); and hence appears the reaſon of drawing D, I, to find the vaniſhing point of the image, for this line repreſents H, *h*, in the geometrical, as D, L, perpendicular to D, I, repreſents *f*, *h*, in the geometrical; H, *h*, *f*, being alſo a right angle, and therefore L, is the vaniſhing point of all the radials in the reflected floor. It may be worth while to examine the correſpondence of theſe lines in the geometrical ſcheme, and the perſpective. The floor reflected in the glaſs, is repreſented at 11, 10, above, which are the images of 11, and 10, below, on the firſt line of the floor, found by drawing lines from the originals to G, (the vaniſhing point of perpendiculars to the glaſs,) and cutting them by other lines from the interſection of the glaſs with the floor; as from P, to L, the vaniſhing point of the radials on the reflected floor, and (therefore) of perpendiculars to the image. Since therefore the reflected image of 11, muſt be in each of theſe lines, it muſt be in their common interſection. Here are three ſets, or pairs of lines, perpendicular to each other; the firſt pair are D, S, the common diſtance, and geometrical perpendiculars to it, for the repreſentation of the room, &c. the ſecond pair D, E, and D, G, for the repreſentation of the glaſs, and the ſeats of objects on it; and the third pair D, I, and D, L, for the repreſentation of the image, or reflection, of the man, and of the floor, at right angles to the man.

The image of the object K, in the glaſs M, is found by lines drawn from each point, geometrically perpendicular to the plane of the looking-glaſs, (which is inclining in the ſame angle from the wall, as the laſt, viz. 18 degrees); theſe points, on the ſurface of the glaſs, are ſeats of the originals, from each of which, an equal diſtance is taken within, or beyond the ſurface, which laſt ſet of points being joined by right lines, become the image ſought. The ſeveral ſeats on this glaſs are found, by drawing lines, from each original point on the floor, parallel to the horizontal line, cutting the ſection of the glaſs on the floor, and thence drawing a parallel to the ſide of the glaſs, and drawing a perpendicular to that parallel from the original point. And for any original point above the floor, find its ſeat firſt on the floor, and proceed as if that was the point, and then draw a perpendicular from the real original point above, to the parallel on the glaſs, as before directed. Or as at

Fig. 74. No. 3. Firſt ſuppoſe the glaſs to be cloſe to the wall, (*i. e.*) to coincide with the line *f*, P, and conſequently perpendicular to the floor, both before and behind.

Then (as the glaſs inclines forwards) the floor, behind, riſes in proportion, (*i. e.*) to the pricked line *f*, O, (18 degrees); yet ſtill 90 degrees will be left, between that line, and the back of the glaſs, from which there muſt now be taken 18 more by the line *f*, *g*, to reduce the angle, behind, to 72, equal to that before, which has loſt 18, by its inclination forwards.

And this is the reaſon of the two angles of 18, behind the glaſs, between *f*, N, and *f*, *g*.

Draw A, B, and its parallels, (from the interſections of b, A, and its parallels) all parallel to *f*, *g*.

Transfer the ſeveral diviſions of the line *e*, *f*, on *f*, *g*, and from theſe laſt, draw to S, croſſing all the parallels of A, B, which finiſhes the reflection of the floor, in the glaſs.

Every particular has been ſo repeatedly explained, in relation to the former objects, that nothing need be here added. If any poſſible difficulty ariſe, a careful inſpection will remove it.—The reader muſt obſerve, that though the glaſs receives but part of the image, yet the whole is deſcribed by pricked lines, that the proceſs may be entirely comprehended.

The ſeveral numerical figures of the image correſpond with thoſe of the originals, reſpectively.

> *N. B.* 1, 3,—2, 4, at the bottom, and top of the image, No. 1. run to the ſame vaniſhing point S, as 1, 3, and 2, 4, &c. of the original, with which they correſpond; and 1, 2,—3, 4, &c. are, alſo, parallel to each other, as in the original, being parallel to the picture.

The floor is chequered on purpoſe, to give occaſion for ſhewing its image, or reflection in the two inclined glaſſes; and in that marked, M, there is alſo the image of ſo much of the window neareſt to it, as could be ſeen, by reflection, in it; as alſo in the oppoſite glaſs over the chimney is the reflection of part of the neareſt perpendicular glaſs, and of the window, and, if the chimney glaſs had been wider, the very image of B, in the glaſs before it, would have been again reflected in that of the chimney, where the pricked touches are made, that being the place in which the diſtance from the image, to the ſide of the room, is doubled, ſuppoſing that ſide continued on, as far (backwards) as the image is caſt.

Though very few deſigners will, perhaps, take the pains to project, by rule, every reflected object; and though it ſeldom happens that very intricate diſpoſitions of ſuch objects occur, yet it may not be uſeleſs to add two or three caſes, in which the principles herein explained, and the methods founded on them, will appear peculiarly advantageous: thoſe who are curious in ſpeculation, and thoſe who deſire to be correct in the execution, will be gratified; and all will be better able to judge of what they ſee, as well as the practitioners will be better able to perform, (even though it be by gueſs) after knowing, and conſidering the rules, than without ſuch knowledge, and conſideration.

Fig. 75. No. 1. P, Q, R, T, is ſuppoſed to be a looking-glaſs ſtanding, perpendicularly, on the horizontal plane; A, B, E, F, an object to be reflected, which is deſignedly made plain, and ſimple, to avoid confuſion of lines; draw A, a,—E, e,—B, b, and F, f, all parallel to the horizon, (which lines will be perpendicular to the plane of the glaſs,) and in theſe lines will be found both the ſeat of the object, on the glaſs, and alſo its reflection, in it. *m*, S, is the vaniſhing line of the glaſs, and *m*, C, of the object to be reflected; but as C, (the vaniſhing point of A, B, and E, F;) is above the horizon, continue *m*, C, till it cuts the horizontal line in *r*, and draw E, *r*, cutting P, Q, S, in *n*, which will be the point where the two planes, of the glaſs and object, meet on the ground; and as their vaniſhing lines meet, above, in *m*,—draw *m*, *n*, which will be their common interſection, and of which, *m*, is the vaniſhing point.

Draw C, L, perpendicular to *m*, S, the vaniſhing line of the glaſs, cutting it in K, then K, will be the vaniſhing point of the ſeats of

A, B,

Plate XLII.

A, B, and E, F, on the plane of the glaſs; for C, is their original vaniſhing point, and K, is perpendicular to it, on the vaniſhing line of the glaſs; and *m*, *n*, being the interſection of theſe two planes, and A, B, C, cutting that interſection in *o*, draw K, *o*, cutting A, a, in 1, and B, b, in 2, then 1, 2, K, will be the ſeat of A, B, C; and as E, F, C, alſo cuts the ſame line *m*, *n*, in V, draw K, V, cutting E, e, in 3, and F, f, in 4; then 3, 4, K, will be the ſeat of E, F, C, and drawing 1, 3, and 2, 4, the whole ſeat is completed; and doubling the four parallels A, 1, to a; B, 2, to b; E, 3, to e; and F, 4, to f; the image is completed, by joining a, b, e, f.

Or, ſince the image or reflection is juſt as far behind the ſeat, as the original is before it, in C, K, L, make K, L, equal to C, K, and then L, will be the vaniſhing point of the image; wherefore draw L, *o*, cutting A, a, in a, and B, b, in b, and draw alſo L, V, cutting E, e, in e, and F, f, in f, and joining a, e, and b, f, the image is completed; and by this method it may be found, even without the trouble of firſt finding the ſeat.

Or, inſtead of drawing four parallels, two will ſuffice, A, a, and B, b; and having drawn L, *o*, cutting thoſe two parallels in b, and a, and continued the ſides of the original A, E, and B, F, till they cut the line *m*, *n*, in *p*, and *q*, draw *q*, a, and *p*, b, cutting L, V, in e, and f, this will complete the image alſo, without finding the ſeat.

Fig. 75. No. 2. Proceed as was ſhewn at large in the former figure, which is the univerſal method recommended. The ſame letters, and numerical figures, are uſed in this, as in that, to ſhew the correſpondence. The only difference is, that, as this glaſs does not ſtand perpendicularly on the horizontal plane, ſo the parallels A, a,—B, b, &c. are not parallel to the horizon, but are *here*, as they muſt be, *always*, perpendicular to the reflecting plane.

Fig. 75. No. 3. In this ſcheme is the ſame general method uſed, as in the two preceding; however, that nothing may be left unexplained, it is to be obſerved, that the glaſs here is oblique, not (as the laſt) on the horizontal plane, but above it, whoſe vaniſhing line is *m*, K, *r*, and the vaniſhing point of the ſides R, T, and P, Q, being K, the lines perpendicular to this plane, are drawn perſpectively (and not geometrically, as in the two former); that is, the vaniſhing point W, of lines perpendicular to it, is found, by the rules heretofore taught, and A, W,—B, W,—E, W, and F, W, drawn, repreſenting perpendiculars, and conſequently K, L, is made perſpectively (not geometrically) equal to K, S: after which the image of the object is found by means of L, the vaniſhing point of its ſides; *m*, L, being its vaniſhing line; and the ſeat (though not neceſſary) is found (as before) to ſhew the conformity of the lines, and of the proceſs, with the preceding ſchemes.

N. B. As the ſame letters ſtand for the ſame points, it is needleſs to enter into the explanation over again, except that here, it became neceſſary to vary two or three; as K, for inſtance, at the ſame time that it is the vaniſhing point of the ſides of the glaſs, is alſo the vaniſhing point of the ſeats of A, B, and E, F, and that the vaniſhing point of the ſame original lines A, B, and E, F, which was marked C, in the former ſchemes, is here marked S, becauſe it coincides with the center of the picture, which is always diſtinguiſhed by the ſame letter, &c. *n*, and V, alſo coincide in this ſcheme; S, D, is the diſtance of the picture; and the point L, is found by drawing S, 5, 6, parallel to W, D, drawing D, K, cutting it in 5, making 5, 6, equal to S, 5, and then drawing D, 6, cutting S, K, L, in L.

Fig. 75. No. 4. This laſt ſcheme is ſtill by the ſame method; but that no difficulty might be avoided, the center of the picture is not the vaniſhing point of either the object, or glaſs, both which are placed obliquely, the one above, the other below the horizontal line; and as E, is the only point of the object that touches the ground (E, C, and conſequently F, being under it) E, *r*, is drawn to the interſection of its vaniſhing line with the horizontal line, and alſo P, being the only point of the glaſs that touches the ground, P, r^2, is drawn to the interſection of its vaniſhing line with the horizontal line, and E, *r*, cutting P, r^2, finds *n*, through which, from *m*, (the interſection of two vaniſhing lines) viz. of the glaſs, and object, is drawn *m*, *n*, the inter-

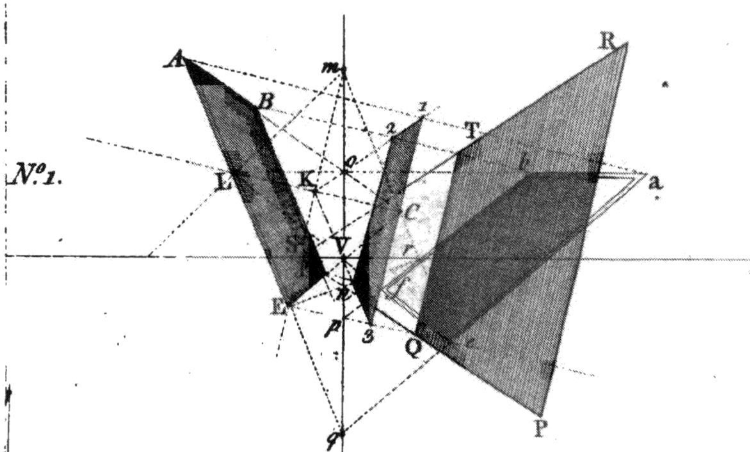

Fig. 75. N°. 2.

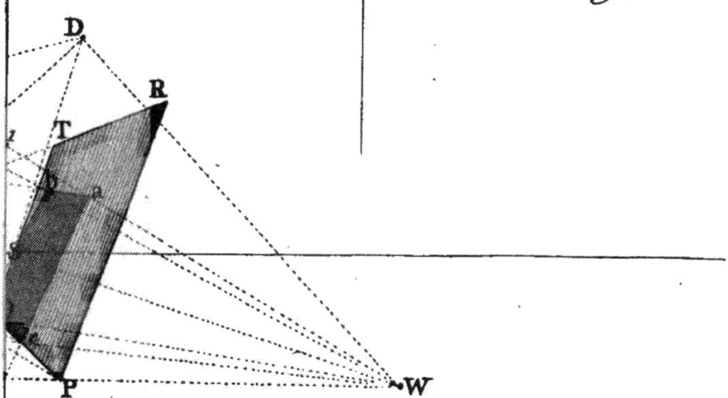

Fig. 75. N°. 3.

interſection of their two planes. The reſt is all as the former, only one letter (viz. Y,) is added here; for S, ſerved in all the former caſes as the vaniſhing point, either of the glaſs, or of the object, one of which coincided with the center of the picture, but Y, is (in this ſcheme) the vaniſhing point of R, T, and P, Q, and Y, S, W, is the vaniſhing line of a plane perpendicular to Y, *m*, (the vaniſhing line of the glaſs) on which Y, D, W, is made a right angle to find W, the vaniſhing point of perpendiculars.

The four laſt ſchemes, Fig. 75. No. 1, 2, 3, and 4, are deſigned to explain, on the principles of *Brook Taylor*, the method of finding reflected objects in mirrors, and have a more particular reference to the laſt ſcheme in his book, where he repreſents the image of a picture as reflected in a glaſs ſtanding obliquely on a table. They are exhibited with all poſſible ſimplicity, and without any ornament, that ſo no lines may enter into the diagrams, but ſuch as are abſolutely neceſſary to the projection of the image propoſed.

This is one of the parts of that work, which is mentioned (in the Preface of this Treatiſe) as attended with difficulty. No. 3, is nearly *Brook Taylor*'s own example, but with all the neceſſary lines; No. 1, and 2, are preparatory, and explanatory of the principles; and No. 4, a caſe ſtill more difficult, but all on the ſame principles.

CONCLUSION.

THE author has, in this work, endeavoured to expreſs himſelf with all the perſpicuity that the nature of the ſubject will admit, and has been leſs ſolicitous to avoid repetition, than to avoid obſcurity. That over ſcrupulous exactneſs, which permits not to repeat an inſtruction (once delivered) though at the diſtance of many pages, makes references backwards continually neceſſary, and not only perplexes and wearies the reader, but diſguſts him more than, now and then, a ſeaſonable repetition; and the getting by heart a great number of definitions, before their uſe can be known, eſpecially when moſt of them will afterwards appear to be unneceſſary, is burthenſome to the memory, and tedious even to patience itſelf; yet every one of theſe muſt be diſtinctly remembered, or the reader muſt be continually turning back to analyze them, which interrupts him beyond meaſure. If, on the contrary, it were thought ſufficient to call a ſhadow, a ſhadow, to call the ground, the ground, and to give the common names to common things, and to treat this ſubject in a more familiar way, it might, undoubtedly, be thereby more accommodated to the apprehenſions of the generality of thoſe, whoſe profeſſions require a knowledge of perſpective. And this is what the author has endeavoured to execute.

He is far from ſaying, or thinking (as the Jeſuit in his Preface) " That perſpective is the very ſoul of painting, and which, alone, can " make the painter a maſter;" or as ſome others, who may have ſet it too high among the requiſites, in forming a painter; ſince many very great maſters have been deficient in it, ſome egregiouſly, who have, notwithſtanding, poſſeſſed the other, and more excellent parts in a high degree; as invention, compoſition, expreſſion, correctneſs of deſign, and colouring; which will produce fine pictures, though the perſpective be, in ſome reſpects, faulty, and much finer, than any, in which the perſpective may be abſolutely true, and theſe other parts but in a low degree.

It is certain, however, that perſpective is an eſſential, and that whatever is erroneous in this reſpect, does not truly repreſent the thing intended; that it is abſolutely neceſſary to the perfection of painting; and that ſome ſubjects, particularly architecture, cannot be repreſented without it. It is alſo certain that a man will invent, and compoſe with more facility, and preciſion, who underſtands it well, than he who underſtands it but imperfectly, ſuppoſing other qualifications equal; that great errors in it are monſtrous, and ſhocking, and that a total ignorance of it is unpardonable in a painter, or deſigner.

The END.

Plate XLIIII.

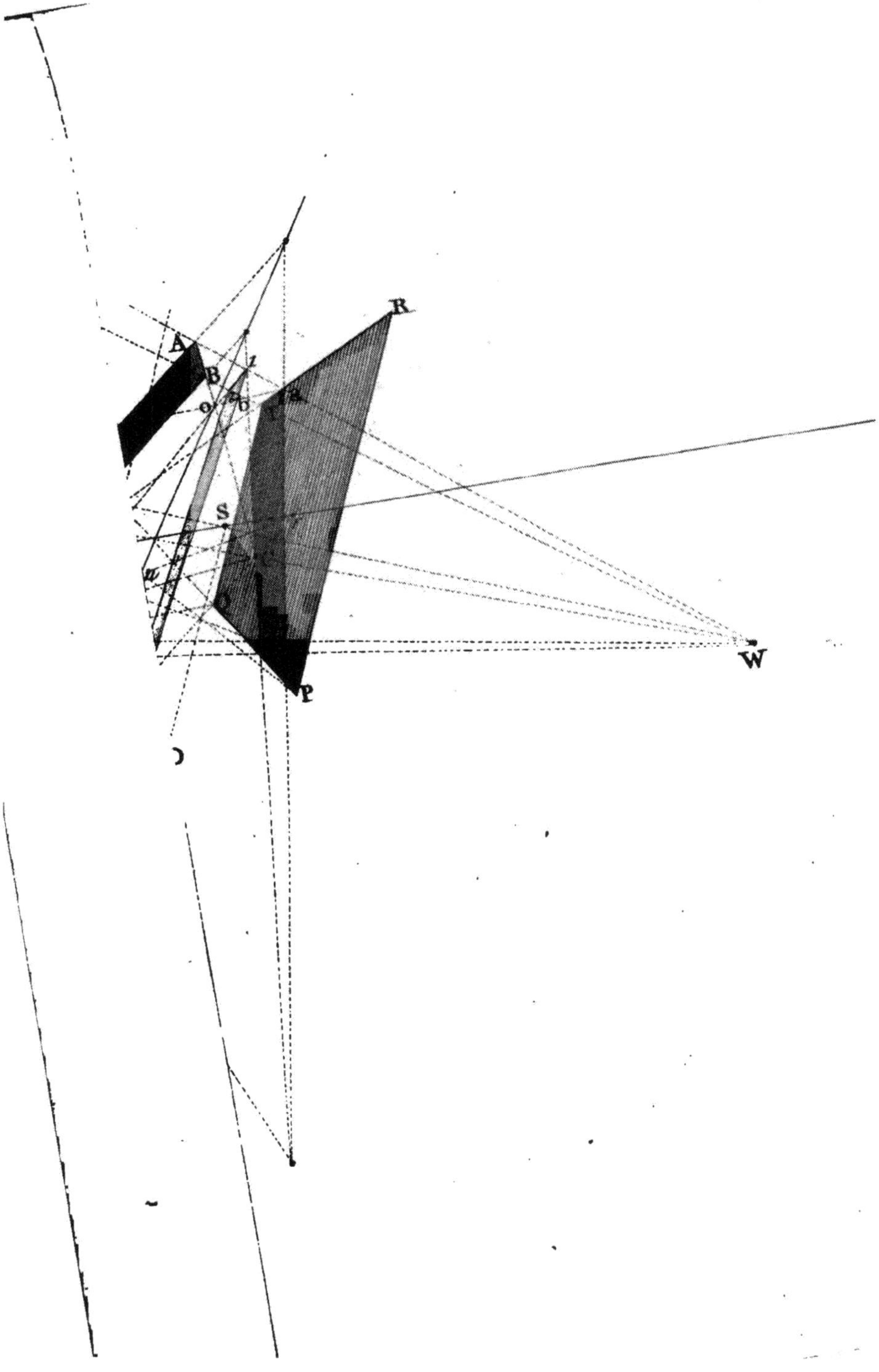

THE

SUPPLEMENT.

THE

SUPPLEMENT:

Added to illuſtrate and explain ſome of the more difficult parts of the foregoing Treatiſe, which, in their ſeveral places, were neceſſarily complicated; but are here ſeparated, in order to their being ſingly, and diſtinctly conſidered. For this purpoſe it has been thought moſt convenient to repeat the ſame figures and numbers as in the body of the work, where the ſame ſubjects are treated (with the addition, only, of capital letters) that reference may eaſily be had to ſuch places.

AND FIRST,

THE reader is referred back, from this place, to Fig. 71. No. 1. where he will find, that the vaniſhing point O, of the poſt 11, 12, is at a conſiderable diſtance below, among other objects, and (on that account) not ſo readily diſtinguiſhed; and, alſo, that the vaniſhing point of its ſhadow is beyond the limits of the plate. For theſe reaſons it has been thought proper to repeat this diagram by itſelf, and in a narrower compaſs, that all the points may be ſeen at once, and ſo their relation more diſtinctly appear, eſpecially as this is a matter of ſome difficulty, and of great uſe.

Fig. 71. No. 1. A.—11, 12, is a line ſtanding obliquely on the horizontal plane, whoſe ſeat is 13, 12, and the vaniſhing point of that ſeat is S.—U, is the given vaniſhing point of the ſun's rays. Firſt find the vaniſhing point of 11, 12, by dropping a perpendicular from S, and continuing 11, 12, till it cuts that perpendicular in O, which will be its vaniſhing point; then draw from O, through U, to the horizontal line, cutting it in X, which will be the vaniſhing point of the ſhadow; then draw 11, U, and 12, X, cutting it in 14; then 12, 14, is the ſhadow ſought. For U, V, cutting the horizontal line (perpendicularly over U,) in V, this will be the vaniſhing point of the ſhadow

of

of any line ſtanding perpendicularly on the ground. Now if ſuch a perpendicular line 11, 13, be drawn, cutting the ſeat in 13, the ſhadow of that perpendicular will be 13, 14, and 14, will be (in that caſe, alſo,) the ſhadow of the point 11; therefore 12, 14, muſt be the ſhadow of the whole line 11, 12, which is a proof, that the firſt operation was true.

All the references are the ſame as in the large ſcheme, and there is no difference in any circumſtance, except that this poſt leans forwards in an angle of 58, and the former in 65; which change was made, only to avoid the too great diſtance of the vaniſhing points O, and X.

So that if the text, relating to the former, be read with this ſcheme, it will anſwer throughout.

And this will be general, for any line, viz. to draw from its vaniſhing point, through the vaniſhing point of the ray of light, to the vaniſhing line of the plane on which the ſhadow is to be projected, whether it be the horizontal plane, or any other; and this interſection, with the vaniſhing line of the plane on which the ſhadow is caſt, will be the vaniſhing point of the ſhadow. For, (in this ſcheme,) imagine the plane D, S, O, raiſed on S, O, till D, S, be perpendicular to the picture; then a line from D, to U, determines the vaniſhing point of the rays; and, conſequently, a line through O, and U, to the vaniſhing line of the horizon, will give the vaniſhing line of the plane of rays paſſing over the whole line O, 12, 11, and therefore, alſo, the vaniſhing point of the ſhadow 12, 14.

Fig. 71. No. 1. E. Is an example of the ſame kind on an oblique plane. Here C, *q*, is the vaniſhing line of ſuch plane; Q, P, a vaniſhing line of planes perpendicular to it; *a*, B, a line ſtanding perpendicularly on the plane C, *q*;—B, its ſeat, on that plane, and P, its vaniſhing point; U, the given vaniſhing point of the rays of the ſun, and V, the vaniſhing point of the ſhadow, found as X, in the laſt; that is, by drawing from P, the vaniſhing point of the line *a*, B, through U, the vaniſhing point of the rays, to the vaniſhing line of the plane on which the ſhadow is caſt; draw *a*, U, and B, V, cutting it in *e*, then *e*, is the ſhadow of *a*, and B, *e*, of B, *a*, on the plane C, *q*.

And if any other line, as *a, b,* be given, on the ſame plane C, *q,* ſtanding obliquely on it (yet being parallel to the plane Q, P,) continue that line *a, b,* to its vaniſhing point Q, and draw Q, U, cutting C, *q,* in *q,* then *q,* will be the vaniſhing point of its ſhadow on the plane C, *q.* Wherefore,

Draw *b, q,* cutting the ray *a,* U, in *e,* and *b, e,* will be its ſhadow.

If *a,* B, were continued to *g,* then *g, b,* would be the ſhadow of *a, g.*

And if *a, b,* were continued to *f,* (or any length) the ſame operation finds the ſhadow; thus *f, b,* is the ſhadow of *a, f,* &c.

. 71. No. 1. F. Here is one more example for the ſhadows of oblique lines. Theſe incline inwards, and therefore have their vaniſhing points above the horizontal line.

O, H, the horizontal line; Y, the vaniſhing point of the four lines A, B;—U, the vaniſhing point of the rays of light, and conſequently U, Y, is the vaniſhing line of the rays which paſs over theſe four lines; and W, (being the point, in that vaniſhing line, which cuts the horizontal line) is the vaniſhing point of their ſhadows on the horizontal plane, (*i. e.*) on the ground. The line A, L, being in a different direction, has another vaniſhing point, viz. *y,* and therefore the rays paſſing over it will produce another vaniſhing line, as U, *y,* which cutting the horizontal line in *w,* that becomes the vaniſhing point of the ſhadow on the ground of this line A, L.

The reſt needs no explanation, only as H, is the perpendicular ſeat of Y, on the horizontal line, and *b,* of *y*; if the perpendicular ſeats of A, are found, then, by means of theſe ſeats, the ſame ſhadows might be determined, as in the caſe of perpendicular lines; for the ſhadows of the point A, would exactly coincide with theſe, here, found, and then the point *o,* perpendicular to U, muſt be uſed as the vaniſhing point of theſe ſhadows on the ground.

The ſeat of any of the points A, is found by drawing a line from B, to H, then dropping a perpendicular from A, to the line B, H, which line is the ſeat of the line A, B, on the ground, as at A, 1, and at A, 2, the ſeat is *a*; and then drawing *a, o,* and A, U, interſecting fecting it in a, this point is the ſhadow of A, which coincides with that already found, and is a proof, that the method, propoſed, is univerſally true.

N. B. The center and diſtance are not given, being no way concerned in this diagram, for wherever the center is placed, in the horizontal line, or whatever be the diſtance, all the ſeveral relations of theſe lines remain the ſame.

It is alſo evident, that two lines, only, are neceſſary to the determining any ſhadow, as appears at A, B, 4, viz. one from the top A, to the vaniſhing point of the rays U, and another from the bottom B, to the vaniſhing point of the ſhadow W; the additional lines at 1, and 2, are merely for illuſtration, or proof; and at 3, there is another line A, L, whoſe vaniſhing point is *y*, and the vaniſhing point of its ſhadow *w*.

The foregoing ſchemes have been introduced, and explained, in order to facilitate the practice, in the perſpective of ſhadows, and principally with reſpect to the members of architecture; for though, hitherto, in ſimple lines, only, (that they may be more eaſily comprehended,) yet their application, and utility will appear by thoſe which follow.

Fig. 69. No. 1. (in the foregoing treatiſe) is the repreſentation of a Doric cornice; now to find the ſhadows of the projecting members, draw from S, (the center of the picture) a line to the extremity of any member, (*e. g.*) to *f*, the extreme angle of the modillion; which line will be (perſpectively) perpendicular to the plane of the picture, and find the point *g*, in which ſuch member touches the naked, or ſolid, of the building, *(i. e.)* the plane on which the ſhadow is to be caſt; and from that point *g*, draw a line *g*, *h*, parallel to S, R, (R, being the given vaniſhing point of the rays of light); then draw *f*, R, cutting *g*, *h*, in *h*, which will be the ſhadow of *f*; and ſo of the reſt.

Fig. 69. No. 1. A. But to explain this operation, unembarraſſed with other lines, is the following ſcheme. Here S, is the center of the picture; S, D, the diſtance; R, the vaniſhing point of the rays of the ſun; *f*, *g*, a line perpendicular to the picture, and alſo to the plane on

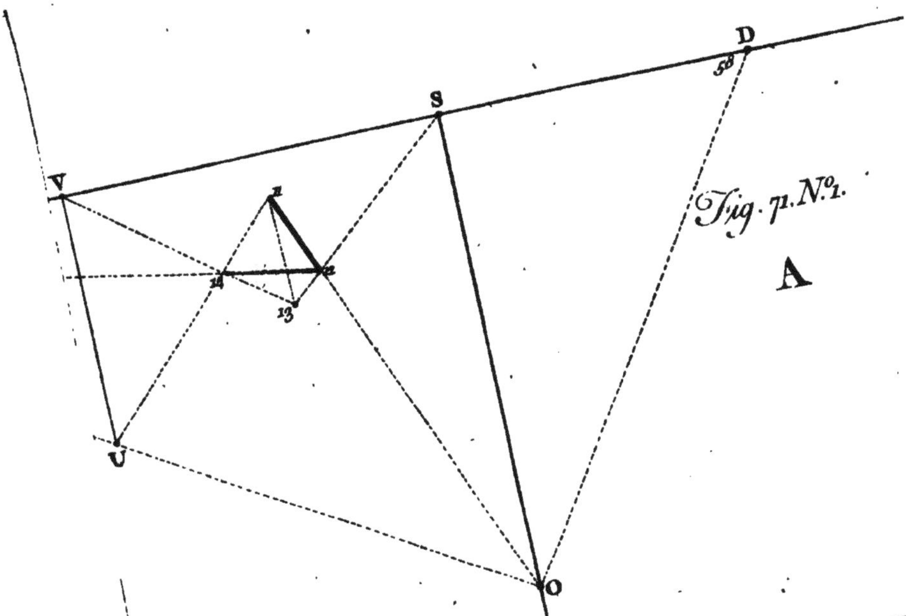

Fig. 71. No. 1.

A

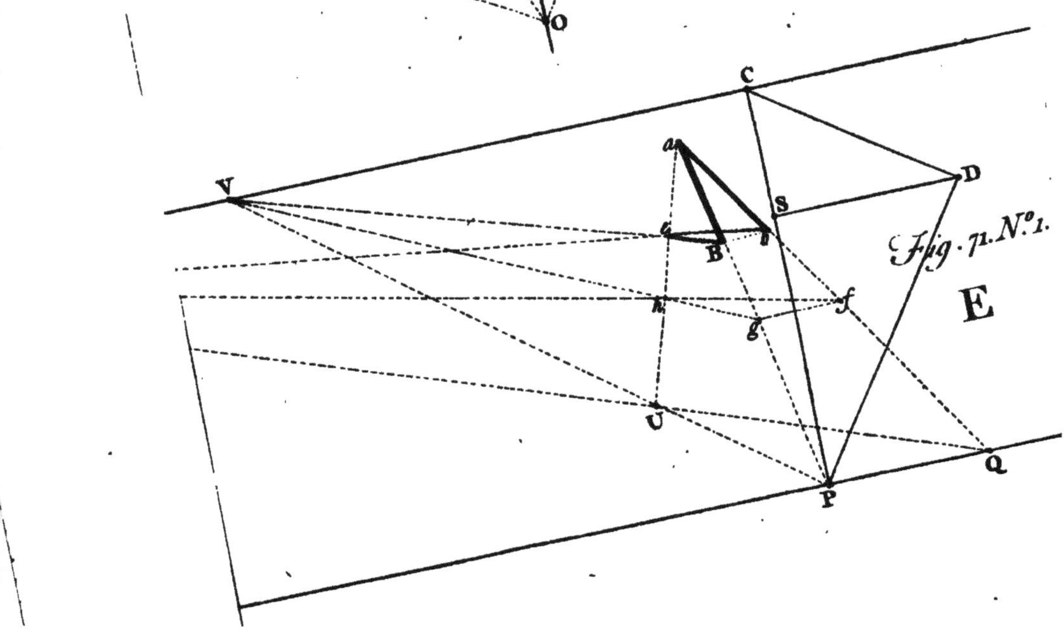

Fig. 71. No. 1.

E

on which the ſhadow is to be caſt, which plane is parallel to the picture. Now, *g*, being the ſeat of *f*, *g*, on the parallel plane, or the point in which it touches that plane, draw *g*, *h*, parallel to S, R, and draw *f*, R, cutting it in *h*; then *g*, *h*, will be the ſhadow of *g*, *f*.

For as all lines tending to S, repreſent lines parallel to D, S, when raiſed up on S, (*i. e.*) perpendicular to the picture; ſo all lines tending to R, repreſent lines parallel to D, R; therefore S, is the vaniſhing point of all the lines *f*, *g*, and R, of all the rays paſſing over them, which rays (though parallel among themſelves) being oblique to the picture, muſt have a common vaniſhing point. And as the plane, on which theſe ſhadows are caſt, is parallel to the picture; and the objects, whoſe ſhadows are ſought, all perpendicular to that plane; the ſhadows muſt neceſſarily be all parallel to each other, and to the ſeat of the rays on that plane, which is S, R, and therefore can have no vaniſhing point; and for the ſame reaſons, all perpendicular objects, that are of equal length, will project ſhadows, on this parallel plane, of equal length alſo.

Fig. 69. No. 1. E. As for the ſide plane of the ſame object, which plane is perpendicular to the picture, the ſhadows will have a vaniſhing point, as Z, perpendicularly under S, for S, Z, is the vaniſhing line of that plane, and R, Z, drawn from R, perpendicular to S, Z, will be parallel to the lines, whoſe ſhadows are ſought, on this plane, which lines are all parallel to the picture. Thus, draw a line from *i*, (the point where *l*, *i*, touches the ſide or profile of the building) to Z, and then draw another line, *l*, R, cutting it, in *m*, which will be the point ſought, that is, the ſhadow of *l*, on the ſolid of the building, exactly as on the horizontal plane in finding the ſhadow of a line ſtanding perpendicularly on it; for (turning the picture) the whole correſponds to that; and having found *m*, the ſhadow of any ſuch point *l*, draw S, *m*, which will determine the whole ſhadow of ſuch projecting member; for S, *m*, repreſents a line parallel to *i*, *i*, and *l*, *l*.

To find the ſhadows on a plane oblique to the picture, ſuch as at Fig. 69. No. 4. (in the foregoing treatiſe) a line muſt be drawn (perſpectively) perpendicular to that plane, (*i. e.* as the modillions are, on this face of the building,) and then the operation will be like the laſt; but as there, ſpace is wanting to introduce the vaniſhing points of the rays, and of the ſhadow, ſee

Fig. 69. No. 4. G.—Draw *b*, A, to its vaniſhing point *g*, and from *g*, draw through R, the given vaniſhing point of the rays, to S, *e*, (the vaniſhing line of this face of the building,) cutting it in *e*, which will be the vaniſhing point of the ſhadow. Now draw *b*, R, and A, *e*, cutting it in *f*, then A, *f*, is the ſhadow of A, *b*, on this plane. Theſe are all the lines that are neceſſary for the purpoſe; and this is the ſhorteſt method.

But the ſhadow *f*, of the point, *b*, might be found by other lines, which are here added merely for illuſtration, and to ſhew a kind of correſpondence.

For, in every method, the truth of the operation depends upon the ſimilarity of triangles, either geometrically, or perſpectively, and in this already explained, the triangles *b*, A, *f*, and R, *e*, *f*, are perſpectively ſimilar, that is, repreſent ſimilar triangles; for *g*, *b*, and *g*, *e*, repreſent parallel lines, as having the ſame common vaniſhing point *g*.

And if R, L, be drawn parallel to S, *g*, (the horizontal line) cutting the ſame vaniſhing line S, *e*, in L, and *b*, a, be drawn parallel to it, then draw a, L, which cutting *b*, R, finds the ſame point *f*, for the ſhadow of *b*, and here the triangles b, a, *f*, and R, L, *f*, are, geometrically, ſimilar.

Again, if a perpendicular from R, be drawn cutting S, *g*, in *r*; draw *r*, *b*, cutting S, A, in *a*, and draw *a*, *f*, parallel to *r*, R, this alſo will cut the ray *b*, R, in the ſame point *f*, and here the triangles *b*, *a*, *f*, and *b*, *r*, R, are ſimilar.

And having found *f*, the ſhadow of *b*, draw S, *f*, which will determine the whole ſhadow of the projecting member; *as in the laſt example.* For S, *f*, repreſents a line parallel to S, A, and S, *b*.

Fig. 72. No. 1. A. This ſcheme is introduced to explain ſome particulars relating to the ſhadow of the ladder at Fig. 72. No. 1. and therefore

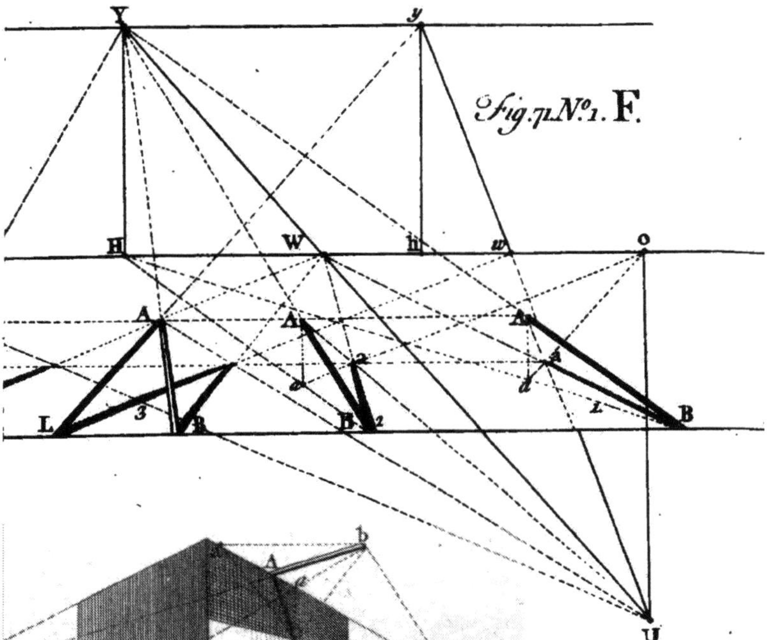

Fig. 71 No. 1. **F.**

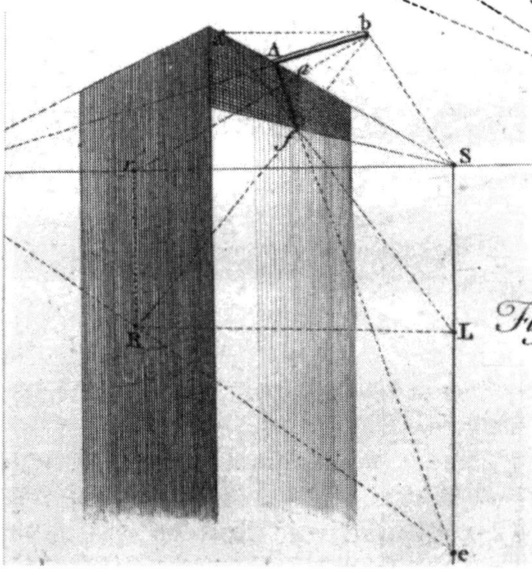

Fig. 69 No. 4. **G.**

fore has the ſame letters, and numerical figures of reference; only inſtead of that object, here is a plank, in order to ſhew the operation and effect more diſtinctly.

G, Θ, 4, is a ray parallel to the plank, and the triangle G, 4, S, is a plane of rays continued to the horizon.—A, 7, is the interſection of that plane, by the plane of the wall againſt which the plank leans: therefore from the point A, (the top of that interſection) drawing A, 5, and A, 6, through the top of the plank, theſe lines will give the ſhadow of it on the wall, but being interrupted by the door, at 13, 14, the ſhadow will thence take another direction. Now ſince the plane of the door (whoſe vaniſhing point is *a*,) cuts the triangular plane of rays in B, 8, (*as the plane of the wall does in* A, 7,) therefore from the point B, draw through 13, 14, which will give the direction of the ſhadow on the door, which ſhadow will meet that on the ground (from the bottom of the plank) in 11, 12. The triangle B, 11, 12, correſponding to the plane of the door, exactly as the triangle A, 5, 6, does to the plane of the wall, and as the triangle 4, *F*, *G*, does to that of the utmoſt diſtance, which, being parallel to the picture, and to the wall, the line 4, *G*, is parallel to A, 6, and 4, *F*, to A, 5, which ſhews the correſpondence of the operation, and proves the truth of it.

And as *a*, is the vaniſhing point of the top, and bottom of the door, ſo *a*, *g*, *f*, will be the vaniſhing line of its plane; wherefore, continuing 11, B, to *g*, and 12, B, to *f*, theſe will be the vaniſhing points of thoſe lines;—and as *a*, *g*, *f*, is at the utmoſt extent, or on the horizontal line, as well as *F*, 4, and *G*, 4, ſo, by continuing *F*, 4, to *f*, and *G*, 4, to *g*, theſe ſame points *f*, and *g*, will alſo be the interſections of the vaniſhing lines *F*, 4, and *G*, 4, with the vaniſhing line *a*, *g*, *f*, which is a farther illuſtration of the whole.

N. B. It ſeems hardly neceſſary to add, that G, (being the point in which the ſame ray 4, Θ, G, touches the ground) anſwers the ſame purpoſe for the plane of the ground, as A, and B, for the planes of the wall, and the door, and that the triangle G, 11, 12, on the ground (therefore) correſponds to that plane, as A, 13, 14, and B, 11, 12, to their reſpective planes.

As

As a farther illuſtration of the two laſt ſchemes, and to render this kind of operation (which is of great uſe) ſtill more clear, here is added a third.

Fig. 72. No. 1. B. Let L, 4, be conſidered as one leg of the ladder, or a pole, continued to its vaniſhing point 4;—L, S, the ſeat of the pole, on the ground, continued to its vaniſhing point S; ſo that L, 4, S, may be conſidered as a triangular plane, whoſe vaniſhing line is S, 4. Draw from 4, through Θ, the light, and from S, through F, the foot of that light, meeting in G, which will be the foot of the light, for the pole, becauſe 4, G, repreſents a parallel to 4, L.

Draw G, L, cutting *a*, 11, (which is the interſection of the plane of the door with the ground) in *b*, and from 8, (the interſection of L, S, with *a*, 11,) raiſe a perpendicular, cutting L, 4, in *d*; draw *b*, *d*, which will be the ſhadow of L, *d*, on the plane of the door; continue *b*, *d*, till it meets *a*, *f*, (the vaniſhing line of the plane of the door) in *f*, which will be the vaniſhing point of *b*, *d*.

Or that vaniſhing point may be found, by continuing G, L, *b*, to *F*, in the horizontal line, and drawing *F*, 4, which will find the ſame point *f*, and then drawing *b*, *f*, which will cut L, 4, in *d*.

And this laſt method will be true for any plane, whoſe vaniſhing line is *a*, *f*.—For ſuppoſe a plane whoſe interſection with the ground is *a*, 7, and which is cut by L, S, in *b*; raiſe, at *b*, a perpendicular up to L, 4, cutting it in *k*, and draw 7, *k*, which will tend to the ſame point *f*; or draw 7, *f*, which will cut L, 4, in *k*, and 7, *k*, will be the ſhadow of L, *k*, on that plane.

And ſo univerſally of any plane, whoſe vaniſhing line is *a*, *f*, from *a*, 11, to *a*, *F*.

Again, ſuppoſe a line drawn through L, parallel to the horizontal line *a*, *F*, cutting 4, Θ, G, in *g*, and *a*, 11, in 11, and S, *g*, cutting Θ, F, in f, then f, will be the foot of the light (removed farther within the plane of the ground); and drawing 4, U, parallel to *g*, L, 11, cutting the vaniſhing line *a*, *f*, in U, then U, will be the vaniſhing point of the ſhadow of L, 4, (or of L, *d*,) on the plane of the door; and drawing 11, U, cutting L, 4, in *d*,—11, *d*, will be that ſhadow;

remem-

Fig. 72. No. 1. A

remembering, that in this laſt caſe, the foot of the light is ſuppoſed to be f, (farther removed within the picture) which occaſions the ſhadow from *g*, to be ſo much longer, than that from G, produced by the foot F, which is nearer; and that, in either caſe, Θ, (the light) is juſt as far within the picture, or the ground, as its foot, whether it be F, or f.

Fig. 72. No. 3. Here the rays of light, are thoſe of the ſun, ſuppoſed to be parallel to the picture, and to H, I; it is required to find the ſhadow of the ſquare projection *a*, *b*, *c*, of this building on the parts contiguous to it.

Firſt, draw *c*, *q*, parallel to K, I, the horizontal line, this gives that part of the ſhadow which is caſt on the ground; at *q*, raiſe a perpendicular to *r*, the edge of the roof; then draw *r*, *n*, parallel to K, L, the vaniſhing line of the plane of the roof, and draw *b*, *n*, parallel to H, I, cutting *r*, *n*, in *n*, which is the ſhadow of *b*; ſo that *c*, *q*, *r*, *n*, is the whole ſhadow of the line *c*, *b*, and is, evidently, in a plane of rays parallel to the picture, and to H, I.

For *c*, *q*, is on the horizontal plane, and parallel to the horizontal line, and *q*, *r*, is parallel to *c*, *b*, and in the ſame plane with that, and *c*, *q*; and *r*, *n*, (joining *q*, *r*,) is on the roof, and parallel to its vaniſhing line L, K; therefore, &c.

Now, in order to find the ſhadow of *b*, *a*, whoſe vaniſhing point is I, let it be conſidered that I, H, is the vaniſhing line of the plane of rays which paſs over *b*, *a*, and L, K, is the vaniſhing line of the roof, and, therefore, that the interſection of theſe two vaniſhing lines E, muſt be the vaniſhing point of the ſhadow of *b*, *a*, on the roof, *for the ſhadow itſelf is the interſection of thoſe two planes*. Therefore draw E, *n*, which will be the indefinite ſhadow of *b*, *a*, on the roof, and drawing *a*, *o*, parallel to H, I, cutting E, *n*, in *o*, this would determine *o*, *n*, the ſhadow of *a*, *b*, (for *o*, would be the ſhadow of *a*, on the roof) if the roof were continued ſo high; but as this is interrupted by the perpendicular plane *l*, *o*, whoſe vaniſhing line is K, H, which interſecting I, H, (the vaniſhing line of the rays) in H, this interſection will be the vaniſhing point of the ſhadow on that plane, *for this ſhadow is the interſection of the rays with that plane*. Therefore

fore draw H, *a*, cutting *n*, *o*, in *p*, and then *a*, *p*, is that part of the ſhadow of *a*, *b*, which falls on the wall, and *p*, *n*, the reſt of it, which falls on the roof; ſo that *a*, *p*, *n*, is the whole ſhadow of *a*, *b*, produced by rays all parallel to the picture, and to H, I.

And to prove the truth of all this, draw from *c*, the ſeat of *b*, on the ground, and from *e*, the ſeat of *a*, two lines, *c*, *g*, and *e*, *f*, parallel to the horizontal line; then draw *b*, *g*, and *a*, *f*, both parallel to H, I, cutting them in *g*, and *f*; then *g*, will be the ſhadow of *b*, and *f*, the ſhadow of *a*, on the ground. And, having continued I, *e*, *c*, and L, *b*, till they meet in *i*, draw K, *i*, and I, *f*, *g*, meeting in X; draw X, L; now raiſe perpendiculars from *g*, and *f*, cutting X, L, in *l*, and *k*; draw *k*, *b*, and *l*, *m*, which will be perpendicularly over *f*, *e*, and *g*, *c*, and parallel to each other, and to the vaniſhing line L, K, and therefore will be the ſhadows of *a*, *b*, and *b*, *m*, on the roof; which lines meeting with the rays *b*, *g*, and *a*, *f*, in *n*, and *o*, theſe rays determine the lengths of the ſhadows; that is, *n*, is the ſhadow of *b*, and *o*, would be the ſhadow of *a*, if the roof reached ſo high; in which caſe, *o*, *n*, would be the ſhadow of *a*, *b*; but as the roof is interrupted by the perpendicular plane above, (which touches the line *b*, *p*, in *p*,) therefore *a*, *p*, will be ſo much of the ſhadow of *a*, *b*, as falls on that plane, and the reſt of it is *p*, *n*, on the roof.

Fig. 72. No. 4. Is a cylinder, lying on the ground, whoſe baſe is parallel to the picture.

S, is the center of the picture; R, the vaniſhing point of the rays of light, which are ſuppoſed to come from the ſun; L, the vaniſhing point of the ſhadow, found by raiſing a perpendicular from R, up to the horizontal line; it is required to find the ſhadow of any point, or points, of the circumference of the baſe of the cylinder, on the inner ſurface of it.

The ſhadow of A, is found on the inner ſurface, by drawing A, a, parallel to S, R, and drawing a, S, and, laſtly, A, R, cutting a, S, in *a*.

For the ſhadow of A, muſt be determined by the ray, paſſing over that point, to the vaniſhing point R, and it muſt be in the line a, S, in in which that ray cuts the inner ſurface, and alſo it muſt be in the point (of a, S,) in which A, R, cuts that line: therefore it muſt be the point *a*.

And ſo for any other point, or points of the circumference: by which operation a number of points in the inner ſurface may be found ſufficient to trace the ſhadow of the circumference, within the hollow of the cylinder.

The ſhadow within the other cylinder is found in the ſame manner; but that is introduced, principally, to ſhew the method of finding the ſhadow caſt on the outer ſurface, by any object, as B, interpoſed between it, and the light. In order to which; firſt find the ſhadow of that object on the ground, then mark any point on the baſe of the cylinder, as b, and find its ſeat c, on the ground: draw c, S, cutting the ſhadow of B, in *d*; at *d*, raiſe a perpendicular, and draw b, S, cutting that perpendicular in *e*, which will be the point of ſhadow ſought. And repeating the ſame operation for as many points as ſhall be neceſſary, the whole ſhadow of the object B, may be found on the outer ſurface.

For, b, c, *d*, *e*, may be conſidered as a perpendicular plane touching the cylinder in the line b, *e*; and *d*, *e*, would be the ſhadow of B, on ſuch plane; but, as the cylinder is circular, the plane of the ſhadow touches it only in the point *e*, which is the reaſon that other points muſt be found, by the ſame method; that is, by marking ſeveral points on the baſe of the cylinder, finding their ſeats on the ground, then drawing lines from thoſe ſeats to S, cutting the ſhadow of B, on the ground, and thence raiſing perpendiculars; and laſtly, drawing lines from the ſeveral points (marked on the baſe) to S, meeting their reſpective perpendiculars in the points of ſhadow.

The END *of the* SUPPLEMENT.

DIRECTIONS to the BOOKBINDER.

The two unnumbered Plates to be placed in the Introduction as paged, to wit, x and xii, and those numbered as follow.

Plate XLVIII.

Fig. 72. No. 1. B.

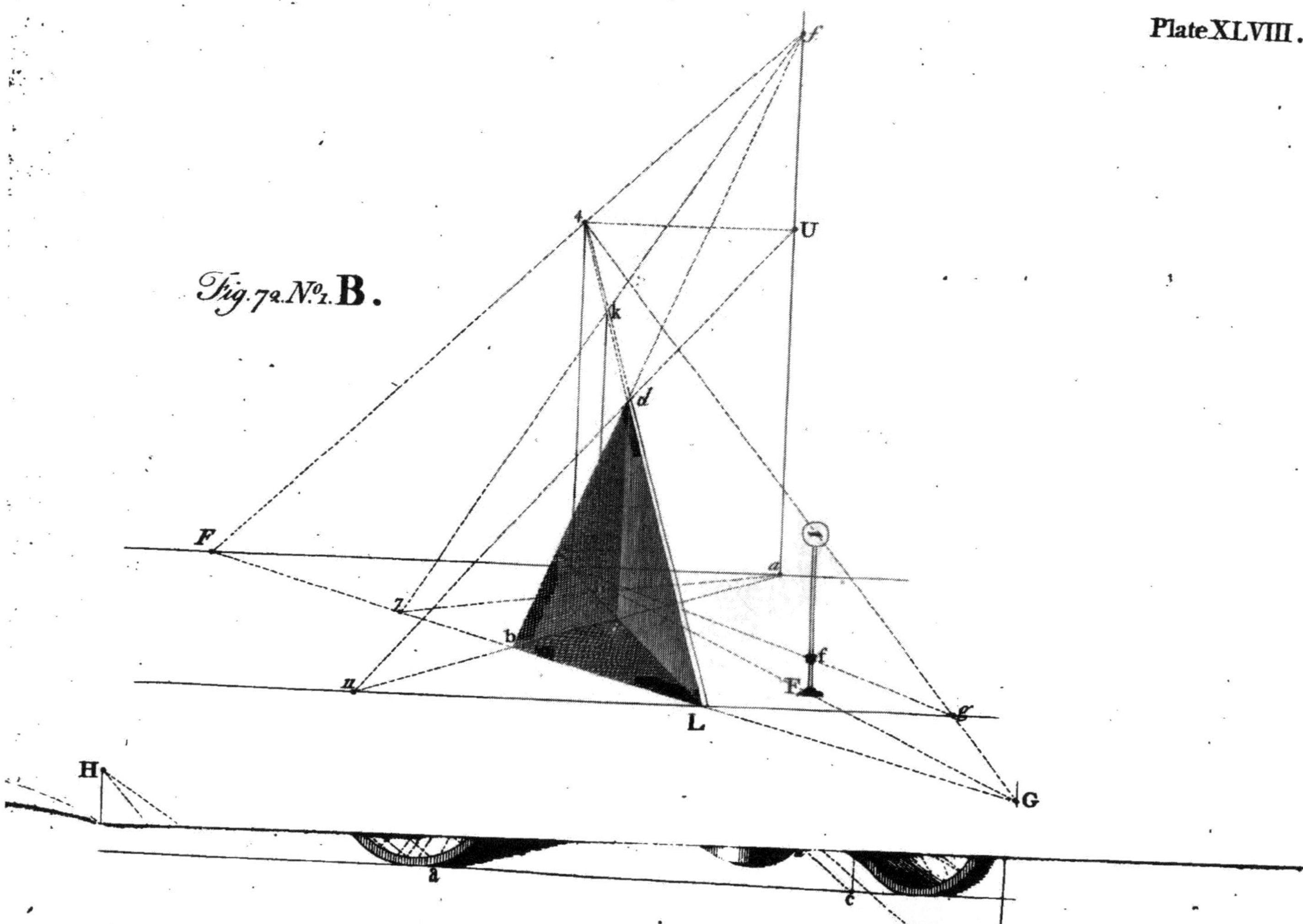

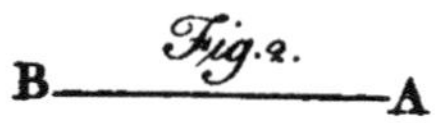
Fig. 2.
B
A

A.
Fig. 1.

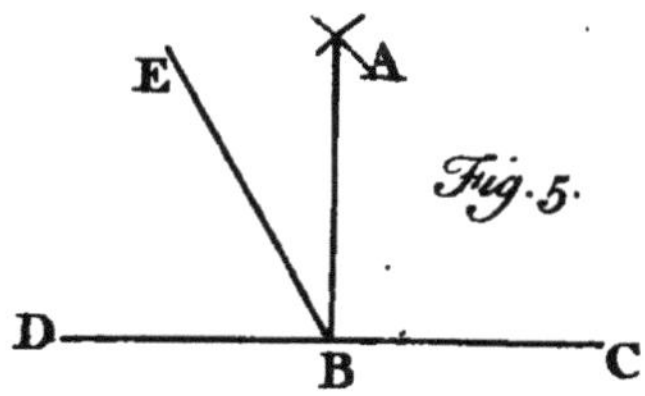
E
A
Fig. 5.
D
B
C

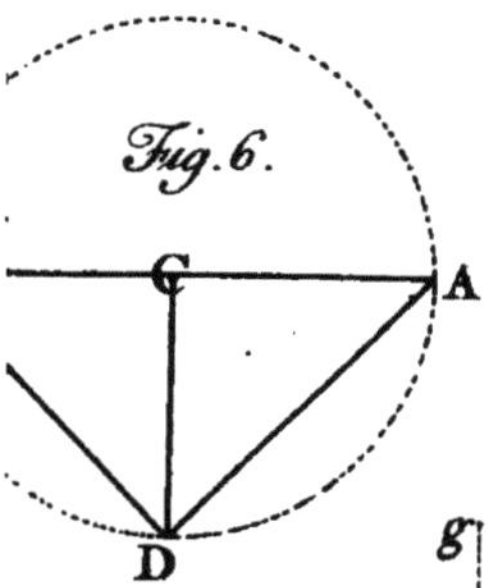
Fig. 6.
C
A
D

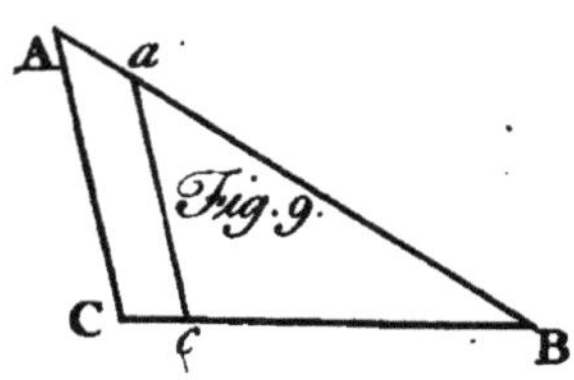
A
a
Fig. 9.
C
c
B

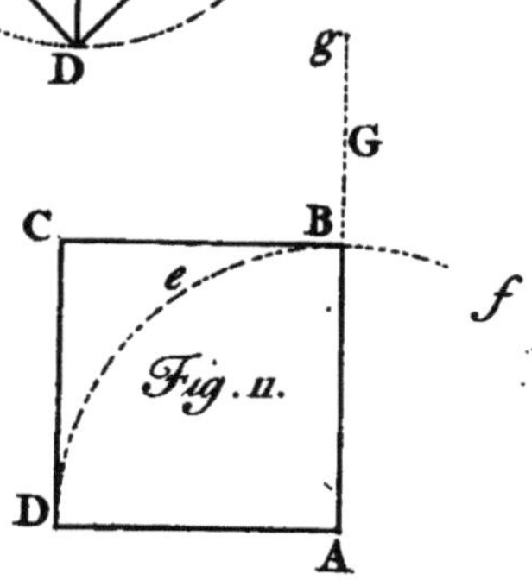
g
G
C
B
e
f
Fig. 11.
D
A

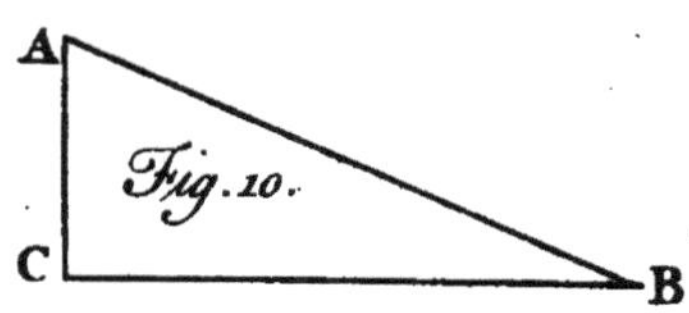
A
Fig. 10.
C
B

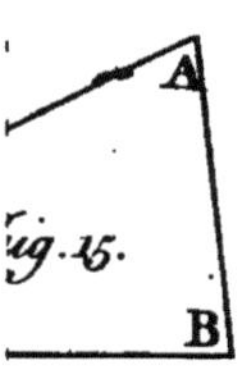
A
ig. 15.
B

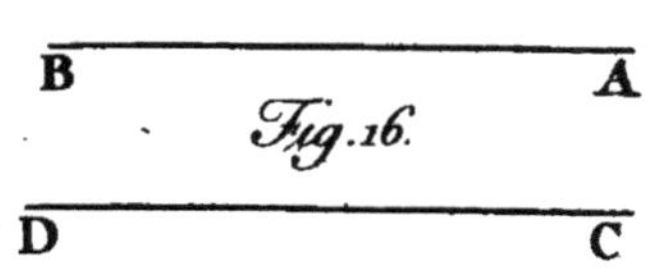
B
A
Fig. 16.
D
C

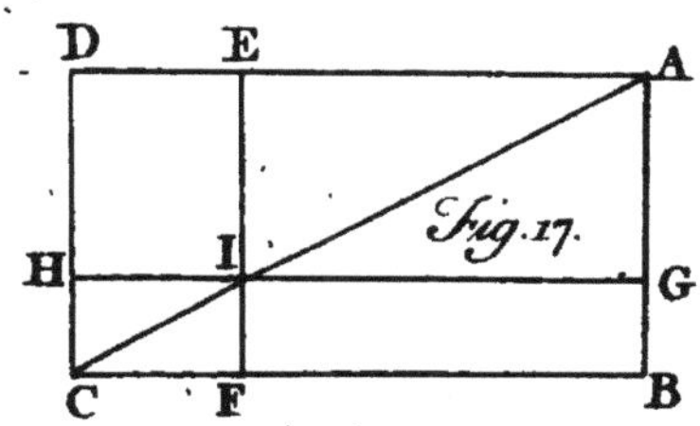

Fig. 17.

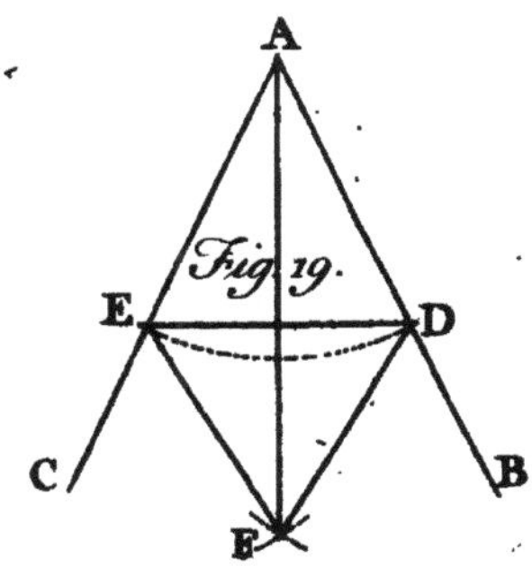

Fig. 19.

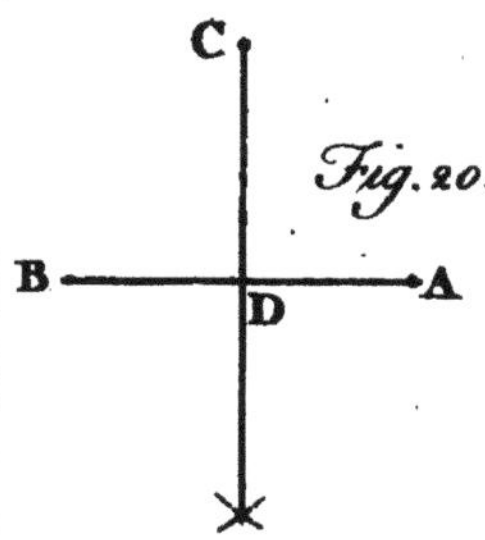

Fig. 20.

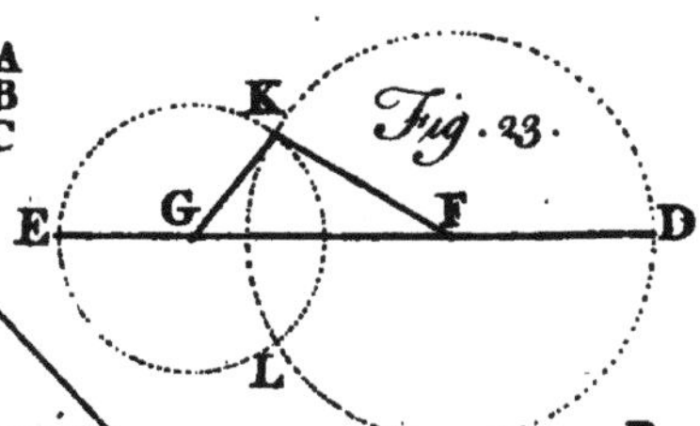

Fig. 23.

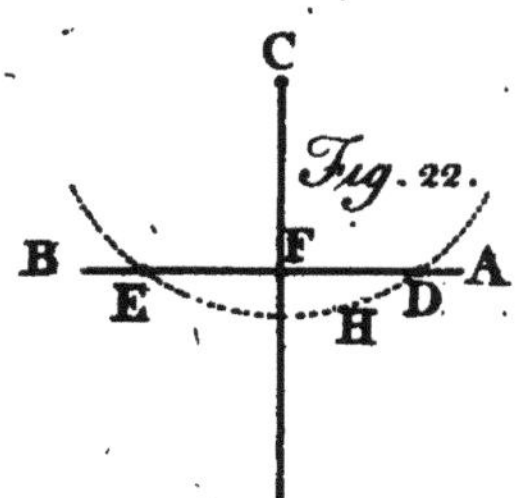

Fig. 22.

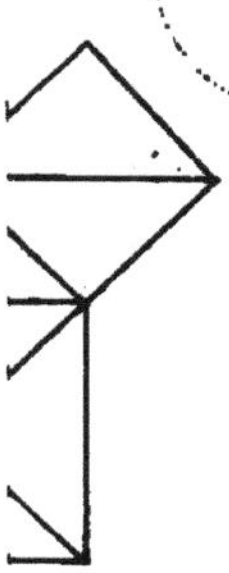

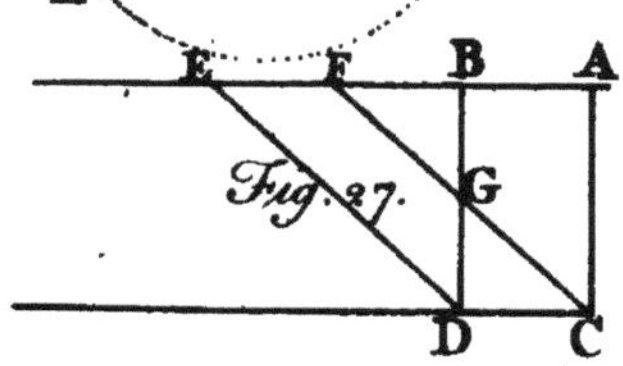

Fig. 27.

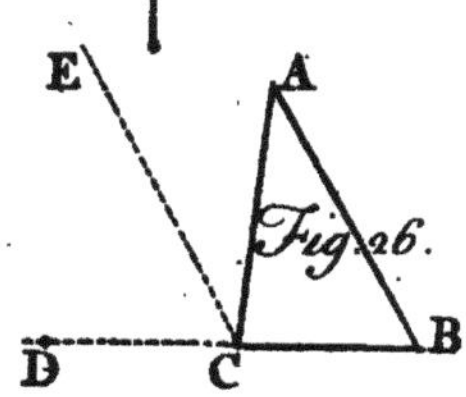

Fig. 26.

Lightning Source UK Ltd.
Milton Keynes UK
UKHW02f1858270518
323310UK00007B/19/P

9 781376 500301